W9-DHU-028

NK3670.L79
The collector's encyclopedia of buttons
3 5029 00020563 1

The Collector's Encyclopedia of Buttons

The Collector's Encyclopedia of Buttons

by

Sally C. Luscomb

BONANZA BOOKS · NEW YORK

Library of Congress Catalog Card Number: 67–27049
Printed in the United States of America

This edition published by Bonanza Books,
a division of Crown Publishers, Inc.
b c d e f g h

ACKNOWLEDGMENTS

I wish to thank the many collectors who, in the past thirty years, have shared with me their button knowledge and their discoveries; those who have sent their buttons to be examined and photographed; and those who have taken apart their buttons to prove certain theories. Their cooperation has provided the background and inspiration for this button encyclopedia.

In the immediate preparation of this book, I want to express my appreciation to those who have offered their assistance, their treasures, and their encouragement: Mrs. Walter Berry, Miss Dorothy Foster Brown, the late Reverend Herbert Cassidy, Mrs. Herbert Cassidy, Mr. and Mrs. J. Harold Cobb, Mrs. E. Burres Eliker, Miss Diana Epstein, Mr. Theodore Gates, Mrs. William Grist, Mr. Edward Gumprecht, Mrs. Kenneth Lydecker, Mrs. Robert Montgomery, Mrs. Gertrude Patterson, Mr. Ralph Sanford, Mrs. Edwin Tarbox, and Mr. H. A. Van Buren.

My special gratitude goes to my husband, Victor E. Luscomb, who has helped and encouraged my every endeavor in the past forty-five years.

CONTENTS

Jasperware buttons. These are on a coat and waistcoat of the eighteenth century. *Courtesy of the Victoria and Albert Museum, Crown Copyright.*

INTRODUCTION

More than almost any other collectible, buttons tell the story of history. Although relatively few buttons are much over two hundred years old, the techniques used to cut, mold, and decorate them had their beginnings before the time of recorded history. The pictures and motifs used in button designs record the facts and fantasies of all ages—the inventions of each generation, historical and political events, stories and fables, economic conditions, scenes of rural and city life. And buttons also demonstrate the arts and crafts of many peoples.

As the number of collectors increases, so do their questions—and who can answer them? How old is the earliest button known? Where was the first button made and worn? There are beautiful and historic gold and jeweled pieces with attachments or links that seem to give them the appearance of buttons, but these were actually worn around the neck on chains. And others made of stone or pottery were seals, which also hung on chains or cords.

Sculpture and paintings are the earliest sources for button data. However, an artist seldom depicted a button in detail; usually it was represented by a small knob or a dot of paint. Early books relate that in the thirteenth and fourteenth centuries, buttons were made of gold by jewelers and bead makers, but these were used as ornaments for costumes; the fastening was done by buckles and girdles. We read of men and women wearing as many as fifty to a hundred small buttons on their garments before the eighteenth century, yet few of these buttons have been preserved, even in museums.

To the collector, it is almost as if buttons did not come into use until early in the eighteenth century—he must be content with the very few that exist from an earlier date. The eighteenth was the century when arts and crafts that had been known for thousands of years began to be employed in the making of garment buttons. Here, again, we read of such costly items as sets of diamond buttons made for important persons. No doubt these treasures stayed in the family, since buttons were like jewelry—rare handmade heirlooms. However, many early and rare buttons are available for collecting.

Famous potters and silversmiths of that century fashioned buttons with the same beauty as their vases and jewelry. Handmade designs were put on copper, brass, and tombac buttons, and silver and gold were heavily plated on these metals. Fabrics for buttons were artistically embroidered with metal threads and beads. Artists painted button tops after the manner of Watteau, Greuze, Boucher, and Van Loo. And late in that century and early in the next, new inventions and materials came into use for button making—the molding of pewter and the stamping of brass, for example.

Europe furnished most of the buttons until almost the nineteenth century. Here and there, records show that a few were made in this country—in New England as early as 1706; in Philadelphia in 1750. Joseph Hopkins made silver buttons in Waterbury, Connecticut, in 1753. A 1770 advertisement announced that Benjamin Randolph was making buttons of apple, holly, and laurel wood. By that same year, the three Grilley brothers had opened a shop in Waterbury, Connecticut, for the manufacture of pewter buttons, and invented a method of including the wire shank. In 1774, the congress of Massachusetts recommended using papier-mâché buttons to reduce imports from the mother country. During this entire period, both horn and pewter buttons were being made in homes, and peddlers were carrying them afar for sale.

By the first quarter of the nineteenth century, buttons were being manufactured everywhere. England, France, Germany, and the United States were in constant competition, especially in the manufacture of metal dress and uniform buttons. Because each country utilized its natural resources and its own craftsmen, materials and techniques varied.

The quality of workmanship and the artistic beauty shown by buttons make it understandable that people became interested in their significance and began to seek them for collections. Among the earliest collectors were young girls of the late 1880's, who sought buttons for charm strings. Of course, they collected with a very specific motivation. The goal was a thousand buttons on a string, and there are several explanations of this magic number. One has it that when the string was completed, Prince Charming would come to claim the girl for his bride. Few completed charm strings have been found.

For generations, countless housewives saved old buttons—sometimes in the expectation of using them again, sometimes out of sentiment, sometimes just because they were too pretty or too fine to throw away. However, it was not until the 1930's that a collection of buttons was organized in a formal way. The first full-fledged button collector—as far as is known—was Mrs. Gertrude Patterson, who spoke over the radio about her collection. This was during Depression days, when many people had more buttons and leisure time than they had pennies. Her talk influenced quite a few of her listeners to turn to the family button box as the source of an inexpensive hobby. Soon, the idea swept the country. From this beginning, button collecting has grown to be one of the most popular hobbies in the United States.

Before long, antiques dealers were hunting for old button boxes full of discarded buttons, hobby magazines started to make space for an occasional column about buttons, books were written on the subject, and a magazine devoted entirely to button collecting was born. Today, little more than three decades later, there are thousands of people hunting for buttons, many dealers who handle nothing but buttons, and a constantly increasing number of button organizations.

There are many bypaths within the broad field of button collecting. Some collectors collect only buttons. Among these are people who build pictures with buttons or collect according to the ABC's; as well as those who collect only George Washington inaugural buttons or politicals beginning with the year they were born or picture buttons showing famous people or places or some one specific type. Others collect buttons as an adjunct to other collectibles of the same materials—pewter buttons as well as other objects of pewter, for example, or porcelain or pottery buttons to enrich their collection of porcelain or pottery objects. However, no matter what kind or category a collector chooses, he needs background information to help him identify, classify, and enjoy the buttons he seeks.

Until now, most button books have either specialized in a single kind of button or attempted to give a quick survey of the whole field. Established as well as beginning collectors have often felt the need of a more comprehensive and detailed book about buttons. The purpose of this present work, which includes the terms used, the means of identification, methods of construction, historical information, data on manufacturers, and so on, is to serve as an encyclopedic source book for all who are interested in buttons.

* * *

To begin a collection today is not quite so easy as it was twenty-five years ago. Still, most families have a button box of some sort, even if it contains no buttons from as far back as Great-Grandmother's day. Buttons also turn up in old jewelry and trinket boxes, in trunks among other mementos, in sewing boxes, on uniforms, and in other places—enough, quite often, to form the nucleus of a button collection.

Relatives and friends from afar, as well as next-door neighbors, may have buttons tucked away that they will be glad to add to your collection, unless the collecting idea takes hold of them too. If it does, there is always the possibility that they will swap their duplicates for some of the extras you have found. In most cases, the age and quantity of buttons a family has depend on whether they have had ample attic and closet space over several generations for keeping family treasures of any kind.

Do not be surprised if antique dealers tell you they "never got into buttons." They are generally telling the truth, for most of them realized quite early that buttons present an entirely different business, too extensive to mix with furniture, glassware, china, or farm implements. Though buttons are small items, they must be displayed to advantage (and therefore require considerable space). They also represent many arts and crafts, and a good dealer would need to learn about all of these, as well as about designs, styles, age, and materials, as he does about each collectible he carries. Still, it is never amiss to ask a dealer in general antiques if he has any buttons. If luck is with you, you may happen to be browsing in his shop just after he has bought the entire contents of a house or cleaned out an attic—he may still have the old button box, or be willing to tell you to whom he sold the last button box he found.

At antiques shows, keep a sharp eye out for little dishes or boxes of oddments and trinkets—there may be buttons among these; or extra-nice buttons may be displayed along with jewelry in small cabinets on the dealers' tables. Now and then, you will find a button dealer at an antiques show. Study his stock well; there is no better opportunity to discover the variety this hobby offers or to learn if there is one type or design that especially appeals to you for specializing, whether this be uniform buttons, politicals, enamels, or glass.

Large cities have button and trimming stores where sometimes there is old dress-trade stock, no longer in fashion. The owners may be glad to clean house if given a little notice. Ask for an appointment at their convenience. Many secondhand clothing stores have already found an outlet for their leftover buttons, but inquire anyhow—they may be looking for a customer.

Because today's new buttons will be tomorrow's antiques, don't neglect department-store button counters. Not all modern buttons are worthy of becoming collectibles, but some have already achieved that status, and others will. Remember, every button in the family button box was once a modern button; and it is always interesting, anyhow, to compare the new with the old, both in materials and designs.

Local auctions in your locality, sponsored by a church, lodge, or some other organization, may also be sources of buttons—especially if you take time to suggest, in advance, to those in charge that the members be urged to donate buttons. Tell them you will be there to bid on them. There are many button boxes of various sizes and vintages still in hiding that may be donated by members.

Political headquarters and conventions yield many collectibles of the historical type. Tell the headquarters staff that you will be glad to have the leftovers, whether their candidates win or lose.

Of course, this personal searching and shopping is a relatively slow method of collecting. It is fortunate for eager collectors that there are dealers specializing in buttons who have their stock thoroughly cataloged and are able to fill many requests without delay. Unfortunately, however, their supplies cannot be replenished like the shelves in a supermarket; but they are glad to help a customer in his search for the particular buttons he wants.

Browse through the ads in antiques and buttons magazines, and make yourself known as a prospective customer to everyone who advertises. Send each one a list of the buttons you want, and ask him to let you know when he can provide any of them.

Many dealers also do business on an approval basis. They are willing to send a prospective customer a box or cards of buttons with a variety from which to choose. If you are new to a dealer, provide him with references and explain your price range and the type of buttons you are most interested in.

When buttons are sent to you on approval, it is only considerate to make your choice reasonably quickly. Promptly return the ones you do not want, wrapping them well and insuring them for their full value. If you want a dealer to send you approvals periodically, tell him so. At button collectors' gatherings, make yourself and your wants known to the dealers present. They seldom have all their stock with them, but they will fill specific requests by mail after they return home.

Gathering buttons for a collection can result in an unexpected bonus for the collector—introduce him to new places and friends, as well as bring him valuable treasures of beauty and historical significance. May your collecting experiences be as rewarding and memorable as mine have been. Good hunting!

Sally C. Luscomb

Southington, Connecticut
November, 1967

The Collector's Encyclopedia of Buttons

A

A. M. PEASLEY. Manufacturer of a fine grade of uniform and other metal buttons, in Boston, Massachusetts, from 1810 to the 1820's.

A. PLATT & COMPANY. Manufacturers of metal buttons, Waterbury, Connecticut, 1840's and 1850's.

ABALONE. A mollusk having one shell. Several species have been used in button making. The one most easily recognized has deep blue and green shades. This "green abalone," or "iridescent," as it is commonly called, has been used for buttons carved in cameo style, for finely carved buttons with gold paint added, and for buttons cut plain and polished. Other shells and other materials were sometimes applied or inlaid to decorate abalone buttons. It is possible to collect many styles of these buttons, all of them appealing because of the natural beauty of the material.

Pink or red abalone shell was also used in buttons. The outer layer of this variety has deep pink streaks, the depth of the color depending on how near the outer surface of the shell the button was cut. In older buttons, the streaks can be more plainly seen on the unpolished backs of the buttons. Frequently, tones of pale green and blue are shaded with the pink. This shell makes more delicately colored buttons than the green abalone.

Abalone buttons have been made for almost two hundred years. It is often difficult to date them. However, those with smooth backs are considered to have been made since 1900. Probably all the carved-cameo style and the more finely carved buttons were made before 1880.

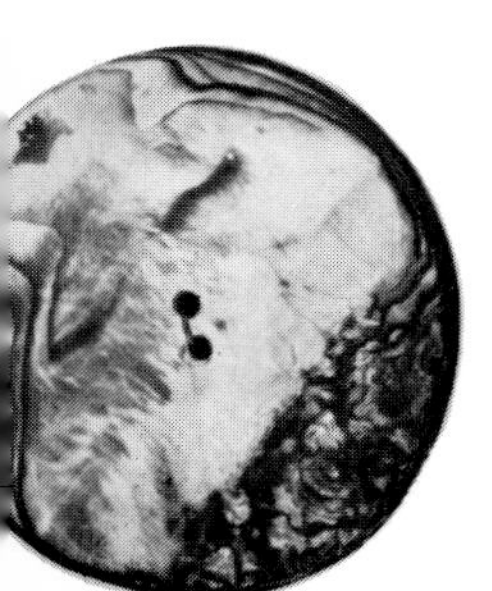

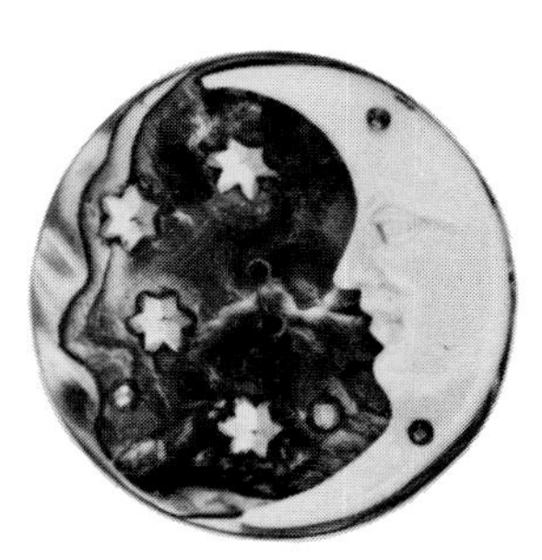

Abalone. (1) Plain; (2) applied mother-of-pearl shell design, cut steel trim; (3) cameo carved; (4) applied mother-of-pearl design, cut steel trim.

ACORN. This nut from oak trees has been used to make novelty buttons. Metal shanks were added to the whole nut, which often was varnished. The cup in which the acorn grows was sometimes filled with sealing wax, and a shank was added. Buttons of this material were made primarily for souvenirs rather than for garments.

ADAMS, GEORGE E. American author. He wrote, and privately published, *Stencils* in 1944, and (with Dorothy Foster Brown) co-authored *Backs of Buttons* in 1946. Many of his articles on Small Chinas have appeared in various publications.

ADAMS, JANE FORD. American author. With Lillian Smith Albert, co-author of *Button Sampler,* 1951, published by M. Barrows and Company, Inc. It was reprinted in 1966.

AGATE. A variegated chalcedony with colors arranged in bold concentric circular bands. These bands often followed the irregular outline of the cavity in which the silica was deposited. Buttons have been made of this material for at least three centuries. Most of those made in the eighteenth century were cut in disks and polished, with pin shanks applied; sometimes pieces of polished agate were used for centers in two-piece metal buttons of this period. In the nineteenth and twentieth centuries, pin shanks were still used, but the stone was also cut on the back for a shank plate to be inserted so the shank would not show on the front. Agate was also mounted in jewel-like settings for small buttons. The banded, or ribbon, agate found in buttons has stripes of several shades of gray or deep reddish-brown.

Moss agate is a translucent chalcedony containing color inclusions, most often green, arranged in moss-fern, leaf, or treelike patterns. Moss agate buttons are not so easy to find as those of banded or striped agate.

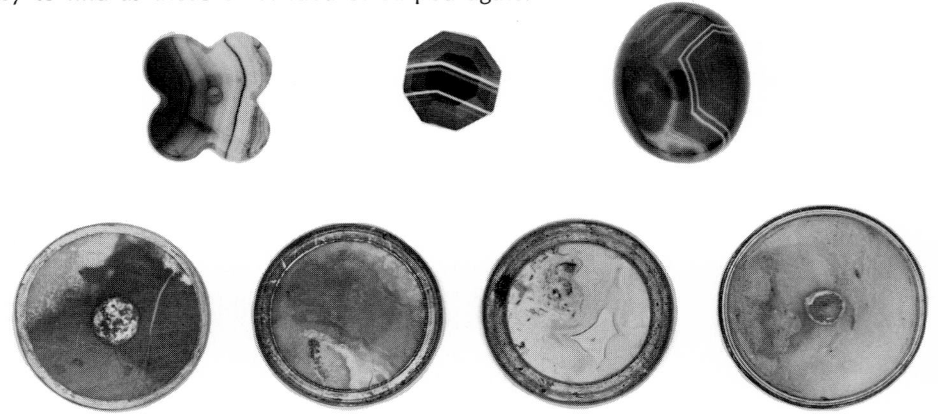

Agate. Top row shows nineteenth-century buttons. In the eighteenth-century buttons at the bottom, the agate is mounted in rims.

AIR CORPS. *See* Armed Forces.

ALBERT, A. H. American author of books on buttons. His *Washington Historical Buttons,* 1949; *Buttons of the Confederacy,* 1963; and *Political Campaign and Commemorative Buttons,* 1966, were all privately published.

ALBERT, LILLIAN SMITH. American author of books on buttons. She privately published *Button Collectors Journal,* 1941, and *Button Collectors Second Journal.* She co-authored the *Button Sampler* with Jane Adams, published by M. Barrows and Company, Inc., 1951, and *The Complete Button Book,* 1949, published by Doubleday & Company, Inc.

ALEMITE. Name of an auto lubricant. It appears on a large black composition overcoat button. On the other side is the slogan "When You Button Up Your Overcoat, Remember Your Car." In the fall of 1937, Alemite, a division of Stewart-Warner Corporation of Chicago, Illinois, sponsored Horace Heidt's Alemite Brigadiers on a national radio hookup. For their theme song, the Brigadiers sang the popular song "Button Up Your Overcoat." Though it is estimated that about 600,000 of the buttons were distributed as souvenirs in 1937, these buttons are seldom found.

Alemite. The front of the button is at the left, the back at the right.

ALLIEN, H. V., & COMPANY. *See* H. V. Allien & Company.

ALLOY. A mixture of two or more metals. Bronze is an alloy of copper and silver; steel is an alloy composed principally of iron. Brass, a combination of copper and zinc, is the most common alloy found in buttons.

ALPHA TYPE. A term used for one-piece buttons with a loop shank. The disks for these buttons were cast or handwrought. The loop shank of hand-drawn wire was brazed to the back. The shank ends were not bent, and so there was very little contact to the button. These buttons were made in the eighteenth century. *See* Omega Type for the improved method of applying shanks.

ALUMINUM. A metallic element refined from various natural ores, mostly from bauxite ore. It has a frosty gray tone. The first known buttons of this material were made in the latter part of the nineteenth century when the methods of processing aluminum were very expensive. Aluminum was then more costly than silver and gold. The early aluminum buttons were one- and two-piece, delicately stamped and chased. Some have been found with pearl background; others, with overlay pearl decorations. Another method of decorating aluminum buttons was to lacquer the disk in tortoiseshell colors, and engrave the lacquered surface to expose a design of aluminum.

In the twentieth century, a few uniform buttons were made of aluminum with stamped designs. Of these, lodge buttons were the most common. Aluminum buttons were made with hand-stamped designs by W. E. Harkness in the late 1940's; the patterns were similar to those found on American Indian silver buttons. In the 1950's, John Eutzy made aluminum buttons decorated by the sand-casting method *(which see).* Most aluminum buttons found by collectors were made in this country—perhaps all of them were. It is known that the Scovill Manufacturing Company made many of the handsome chased ones.

Aluminum buttons. Nineteenth century.

Aluminum buttons. Made by W. E. Harkness in the 1940's.

ALUMINUM STENCILS. A term used for an almost flat aluminum button having several coats of paint, enamel, or lacquer, with patterns similar to those on the ceramic buttons called China Stencils. A patent was granted in 1931 to Forrest G. Purinton, assigned to the Patent Button Company of Waterbury, Connecticut; it stated, ". . . to new and useful methods of improvements in ornamental buttons, and has for an object to provide a metal button that will simulate in appearance a glass or porcelain button but at the same time, will not crack or break if run through a mangle after same has been applied to a garment. Still another object is to provide a button made preferably of aluminum so that the same will be relatively light in weight. . . ."

These aluminum buttons with stenciled designs were made by the Patent Button Company in the 1930's. A base coat of "paint or enamel" in color was sprayed over the entire button, and baked. Then a stencil design of contrasting color was applied and baked. Finally, a coat of clear lacquer was sprayed on to protect the design. The colors used for the base and designs were black, blue, brown, cream, gold, green, lavender, orange, red, and white. Only about five patterns were used. All have two holes, and range in size from 5/16" to 7/8". Aluminum buttons made similarly to the stencils were also manufactured by this firm; they were covered with the same bright colors but had no stencil designs. Since the lacquer did not hold up well on any of these buttons, very few are found in good condition.

Aluminum stencils.
The sales card dates from the 1930's or 1940's.

AMASA J. GOODYEAR (also A. Goodyear & Son). American button makers, 1812–27. These names appear on both early pewter and one-piece gilt buttons. The buttons identified as being made by these men are extremely rare, especially the gilt ones. Little is known about the son who was in business with the senior Goodyear, but Amasa was the father of Charles and Nelson Goodyear of hard-rubber fame. It is quite likely these boys were apprentices in their father's button business many years before their experiments and success with rubber.

AMBER. A translucent to transparent fossil resin, ranging from yellows to browns. Not many buttons of this material have been found. Most are dome-shaped; some have faceted designs. Pin shanks or applied wire shanks were used.

AMERICAN BUTTON MANUFACTURING COMPANY. Makers of fancy metal buttons in Boston, Massachusetts, in the 1860's.

AMERICAN BUTTONISTS SOCIETY. Organized by a handful of men who were interested in digging artifacts at campsites. The society was organized in 1901, and their first regular meeting was held in New York City, February 15, 1902. The digging was under the direction of the New-York Historical Society, which received the best and the most of their findings. Why these men who enjoyed a few get-togethers and exchanged research findings chose "Buttonists" for their name is not known. They dug up and preserved as many bullets, buckles, hat pieces, and cooking utensils as buttons. Most of the few articles they kept for themselves have been scattered far and wide. A very few have been included in the Luis F. Emilio collection, now in the Essex Institute, Salem, Massachusetts.

AMERICAN POLITICAL ITEMS COLLECTORS. An organization formed in 1945 by five collectors. It was reorganized in Chicago, Illinois, during the 1960 Republican Convention, and plans were laid for an expanded and more active organization. The purpose of the organization is to elevate political Americana into its proper historical perspective. Although some members collect and preserve all mementos of political campaigns, such as torchlights, banners, cartoons, and so on, almost every member collects the buttons that were made to be sold or given away as souvenirs during campaigns. Membership is by invitation.

AMES SWORD COMPANY. An outgrowth of the Ames Manufacturing Company, founded in 1834 in Chicopee, Massachusetts. The Ames Sword Company was sold (1922–23) to the Lilley Company of Columbus, Ohio, manufacturers of regalia. Although to date there is no documented record of buttons in the long list of regalia items by the Ames Sword Company, the company name is found on the backs of buttons. This may mean that the buttons were made for them by another company.

AMETHYST. A transparent variety of crystalline quartz, ranging in color from pale violet to deep purple. Amethyst was used sparingly in button making; even glass of this color is not often found in buttons.

ANIMAL DESIGNS. Button designers have found animals, both domestic and wild, a popular subject. They have used almost every animal as a single figure on a button, or pictured them in natural surroundings. Since designers sometimes used their "artists' license," it is not always possible to know whether a given design is a boar or a pig. Though the rat seems a strange subject for a design for women's wear, rat designs can be found on glass, horn, and metal buttons. *See also* Livery; Mythological Designs; Picture Buttons; Story Buttons.

Animal designs. Nineteenth and early twentieth centuries, all metal.

ANTIQUARIANS. A term coined by David F. Johnson, a button authority and author of button books, for a glass button with a U-shank. A fault of this construction was that the glass dropped down between the ends of the U-shank and made sewing difficult; therefore, many of these buttons are found with the piece of glass broken off. These buttons of clear or opaque colored glass are usually small, with a slightly flat back and faceted front. They are considered among the oldest of glass buttons—the reason why Mr. Johnson named them "Antiquarians." An English glass consultant thought that they were probably made in the eighteenth century of Bristol glass. Some of the newer collectors have called the shanks "staples."

Antiquarians. Glass, nineteenth century.

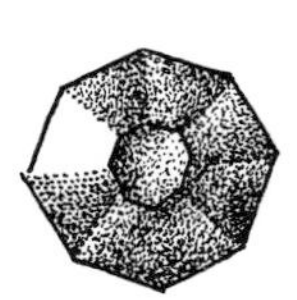

ARCHITECTURAL DESIGNS. Structures of all kinds have been pictured on buttons in the past four centuries. Button designers have missed hardly a building of any type, from doghouses to famous castles. Roman and Greek buildings and the ruins of buildings were often the subject of designs on the large handsome buttons used for men's wear in the

Architectural designs. A set of architectural-design buttons dating from the eighteenth century. The designs are painted on ivory, under the glass.

eighteenth century. Buildings were carved, molded, painted, printed, sketched, stamped, or transferred—on everything from paper to silk, iron to gold, plastic to glass, linoleum to ivory. Since button designers copied actual buildings, the buttons have historical significance for everyone and a special interest for architects. The designs include the Eiffel Tower, Statue of Liberty, Doge's Palace, Aeolian Bridge in Rome, the Tuileries, "Barnum's Folly," and many others. Some designers built "dream houses" such as "A Cabin on the Range" on button disks, and these are equally attractive to the button maker and the collector.

Architectural designs. The first and third buttons in the top row date from the eighteenth century and have the design painted under a glass face. All the others are nineteenth-century metal picture buttons.

ARISTOCRATS. A term coined by Mrs. Edith Fuoss, author of two books on black glass buttons. Aristocrats have a particular type of decoration on a flat polished surface. The design was incised on the mirror-like surface, and filled with either gold or silver. Silver or gold was then brushed on the main design—often, petals of flowers, leaves, hands, birds, or insects. When the outline was gold, the leaves were painted silver; when the outline was silver, the flat part of the design was painted gold. These designs were used on several sizes of black glass buttons. Aristocrats are considered rare; they are fairly difficult to find now.

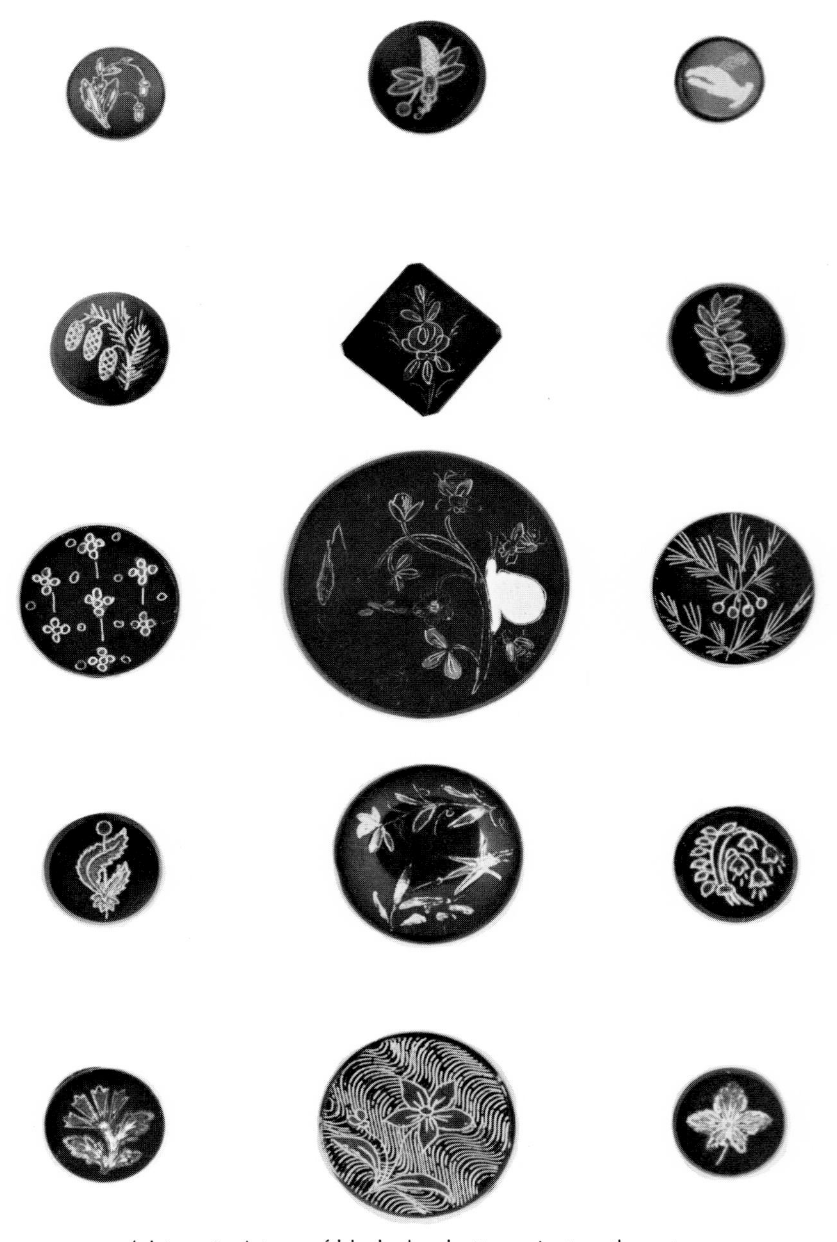

Aristocrats. A type of black glass button, nineteenth century.

ARITA PORCELAIN BUTTONS. Arita is a Japanese town, in the western part of Kyushu, famous for its pottery works dating from the end of the sixteenth century. In the 1960's fine porcelain buttons, called Arita porcelain, were brought to this country. Porcelains from this area were usually made in small family shops, and seldom exported; they were brought to this country by American shop owners and tourists, who were reluctant to tell their sources.

In the sixteenth century, a Korean potter at work in Japan discovered on Mount Izumi (in Hizan Province), a peculiar clay needed to reproduce particular porcelains of China. This "Hizan" ware, known also as Arita from the town of its manufacture, is now one of the finest wares in Japan.

Most Arita porcelain buttons have realistic shapes and self-shanks; a few Arita medallions have been put into metal mountings. The back markings have not been authentically identified.

Arita porcelain buttons. Twentieth century.

ARMED FORCES BUTTONS. Buttons made for uniforms of the various branches of the United States Armed Forces date from about the 1700's to the present. However, according to the Department of Defense, the Army, Navy, Marine Corps, National Guard, and their components were not officially designated as the "Armed Forces of the United States" until the National Security Act, effective July 26, 1947. Since that time, the Air Force has also become a separate branch of the service.

The Army, Navy, and Air Force each has a Secretary who serves under the Secretary of Defense. The Marine Corps is a branch of the Navy; the Coast Guard is directed by a Commandant who is under the Treasury Department. The National Guards are directed by the Governors of the individual states, except when called by the President; they are financially maintained by the United States Government. Today there are very few militias, and they hold mostly honorary positions—for example, the Foot Guards and Horse Guards in Connecticut. *See under* Armed Forces, Women's Army Auxiliary Corps.

The first American regiment (infantry), formed from a remnant of the Continental Army, which was disbanded November 2, 1783, consisted of eighty men and one officer. It constituted the entire "army" of the United States. At the same time the Massachusetts and New Hampshire Continental lines had been retained to take care of public property stored at several places, mainly at Fort Pitt and West Point.

In 1789, after much controversy, Congress agreed that there should be a peacetime army. There were to be eight companies of infantry and two companies of artillery. To raise these troops, quotas were assigned to four states in which it was considered troops might be needed. The six ranking officers who formed the General Staff were chosen from those states.

Very little has been learned about the uniform and buttons worn by these early companies. The best source of information is *Uniform Buttons, 1784-1948* by David F.

United States Army buttons. The first two rows at the top date from 1792 to the 1820's. Rows 3 and 4 are artillery buttons. Row 5 shows buttons belonging to dragoons and riflemen, and the bottom row contains militia buttons.

Johnson, published in 1948, which has been reprinted several times. Since that book was written, a group called Collectors of Historical Buttons has issued brochures of newly found, early uniform buttons. Mr. Johnson, in his book, emphasizes the need for more extensive research and cataloging.

United States Navy and Marines buttons. The buttons in the top row date from 1800 to the 1830's. Those in the middle row are from the 1830's and 1840's. The bottom shows Marines buttons of the 1800's.

United States Army buttons. From 1850 to the 1900's. Those in the top row with a "D" are from dragoons' uniforms; with an "R," from riflemen; the "V" on the last button stands for "Voltigeur." The first button in Row 2 is an engineer's; all the remainder in that row and the next are from other enlisted men. The first three buttons in the bottom row are post-1902; the last two are Air Force.

Early records of buttons ordered by the government for the various branches of service are very sketchy, and manufacturers' records are similarly scanty. Often, manufacturers get in touch with collectors to find buttons that they made in their early days, the back marks serving as the only means of identification. The descriptions of uniforms in most records merely state that the buttons were gold or silver, yellow or white metal. The sizes of the early uniform buttons varied, often by a fraction of an inch. In button books, a design will be listed as 22 mm., 23 mm., or 24 mm. (Approximately 25 mm. make an inch.) Back marks usually show that each size was made by a different manufacturer; the reason for the slight variation is not known.

The first Armed Forces buttons were one-piece, except for the very few metal-covered buttons that have been found (*see* Covered Type). The buttons excavated from early campsites are mostly pewter. About the earliest uniform buttons collectors can find, and identify, are the one-piece brass buttons made about 1800. Very often, back marks help to date a button, as in many cases the early manufacturers were in business only a short time. It was about 1830 before two-piece uniform buttons appeared, but since then all Armed Forces buttons have been made with at least two pieces; the slight variation in sizes continued for several years.

Often, collectors divide the early buttons of the Armed Forces into separate groups: Army buttons; Navy buttons; militias. (Since the militias formerly played a more significant role than they do today, there are many militia buttons.) The Army group of buttons includes those for the General Staff; the Staff Corps and Departments; the Artillery; the Light Infantry; the Infantry; the Mounted Troops, which included Dragoons, Rifles, Voltigeurs, Cavalry; the General Service; and minor arms. The Navy group of buttons includes Naval Officers, Chief Petty Officers; Sailors; the Marine Corps; the Coast Guard, and allied services. The third group consists of the militias of the several states.

United States Armed Forces buttons were made mostly in this country, but during wars they have been made in other countries; the names of the manufacturers serve to identify them. (See separate entries for the individual manufacturers' names.) All buttons were made according to government specifications. A distinguishing feature is the wire loop shank. There are also buttons with similar front devices but having self-shanks, which were made for the dress trade. These have sometimes been found on uniforms. Whether an unofficial button was put on by the uniform maker, or the serviceman replaced a lost button, is not known. During wars, uniforms influenced fashions and buttons for the dress trade, and the cheaper uniform-type buttons were made for women's and children's garments.

Women's Services Buttons. Most of these buttons were worn during World War II. Although women served in the Civil War and World War I, their number in the services was small until World War II; few buttons were made especially for women's uniforms until this time; soon these were changed to the same buttons worn by the men in similar services. *See also* Women's Land Army of America Buttons.

Marine Corps. During World War I, 305 women were enlisted in the Marines, but the group was disbanded in 1919. The Marine Corps Women's Reserves was established in 1943. It is now a permanent part of the Marines. Their buttons were the same as the men's.

Women's Air Force (WAF). The women wore the same buttons as the men. The WASP, Women's Air Force Service Pilots, was created in 1942 and discontinued in 1944. In 1948, women were permitted to join the Air Force. The buttons were the same as the Air Force buttons worn by men.

Women's Army Auxiliary Corps (WAAC). Created in 1942. The name was changed to Women's Army Corps (WAC) in 1943. It became part of the Regular Army in 1945.

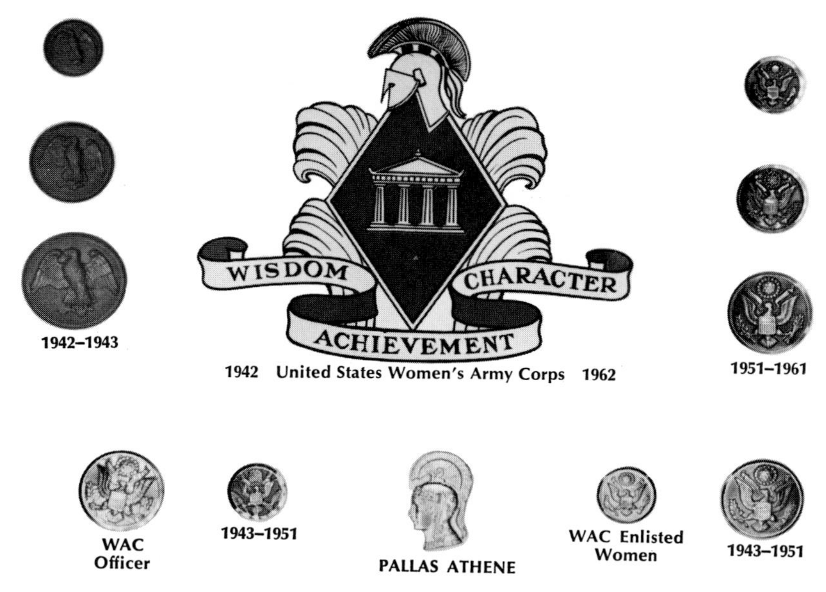

Women's Army Auxiliary Corps. 1942–62.

The WAAC wore light-brown plastic buttons with a raised eagle design. Before 1951, the WAC wore the regular buttons of the Army. From 1951 to 1961, the women wore a brass button darkened by an "antique" finish. In 1961, buttons for their new green Army uniform were changed to the regular polished brass buttons.

Women's Reserve of the United States Coast Guard (SPARS). Name taken from the Coast Guard motto, *Semper Paratus.* The Women's Reserve was organized in 1942, and disbanded in 1945. They wore the Coast Guard buttons on their uniforms.

Women's Reserve of the United States Navy. Called WAVES from the initial letters of Women's Accepted for Volunteer Emergency Service, this group was created in 1942. The Waves wore blue uniforms with blue plastic buttons bearing the raised eagle and anchor design; in hot weather they wore a white uniform with white plastic buttons, the same design as the blue. The Corps is now a permanent part of the Navy, and the women wear the regular metal Navy buttons.

ARMITAGE, GEORGE. Philadelphia, Pennsylvania, maker of stamped button blanks. He worked in the Philadelphia Arsenal from about 1800 into the 1830's. His name appears on buttons.

ARMY. *See* Armed Forces Buttons.

ARMY SPECIALIST CORPS BUTTONS. Plastic buttons made with an eagle insignia and the letters "A S C" at the top. They were originally designed and approved for the use of the Army Specialist Corps in the 1940's. This special corps was authorized by the Secretary of War "to do special duties in connection with the prosecution of the war, such as obtaining certain materials, developments, etc."

Some shipments of the buttons were made to certain colonels and also to the Philadelphia Quartermaster's Department, which had placed the contract. While the

Army Specialist Corps. 1940's.

buttons were in production, the contract was canceled, and the Army Specialist Corps was discontinued by authorization of the Secretary of War. The buttons, therefore, never came into common use on uniforms. The officers and members of the ASC were then inducted into the regular branches of the United States Army, and the buttons they wore from then on were the same as those of the United States Army.

The buttons were made in two sizes, one for sleeves and one for the coat front. Light brown and gray plastic were made for regular service, silver-plated plastic for officers. A dark-brown plastic button was made for a sample and submitted to the United States Government, but it was rejected for the self-rim style. All these buttons are extremely rare.

ART NOUVEAU. A style of art, popular mainly from the end of the nineteenth century to the beginning of the twentieth, characterized by flowing, curving, and interlacing lines. *Art nouveau* was a protest against the old styles. In contrast to the heavy, rigid, dark art of historicism, it offered a slender, supple design in light cool colors. *Art nouveau* flourished in London, New York, Vienna, Barcelona, Brussels, and Munich, each city contributing distinctive features to the style as a whole.

Art nouveau buttons in the style and from the period, usually of fine workmanship and quality materials, were generally of three main designs: nonpictorial, composed of interturning ribbon-like lines; pictorial, chiefly flowery portraits or stylized figures of women or sinuous flowers; and (in the later phase of *art nouveau*)abstract geometrical, the designs often of Celtic inspiration.

Many *art nouveau* buttons were made of hallmarked silver; numerous examples of these have been found in their original jewelers' boxes (commonly six matching buttons in a set), bearing the name of their source, often fine stores such as Tiffany's or Liberty's. The silver buttons are generally pictorial, with heads of women with long flowing hair that continues into flower or leaf design, or highly stylized figures of women in flowing toga-like gowns. Often the buttons are not circular, but of an irregular shape determined by the *art nouveau* rhythm of the border design. There were also many *art nouveau* buttons in enamel; these were commonly fluid flowers or leaves, set off by a typical serpentine line design.

As a result of the current vogue for *art nouveau* among designers and collectors, *art nouveau* buttons are often priced above their intrinsic value to a button collector.

ASHLEE COMPANY. New York button manufacturers, 1903–1950's. The Ashlee Company was the outgrowth of the button manufacturing firm Edgar S. Asch Company. In 1903, Asch Company, headed by O. S. Gundlach and Edgar Asch, took over part of the stock and fixtures of Steel & Taylor, a button firm established in the 1870's. After the death of Mr. Gundlach, Mr. Asch bought out his share and continued to employ his son, George Gundlach. In 1931, Mr. Asch retired, turning the business back to George Gundlach. In 1945, because of ill health, Mr. Gundlach turned the business over to his wife, Mrs. May Gundlach.

It was during Mrs. Gundlach's ownership, in the forties, at which time the firm had converted from button manufacture to jewelry engraving, that button dealers discovered that the Ashlee Company retained a leftover button stock from the E. S. Asch Company and the Steel & Taylor firm. Although some of the stock was finished buttons, most of it was unassembled parts. The dealers first purchased the leftover completed buttons, and then engaged the Ashlee Company to assemble, or create from the findings, finished buttons, often intermingling parts from the two companies. There has been controversy among collectors in classifying these newly assembled buttons because of their composite construction, as well as the discrepancy between the early date of the materials and the later date of their assembly.

ART NOUVEAU

Row 1, left to right: (1) brass, with a flower capping the head; flowing leaves form the border; (2) gunmetal-luster black glass, hatpin top, stylized cattails in the symmetric, architectonic *art nouveau* style; (3) brass, romantic portrait in irregular shape, bordered by curvilinear lines.

Row 2: four glass buttons that exemplify stylized flower designs with the stems and leaves flowing or interlacing to create the borders.

Row 3: (1) painted metal, flowers and twisting lines; (2) hallmarked silver; an excellent example of interweaving of hair, flowers, and leaves, their lines dictating the irregular shape; (3) hallmarked silver; classic portrait with stylized hair flowing into and forming the border shape; (4) hallmarked silver, from a boxed set of six, by Liberty & Co., London; has back stamp "Cymric" (meaning Celtic), a trademark used by Liberty on some *art nouveau* pieces; abstract geometric lines in a Celtic motif, including a turquoise stone.

Row 4: (1) enamel, painted flowers set off by a curvilinear design stamped in the base; (2) enamel, stylization of the peacock eye, a popular subject of *art nouveau* designs; (3) enamel, geometric design of interlacing lines stamped in the base; (4) glass, free-flowing organic design.

AUBURN BUTTON WORKS, INC. Button manufacturers in Auburn, New York—1876 to date—founded for the manufacture of pearl buttons. When plastic materials became available around the turn of the century, the Auburn Button Works switched to the manufacture of plastic buttons. First they made buttons of celluloid, then Bakelite *(which see)* and urea. They no longer manufacture buttons.

AVENTURINE. Usually referred to as goldstone. Aventurine was discovered by chance about 1810 and manufactured for a long period at the glassworks of Murano, Italy. The golden iridescence of the glass is caused by a crystalline separation of metallic copper from the mass, colored brown by peroxide of iron. The molten glass was allowed to cool slowly to facilitate the formation of crystals. Trapped air formed bubbles, which help to reveal the true character of the goldstone. Frequently, the polished surface of the finished product is pitted where the polishing cut through air bubbles.

About fifty years later (1858), a variety of quartz was discovered that was spangled throughout with minute scales of mica. It was named aventurine because of its similarity to the goldstone glass. The manufacturers' goldstone far exceeds the natural in brilliancy and in every desirable feature except hardness. There are no known buttons made of this quartz.

Buttons made of the manufactured goldstone have wire shanks or holes for sewing. Some jewel-type buttons have goldstone centers, and these buttons range from $^{3}/_{8}$" to $1^{1}/_{4}$". Goldstone has also been used as inlay in other glass buttons, and mixed with other glass in mottled and swirl designs.

B

B. BLUMENTHAL & COMPANY, INC. Wholesale importers and distributors of buttons, New York City, 1877 to date. August, Isaac, and Benjamin Blumenthal, three brothers, came to America in the 1840's to engage in the importation of "fancy goods," which included beads, bags, buttons, and cutlery.

In 1877, Benjamin Blumenthal and E. R. Blanchard, a Frenchman, established partnership in New York City. Although the infant button industry of New England was expanding, particularly the manufacture of cloth-covered metal buttons, the "carriage trade" of New York, Boston, Philadelphia, Baltimore, and the larger southern cities still looked to Paris for style. Annual buying trips to Europe were a necessity for the Blumenthal Company, to meet the needs of their growing list of customers.

In 1880, E. R. Blanchard withdrew from the partnership. Since that time members of the Blumenthal family have been partners of the concern. Benjamin Blumenthal retired in 1897.

In the past several years, a large share of the company's production has been designed by its own people in the New York offices. Their American product is exported to Europe as well as to South America, Africa, and the Near East. The importing of buttons dwindled as tremendous gains were made in domestic manufacture. The major exception is glass buttons. Although American glass factories have materials and facilities to manufacture buttons, the industrial and domestic demand for other glass products is so large and varied that there has been no serious effort to compete with the glass-button processes of Europe.

"LaMode" is the Blumenthal trade name found on many cards of their buttons. Sometimes the trade name for their finer buttons is molded on the back of the buttons.

In 1932, this concern opened up a new avenue for selling their less expensive buttons. Cards of their buttons bearing the trade name "Le Chic" were soon in every F. W. Woolworth Company chain store across the country. In these stores, early button collectors found the bright realistics sometimes called "goofies."

Buttons have been made for the Blumenthal firm in almost every button factory in this country, though Blumenthals have, at various times, maintained factories of their own.

B. SANDERS. (Father and son.) Inventors and button manufacturers of Birmingham, England, in the early nineteenth century. B. Sanders started a business in an unsubstantial way, and startled the button trade by introducing a covered button made of cloth and possessing a metal shank. His son, B. Sanders, Jr., improved the iron shank to make what is called the "flexible shank button." This was patented in 1825. A piece of canvas protruded through the back of the button, taking the place of the wire shank; a needle could pass freely through the canvas in any direction.

Later, came the application of Sanders' principle of making metal buttons: The upper blank was driven, by heavy pressure, into a die of hardened steel that gave it the desired shape and pattern; the under blank was similarly pressed in another die, which also "riveted" the shank into the plate. The two dies were then pressed together, and the button was complete except for the finishing. Buttons made in this manner, especially uniform buttons, are referred to as the Sanders type.

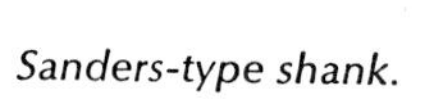
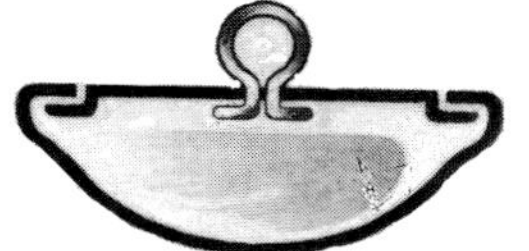

Sanders-type shank.

B. SCHWANDA & SONS, INC. Manufacturers and importers of buttons, 1882 to the present, Long Island, New York. The business originated in Czechoslovakia in 1882. In 1892, Benedict Schwanda emigrated to the United States with his family and two mechanics, bringing along three foot-power lathes. In 1894, he started the manufacture of ocean pearl buttons in New York City. New and improved power-driven lathes replaced the foot-power lathes about 1896.

In the early 1900's, Schwanda's two sons entered the firm as apprentices, gaining experience as the business expanded and improved. The firm's first manufacturing plant was built in Winfield Junction, New York, in 1902; subsequently, extensions were added. Branches were also established in Staffordsville, Connecticut, and Denton, Maryland, and a warehouse in Bohemia, Long Island. In 1903, the main plant, now the headquarters, was established in Long Island City, New York. It was during this period that Schwanda began importing other kinds of buttons from Czechoslovakia and the various major European button centers. In 1961, the partnership was incorporated, and the organization was put under family management.

In their early button-making days, the Schwandas made exquisitely carved shell buttons for the fancy and elaborate dress trade. After the turn of the century, their buttons were sold under the trade name "Buttons by Schwanda." By this time, their line included a full range of patterns, sizes, and colors in polyester, metals, Galalith (*which see*), rhinestones, vegetable ivory, horn, leather, black glass, opaques, and crystals.

BABINGTON, HELEN. Ceramist, Detroit, Michigan. In the 1940's, she made porcelain buttons, mostly in realistic shapes, usually with much gold.

BACK MARK. A term used for any stamping found on the back of buttons: words denoting quality, such as Extra Rich or Superfine; manufacturers' names; uniform makers;

stars, dots, eagles. The name of a known maker and recorded facts regarding his business career can be associated with contemporary activities and events to determine with reasonable accuracy just when a specific item was produced, and for what purpose. Even the lack of a back mark will often establish the period of use, since it was not until the early 1800's that button makers began to stamp firm names, trademarks, and other devices on backs. But there are exceptions to the helpfulness of back marks; sometimes the makers' names have been spelled incorrectly, or a motto does not seem to be related to the face die. *See also* Quality Marks; Registry Marks.

BACK MARKS

(1) One-piece plated General Army Button (1812), with motto on back. (2) Two-piece Engineer Corps button with name of maker on back. (3) Two-piece button (1850's–60's) with early state seal of Georgia. Back: "W. G. Mintzer, Phila." (4) Two-piece, Eagle—Infantry. Back is a possible die error; records show Young, Smith & Co. (5) A plain one-piece gilt button showing a political inscription on the back. (6) "H & T. Britannia Metal" could be a "back mark" on the front of a button. The back is flat and plain. (7) The name of the organization appears on the back of a plain-face two-piece button. (8) Front shows the bust of Dr. Phillippe Pinel, partially encircled by the name of the institution, St. Elizabeth's. Buttons of federal agencies and municipal departments often carry this type of marking. (9) British Registry Cipher. The face pattern is the British coat of arms with a garter bearing the words "The Royal Mail Packet Company." (10) Hallmark, unusual on uniform buttons. Face carries a design of four lances, with pennons crossed in pairs, separating "2" and the initials "B" and "L" (Bengal Lancers). (11) Gold-plated copper, two-piece, with floral face designs. Back has a dove, thistle, and "Victoria I." (12) The face offers no help in clarifying this strange back mark: "Secure Amidst Perils."

BACKGROUND. A contrasting material serving as a visual surface to better show off the design of a button. For example, in a button made of metal, there may be a thin layer of wood, or pearl, and on this a metal design; the wood or pearl piece is called the background. When the button has a pearl background, the collector sometimes refers to the button as a "Pearl Background" button.

Steel buttons. Shell supplies the background of these steel buttons, which have brass escutcheons.

BAILEY, GREEN & ELGER, INC. Wholesale importers and distributors, New York City, 1880's to date. Their trade name, B.G.E. Originals, may be found on sales cards and/or the backs of buttons.

BAKELITE. A synthetic plastic invented by Dr. Leo Hendrick Baekeland, between 1907 and 1909, a Belgian chemist living in America. The discovery of Bakelite is considered to have laid the real foundation of the synthetic plastics industry. It is a combination of carbolic acid, formaldehyde, and lye. Today, rather than referring only to a specific plastic, Bakelite is the trade name for the compounds sold by the Bakelite Corporation. Buttons found with the word "Bakelite" molded on the back are usually in plain and drab colors.

Bakelite buttons. Twentieth century. (1) A sew-thru with flower decoration. (2) Molded cameo-type head, with self-shank.

BALL & SOCKET MANUFACTURING COMPANY. Manufacturers of buttons and other fasteners, Cheshire, Connecticut, 1901 to date. In 1901, The Cheshire Manufacturing Company combined with Ball & Socket Fastener Company, Portsmouth, New Hampshire, adding snap fasteners (ball-and-socket type) to their line of buttons. In 1902, this firm merged with the Consolidated Fastener Company of Boston, Massachusetts, to form a new company known as the United States Fastener Company. The manufacture of ball-and-socket fasteners was taken over in 1919 by the Boston concern, and the Ball & Socket Manufacturing Company in Cheshire resumed button making.

BAMBOO. A grass that, when dry, is harder than oak and usually tan in color. One feature that distinguishes it is the porous ends. The designs on bamboo buttons are painted on or burned in with hot instruments. Bamboo has also been combined with plastic and celluloid to make buttons. As far as is known, all bamboo buttons have come from the Orient since 1900.

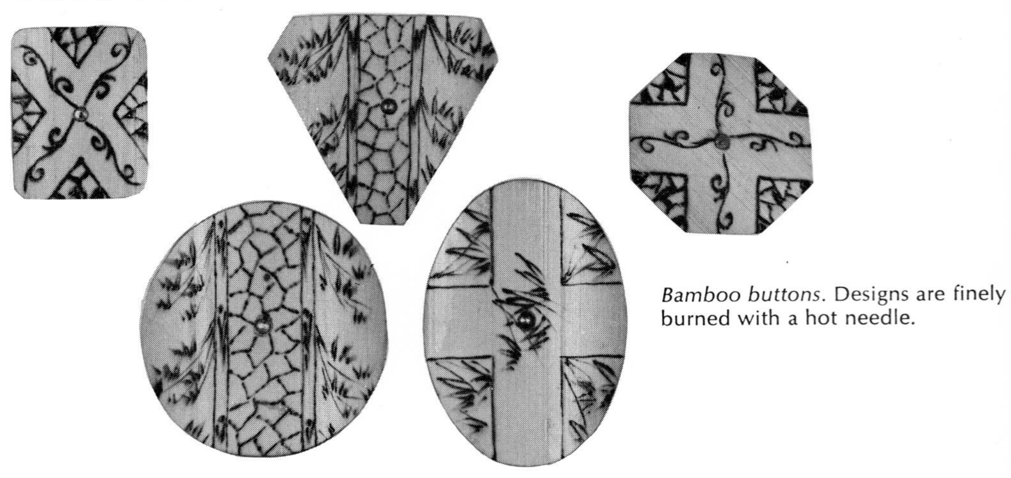

Bamboo buttons. Designs are finely burned with a hot needle.

BARK. The outside coat of wood or vegetable ivory nuts that has been left on as part of the decoration on buttons.

BAROQUES. *See* Pearls.

BASSE TAILLE. *See* Enamels, Enameling.

BASSOT, EMILE. He invented and received the patent in 1830 for the process of softening and molding hoof and horn.

BASSOT TYPE. Buttons named for Emile Bassot, molded from hoof or horn. They are distinguished by their embedded wire shanks, and often have stamped designs. Some are in the natural colors; a few were dyed in dark colors, but most were dyed black.

BATTERSEA. A town in England where a factory for making enameled articles was founded about 1750 by Theodore Janson. Many beautiful enamel pieces, often referred to as Battersea enamel, were made in this factory during its short existence. Records of the bankruptcy sale in 1856 listed buttons, and so buttons were evidently made there; but, to date, no buttons have been authentically credited to this firm.

BAUXITE. An ore named after a town in southern France, Les Baux, where one of the first deposits was found. Bauxite buttons were made for the tourist trade and brought to this country from Moengo, near the border of French Guiana. It is not known that any buttons were made of bauxite in the United States. Here, the principal bauxite producing states are Arkansas, Georgia, Tennessee, and Alabama.

Bauxite appears in shades of creamy pink to deep mahogany red; the natives of Moengo chose the prettiest pieces to make into buttons. The work was done with crude tools, files, saw blades, sandpaper, and powdered bauxite. All such buttons are thirty or more years old.

Bauxite buttons. (1) creamy pink with spots of red; (2) cream and red; (3) light red; (4) deep mahogany red.

BEADS. Beads of all materials have been used to decorate buttons. Sometimes they were sewed to fabric-covered buttons. In the eighteenth century the beadwork on buttons matched that on the coat.

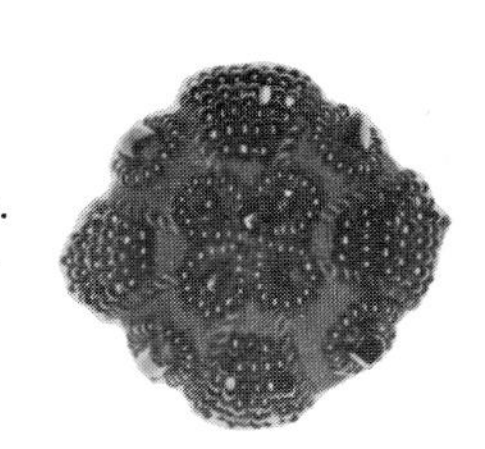

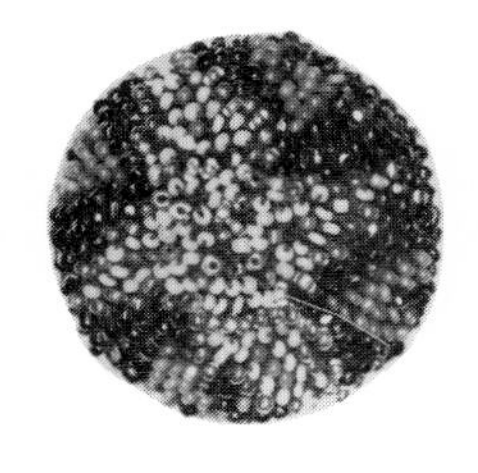

Beaded buttons. Nineteenth century. The beads were sewed to the fabric.

BEN L. STUDIO BUTTONS. Plastic buttons made by Benjamin Lang, Michigan, in the 1960's. The clear plastic buttons encased bright cutout pictures. The designs included such various subjects as religious themes, plant life, animals, and scenes.

Picture buttons. Plastic; twentieth century. Made by the Ben L. Studio.

BEN SILVER COMPANY. New York, 1900's. Most of the buttons made by this concern have stamped designs, the backgrounds being filled in with bright enamels. Of interest to collectors are the college blazer buttons sold in sets through college shops in the 1960's.

BENEDICT, AARON. American pewterer, made pewter buttons in 1812, and yellow metal (brass) buttons from 1823–29. "A. Benedict" is found on the backs of some of his one-piece buttons, though these are very scarce.

BENEDICT & BURNHAM. American manufacturers of brass buttons, 1834–43. The manufacturer's mark, "Benedict & Burnham," appears on one-piece buttons. The firm became the Waterbury Button Company.

BENEDICT & BURNHAM MANUFACTURING CO. American manufacturers of brass buttons, 1843–49. The back mark under this name appears on one-piece and two-piece buttons. The company became the Waterbury Button Company.

BENNETT, MARIE LA BARRE. American ceramist, 1952 to date. Mrs. Bennett made glass and ceramic articles for some years before she began making buttons. After becoming a button collector, she concentrated on the making of jasperware buttons. Since 1952, when she first showed her beautiful cameo-type buttons—"in the manner of Wedgwood," she called them—her buttons have become popular with collectors of buttons and collectors of jasperware. To prevent her buttons from becoming confused with the works of other makers of jasperware, Mrs. Bennett cut her initials, "M B," into the back of each of her buttons, sometimes including the date. Mrs. Bennett's buttons come in the popular shades of blue, as well as red, green, lavender, brown, white, and black, with white heads or figures; all the buttons have self-shanks. The cameo designs for her molded buttons include classic figures, and copies of Thorwaldsen's sculpture, Kate Greenaway's illustrations, and nineteenth-century picture buttons. The buttons range in size from an inch to two or more inches, and are usually round or oval. *See also* Jasperware.

Jasperware buttons. Twentieth century. Made by Marie La Barre Bennett.

"BENNINGTON" POTTERY. A term incorrectly used for pottery buttons having similar color and glaze to that of a particular ware made at Bennington Pottery (Vermont). The buttons of this ware known to date were made in Norwalk and Prospect, Connecticut. *See also* "Norwalk" Pottery Buttons.

BERRY TIP. A term used for the premolded glass tips fused to the top of round or cone-shaped glass buttons. The tips, mostly found on glass buttons that have a swirl back with wire shanks, resemble the ends of raspberries. They are usually molded of a contrasting color. *See also* Glass Buttons: Mechanical Makeup, Coronets.

BIAS SAWTOOTH. A term for Small China buttons that have tiny bias lines molded at the edge. *See also* Sawtooth Buttons; Small Chinas.

BICYCLE BUTTONS. Bicycles were used as designs on picture buttons made in various materials and techniques (*see* Transportation Designs). And bicycle makers were very generous with souvenir buttons advertising their product. The League of American Wheelman had buttons on which bicycle wheels formed the design. All these buttons were made in the late nineteenth and early twentieth centuries. Wheelman's League buttons were made in all metal, and enameled.

Enameled button.
The League of American Wheelmen.

Souvenir bicycle buttons. Nineteenth and twentieth centuries.

BIDDERY METAL. An alloy of copper, zinc, lead, and sometimes a small portion of tin. This metal resembles pewter. Since 1950, most of the buttons made of biddery metal have come from India. The Indian artists first cover the button disk with a velvety black finish. They decorate this by cutting a line design through the black surface, and then laying fine silver and gold wires into the lines. The gold and silver wires are pressed in by means of burnishing tools.

BIEBER, OTTO. Maker of clear plastic buttons containing real flower arrangements. The real flowers, arranged by Alma Wright, were enclosed in clear plastic with a metal shank embedded in the back. (A very few of the first ones had plastic shanks cemented on the back.) The plastic was guaranteed not to discolor, and was washable and heatproof. A few buttons were made with bright fishing flies enclosed. Bieber buttons were made in sizes from $3/4$" to $1\frac{1}{2}$". Mr. Bieber first put them on the market in 1948, but he produced them for only a relatively short period.

Clear plastic button.
This twentieth-century plastic button with real flowers was made by Otto Bieber.

BIRDCAGE. A term used for one of the Small Chinas. It is derived from the shank. Birdcage buttons are one of the two-piece all-china buttons. The back, made separately, is V-shaped; it has four holes and was fired into the front of the button, which was hollow. Some fronts are plain, but others have conventional designs, such as narrow or wide borders, insets of mottled china, or "piecrust" edges. The painted color trims are pink, blue, green, black, and brown. Birdcage buttons range in size from less than 1/2" to 3/4".

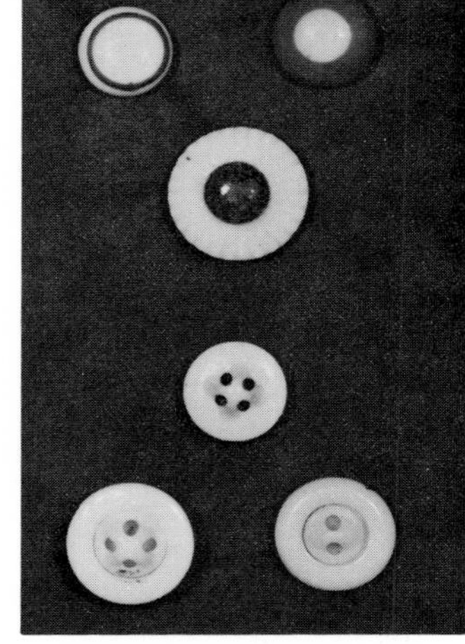

Birdcage. The buttons at the top are given in front view. The back views are at the bottom.

BIRDS. One of the most popular designs painted, transferred, inlaid, or carved on buttons, especially those made in the nineteenth and twentieth centuries. Birds can be found in the designs on buttons made of almost every material. Probably more than half the birds in these designs cannot be identified even with the keenest imagination.

Buttons with bird designs must have sold well: button boxes yield many with birds on them—buttons of all sizes, from those small enough to have been worn on the fronts of basques to large coat buttons. However, when the collector tries to find a robin, bluebird, or sparrow, if the design is not colored, classification may be impossible. The bird easiest to identify, and of enough variety in design to make a good showing, is probably the owl; peacocks might rate second among birds that can be identified on buttons.

BIRD'S EGG. A term for glass buttons that have a speckled overlay similar to a bird's eggs. The buttons, usually ball-shaped, have a swirl around the wire shank.

BLACK GLASS. *See* Glass Buttons.

"BLACK GLASS BUTTONS." The title of a book written by Mrs. Edith M. Fuoss and Mrs. Nora O. Jones in 1945. It was the first book written about the many types of these buttons, and was well illustrated. Now out of print.

"BLACK GLASS BUTTONS—RETURN ENGAGEMENT." A book written by Mrs. Edith Fuoss and Mrs. Caroline Smith in 1952. Although written with another co-author, this book was really a sequel to *Black Glass Buttons*. It too is now out of print.

BLACKOUT BUTTONS. These buttons, made in England to be worn during air raids, looked like ordinary white cloth buttons, but they would radiate light in darkness. They were sold on cards of two that specified one was for the lapel and one to be worn on the back. Large letters on the card were A.R.P., which meant Air Raid Prevention.

BLOOD BUTTONS. Although the difference between buttons made of blood and those made of other compositions cannot be noted, some collectors persist in using the name. Patents were granted in 1879 and 1880 to William Niles of New Jersey and Wilford

Palmer of New York for the manufacture of articles, including buttons, made of blood and other materials, but no buttons are authenticated as made by them.

BLOWN GLASS. *See* Glass Buttons.

BLUMENTHAL, B., & COMPANY, INC. *See* B. Blumenthal & Company.

BOAT DESIGNS. *See* Transportation Buttons; Transportation Designs.

BOEPPLE, J. F. The first person in the United States engaged in the manufacture of buttons made from the shells of freshwater mussels. In 1887, Mr. Boepple, who formerly had been engaged in a similar business in Hamburg, Germany, settled in Muscatine, Iowa. In 1891, he began the manufacture of buttons from shells found along the Mississippi River in the Muscatine area. Buttons are still manufactured in Muscatine, Iowa.

BOGATAY, PAUL. American ceramist and sculptor. In addition to his sculpture, in the 1940's he made a few pottery buttons, mostly realistic head designs, heavily glazed.

BOGWOOD. The wood of oak or pine trees that has been preserved in bogs for centuries. Bogwood is found mostly in England and Ireland. The designs on bogwood buttons and jewelry indicate that most of the pieces came from Ireland and were made in the nineteenth century. The few extant bogwood buttons have carved fronts and plain backs with metal shanks. (Pieces of bogwood jewelry are found most commonly; the bracelet pieces, which were made to be strung on round elastic, are sometimes mistaken for garment trimmings.) The most common design was shamrock leaves, intricately carved. Also popular were castles, doorways, and gates. All have a soft black finish.

BONE. That used for buttons usually came from cattle. It was boiled, cleaned, and cut into lengthwise slabs from which disks were cut in varying sizes. Many bone buttons were strictly utilitarian, such as underwear and trouser buttons; however, there were beautifully carved and inlaid examples. Most of the utilitarian and sew-thru's with two, three, four, or five holes were made during the past three centuries. Some of the eighteenth-century bone buttons have pinhead shanks with self-rims, frequently with a concentric design. A few have metal rims.

Carved and inlaid bone buttons have been made mostly since 1850. At the same time other bone buttons were decorated with transfers, metal escutcheons, or centers of various materials. Bone buttons from the East were carved with typical Oriental designs.

A few bone buttons were made in Alaska, mostly for the tourist trade. Many of these were shaped like a walrus. Others had finely cut line designs, which were filled with black pigments. This decoration resembled the native carving done in many countries—similar to, but distinctly different from, New England scrimshaw.

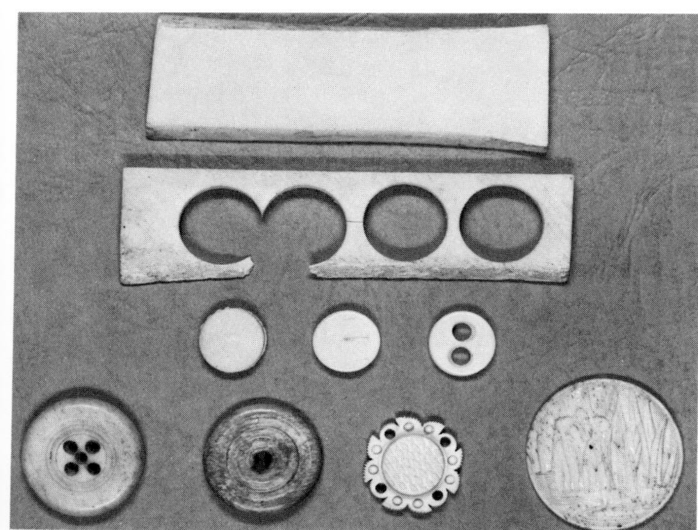

Bone. At the top is a cut slab of bone, followed by a similar slab from which button disks have been removed. The first two buttons at the bottom are eighteenth century; the two at the right are carved bone.

BOULTONS, The MATTHEW. Father and son, manufacturers, Birmingham, England. The Boultons' manufacturing was begun by the senior Matthew early in the 1700's; in 1745 the junior Matthew, at the age of seventeen, entered his father's business. When the son became of age, his father made him a partner. The elder was called a toymaker. In the eighteenth century, the term "toy" referred to such articles as trinkets, seals, tweezers, smelling bottles, inkwells, corkscrews, buckles, and buttons. The younger Matthew Boulton became an inventor of small articles made of pewter and silver, and the Boulton wealth came from these inventions. The Boultons' products included button settings for the well-known Wedgwood jasperware medallions.

BOX SHANK. This square hollow metal shank is also sometimes called a "square shank" or a "four-way shank." It is box-shaped, as its name suggests. The shank has a hole drilled or stamped through either two or four of its sides so that a needle and thread can be passed through the shank to attach the button to a garment. Box shanks are found only on buttons of molded materials such as glass, celluloid, and plastics.

Box shank. Metal, with four holes. Nineteenth and twentieth centuries.

BRACELET. A term used for the wire ring embedded in the top of glass buttons while the glass was soft. Sometimes the wire was twisted.

BRAND DESIGNS. These were originally made for the irons used to burn identification marks of ownership onto animals and articles. Apparently, the custom of imprinting designs by burning with hot iron began thousands of years before Christ. Old brand designs have been used to decorate twentieth-century metal and leather buttons.

Leather buttons. Twentieth century, with brand designs.

BRASS. More buttons have been made of this material than of any other. Although brass was used sparingly for buttons in this country before 1800, many brass buttons were made in Europe and sent here—on garments or in sets. Eighteenth-century brass buttons were mostly large and handsome, each dot and dash made by a single hand punch. Very few brass buttons of this period were small; most small ones were worn on the leg of the breeches, or sometimes on the waistcoat. At the turn of the eighteenth century fashion called for more brass buttons, although smaller ones, still one-piece with a loop shank. Soon after 1800, gold-plated brass buttons appeared. At first, they were one-piece; then, by 1830, the two-piece buttons appeared, and men continued to wear these until 1850.

Brass began to be used for uniform buttons in the United States about 1802. In the beginning, these were one-piece buttons; later, two-piece. Brass buttons have been made constantly since 1800.

"BRASS ROOTS." A book published by the Scovill Manufacturing Company, Inc., covering 150 years of craftsmanship in metals. It is a history of their company, dating from Abel Porter's humble beginning in making pewter buttons in Southington, Connecticut (1802), to their mass production of all kinds of brass articles, including buttons, in Waterbury, Connecticut, factories in 1952. *See* Scovill Manufacturing Company for additional information.

BRITANNIA METAL. An alloy introduced in England about 1770. The best grade was composed of 90 parts tin and 10 parts antimony. Just when buttons of Britannia were first made is not known. In appearance and grade, Britannia metal is very much like hard pewter. Unless a button has "Britannia" on it, it is impossible for a collector to tell accurately if it is made of the Britannia formula. The collector usually places all the early 1800's white alloy buttons in one group. *See* Pewter Buttons for more on these white alloy buttons.

BROCADE. A fabric woven with a raised design. For use on buttons, the designs were often woven in medallions, with space between them for cutting them into button covers. Although brocade-covered buttons were made in several colors, most of them were dark—brown, dark blue, and black. They were made with metal backs, and either wire shanks or flexible shanks, and ranged in size from $\frac{1}{2}$" to 1". Brocade buttons were made for several years after the 1850's.

Brocade buttons. A salesman's sample case.

BROOKS, EDITH and ALAN. Painters, England. They decorated opaque glass and white plastic buttons in 1960's. Their subjects were often children's toys, animals, flowers, or seasonal themes. Two sets of their buttons were accepted by Queen Elizabeth II as gifts for Prince Charles and Princess Anne. The set for Prince Charles had bright pictures of toys; the set for Princess Anne had various dainty flower designs. The buttons,

$^1/_2$" to $^3/_4$" in size, were decorated with fine camel's hair brushes; then a clear lacquer was added to make the design permanent. The Brookses primarily made paintings, and only occasionally decorated buttons. Brooks buttons were imported into this country by the button dealer Mrs. Marion Radosh.

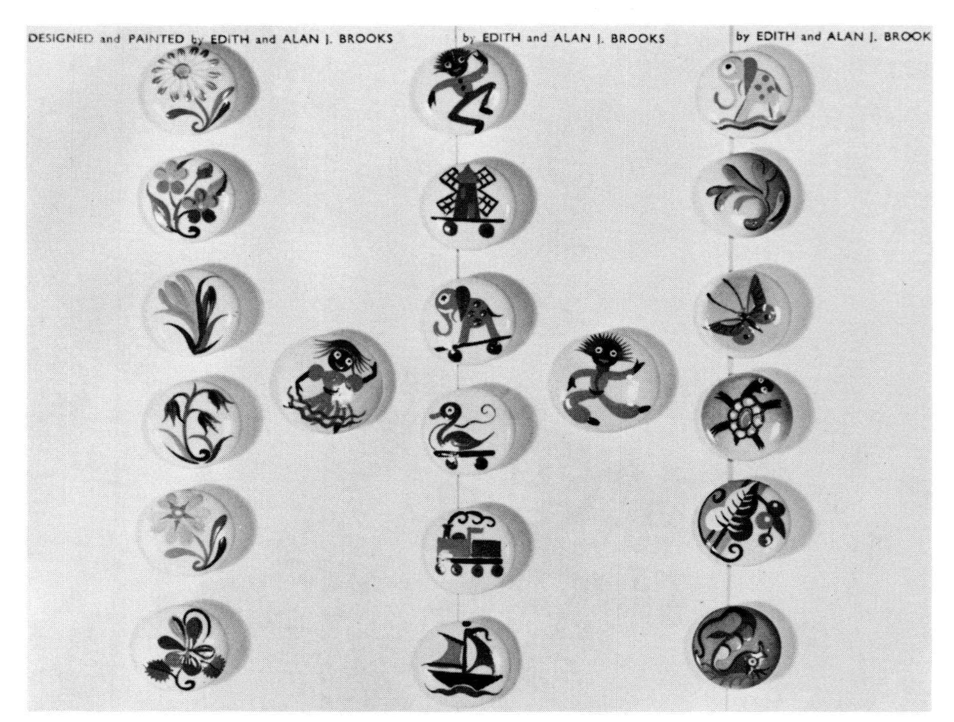

Plastic buttons. Designed and painted by Edith and Alan Brooks, in the 1960's.

BROWN, DOROTHY FOSTER. American author and columnist. Her book *Button Parade* was published in 1942 by the Lightner Publishing Co., and she co-authored and illustrated *Backs of Buttons* with George E. Adams, 1946. She has been the button columnist for *Hobbies* magazine since 1938.

BULLET. A term used for plain ball-like uniform buttons with a flat back and loop shank.

BULL'S-EYES. These are Small Chinas that have a white body with a colored design of concentric circles, a dome shape, flat or slightly rounded back, and a metal shank plate and wire shank. The pattern resembled the bull's-eye on a target. The circles were either fine lines, wide lines, or a combination of both. Occasionally two colors were used on one button; the usual colors were blue, green, lavender, yellow, pink, black, or brown. Bull's-eyes range in size from $^3/_8$" to $^3/_4$". Most of the patterns are scarce, and the largest ones are seldom found. These buttons have also been called "gaiter buttons." Although probably never worn on a gaiter, they do resemble gaiter buttons in shape and construction. *See also* Gaiter Buttons.

Bull's-eye chinas. Nineteenth century.

 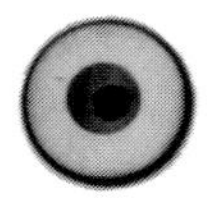   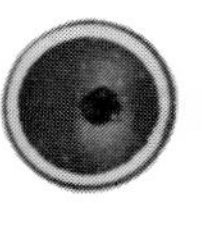  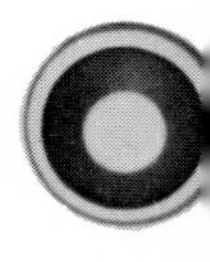

BURWOOD. A trade name given to a wood product made by the Burwood Products Company of Traverse City, Michigan. Many small articles, including buttons, were made of this material, but the firm discontinued the making of the buttons and buckles in 1937. Burwood, a cold-molded plastic material, was developed about 1920 by a group of men interested in the furniture business. At that time, carved wood overlays were very popular on furniture, and these men sought a means of making a plastic material from fibrous ingredients that would simulate wood and stand up as well as genuine wood carving. Wood pulp was used as the base, to which was added flour, rosin oil, some color, and an ingredient they called "lithopone." The mixture flowed with comparative ease into molds. It was then baked for a number of hours, and became very rigid.

Burwood buttons have a brownish color when new, but many lose their original shiny finish. Their designs include boats, dogs, flowers, and conventionals (*which see*). They range in size from 3/4" to almost 2".

Burwood. Twentieth-century buttons made of a wood-pulp composition known as Burwood.

BUSTLE BUTTONS. Froglike ornaments that were used on the bustle of a dress or on the tails of a lady's suit. The buttons were covered with fabric or braid. They were sewed on as a double row of trim, the buttons in one row having loops that hooked over the buttons in the other row.

"BUTTON CLASSICS." A book written by L. Erwina Couse and Marguerite M. Maple, in 1941; now out of print. The book has full pages of pictures, mostly pictorial buttons of different materials, with each button being described on the opposite page.

"BUTTON COLLECTING." The first book written for button collectors after the early organizations were founded, 1939. It was written by Polly deSteiger Crummett, and is out of print.

"BUTTON COLLECTOR'S HISTORY." A book written by Grace Horney Ford, 1943. This book gives much button history of interest to collectors. It contains information on the materials and crafts used in making buttons, and tells when and how many of the early buttons were worn. It was privately published, and is now out of print.

"BUTTON COLLECTOR'S JOURNAL, The." A book written by Lillian Smith Albert, 1941. As the title indicates, it was written as a journal—a collector's records of her activities, the places she visited and the buttons she saw, the bits of information she accumulated. It is now out of print.

BUTTON COLLECTORS' ORGANIZATIONS. The first to organize in the United States was the National Button Society in 1939 at Chicago, Illinois. It was fostered by the show manager O. C. Lightner, who gathered a few interested dealers and collectors together at an antiques and hobbies show in Chicago. Its membership was at once opened to any button collector, dealer, museum, manufacturing company, library, and so on, in the world. Still in existence, it is the largest button organization, and holds annual conventions and shows in different sections of the country. Since 1940, when societies were formed in Indiana and Michigan, state and local clubs have come into being all over the country. Some states have as many as fifteen small clubs. There is no official affiliation between the organizations; none have headquarters or permanent addresses.

These organizations present programs and displays at their meetings, and some publish bulletins. Your local public library or museum is the best source of information on the organizations nearest you.

"BUTTON COLLECTOR'S SECOND JOURNAL." A book written by Lillian Smith Albert, 1941. Like her first book, *The Button Collector's Journal,* it is a record of visits and buttons.

"BUTTON HANDBOOK" AND SUPPLEMENTS. Books by Mrs. Florence Zacharie Nicholls, published between 1943 and 1949. The book and its three supplements have pages of button illustrations, each button numbered. On another page they are identified, and descriptions and prices given. All except Supplement III are out of print.

"BUTTON INDUSTRY, The." A book written by W. Unite Jones, Birmingham, England, 1924. This edition has been out of print since 1933. *The Button Industry* is the story of the early button industry in England, with some mention of American button making from the beginning of the eighteenth century. Though the book was reprinted in the United States (with permission of Mr. Jones's family) by Mrs. Edith Fuoss (Michigan, 1947), it is again out of print.

"BUTTON PARADE." A book written by Dorothy Foster Brown, 1942. Most of the illustrations were drawn by Miss Brown, who included conventional designs as well as pictorials in her book. The term "goofies" first appeared in this book.

BUTTON PRICES. *See* Values.

"BUTTON SAMPLER, The." A book by Lillian Smith Albert and Jane Ford Adams, 1951; reprinted in 1966. It was a small book, one of the series Collectors' Little Book Library. It contained brief paragraphs on many button subjects and numerous illustrations.

"BUTTON STRING, The." A book written by Thelma Shull, 1942. It is a pleasing story for juniors, written in prose and verse, about two children visiting Grandmother and being given an old button string that she had made many years before. Many buttons are pictured, and bits of history, stories, and information are mingled. Now out of print.

"BUTTONS ARE ART." A compilation of pictures with descriptions by Louise Huntington Jarvis. It was presented in two separate sections in loose-leaf form. The illustrations show buttons, and also copies of pictures that influenced many button designs. In some cases, the designs on the buttons shown are almost exact copies of paintings, sculpture, and architecture.

"BUTTONS OF THE CONFEDERACY." A book by Alphaeus H. Albert, 1963. It is a catalog of the Confederate buttons known at the time, each button illustrated and priced.

C

C.M.R. MANUFACTURING COMPANY. *See* Coin Buttons.

CABOCHON. An unfaceted cut stone, or piece of glass imitating stone, dome-shaped and polished. The back or base of the stone was usually left flat. The cabochon used in buttons is set in a metal mounting or has had a shank added to the flat back.

CAEN. Name found on the back of molded horn buttons, for Caen, France, the place where these buttons were made.

CALICO BUTTONS. These are china buttons with decorative patterns that are similar to, sometimes identical with, those on the cotton fabric called calico. Calico fabrics had very small designs, sometimes tiny flowers and leaves, often little geometric dot-and-line designs. Calico got its name from the fact that it was first brought to Europe in the seventeenth century from Calicut, India. In Europe, calico patterns were first printed on cloth by block printing; later, yards at a time were printed between rollers.

Calico cloth became very popular in America, and by the 1840's small china buttons were being made to match the fabrics. The designs on both fabric and buttons were either in a single color—pink, red, yellow, orange, green, blue, lavender, brown, black—or in a combination of colors. Nearly all the buttons had the colored design transferred onto a white-body button, though a very few had white designs on a colored body. Garments of calico with calico buttons were made for the whole family—baby, daughter son, mother, and father. There are stories that tell how Father went to market with potatoes and grain, and came home with a bolt of calico with calico buttons to match; then Mother proceeded to make clothes for everyone in the family.

The original cards of calico buttons that have been found indicate that the buttons were made abroad in both France and England. In America, Charles Cartledge & Co., of Greenpoint, Long Island, New York, first made calico buttons in July, 1848. About a hundred different patterns were manufactured by them before their pottery closed in 1856. Altogether, nearly 600 patterns have been found. Most calicoes have two, three, or four holes; a few have pin shanks, and some are rimmed, or mounted like jewels. They range in size from less than 1/4″ to 1 1/4″. In shape, they are identified as "dish," "saucer," or "inkwell."

Calicoes. The buttons in the top row are jeweled and rimmed. Row 2 shows buttons with dark bodies and white patterns. All the remaining buttons have white bodies and colored patterns.

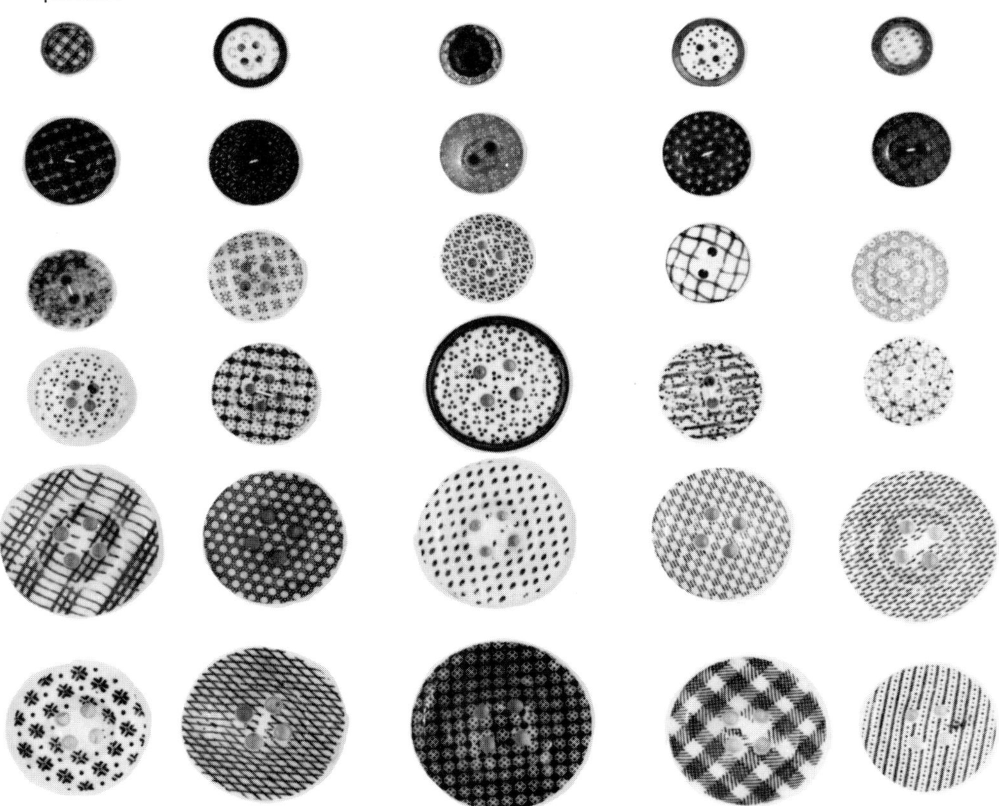

CAMEOS. A term sometimes broadly used by button collectors for buttons with cut or molded raised designs. Genuine cameos have a design produced by cutting away portions of the upper layers of stone or shell and leaving an underlayer as a background. According to a definition jointly prepared by the National Better Business Bureau and the American Gem Society some years ago, it was suggested that cameos should be distinguished as stone cameos or shell cameos. If the cameos are molded or pressed, they should be described as such; for example, one molded of glass should be called a glass cameo, molded cameo, or imitation cameo.

Shell buttons with cameo designs are frequently found; shell cameos also were mounted. The designs on shell buttons are mostly heads, scenes, or small figures. These cameos are generally intricately carved. Sometimes the artist cut his design into the light layer of shell, leaving the dark layer for the background; or he cut a dark design on a light background. The background of some shell cameos has a finely incised design filled with "gold." Shell cameos mounted like gems have prong settings, or a band with a row of cut steel for a border. These shell buttons were made in the nineteenth century. Only a few stone cameo buttons have been found.

Molded glass or composition buttons with head designs are sometimes called "cameos." The glass ones were made in the nineteenth and twentieth centuries, but the composition cameos, including those of plastic, were made in the twentieth century.

Shell cameos. Nineteenth century.

CAMPAIGN BUTTONS. These are made to publicize candidates for governmental office. Though they were originally made for presidential candidates only, later they appeared for senators, governors, and others as well.

At first, campaign buttons were made like men's garment buttons of the day—one-piece and two-piece brass buttons with loop shanks. A few were made of horn or rubber, with stamped or molded designs. Those with heads, with or without names, are easily identified. Those with pictures of log cabins are sometimes taken to be Lincoln campaign buttons; but all the log cabins, with or without cider barrels, flagpoles, men, or garden tools, must be credited to the campaign of William Harrison. To date, over fifty varieties of these are known.

When ferrotypes came into vogue, campaign buttons began to appear bearing the candidate's picture. Then came photography, followed by bright paint on metal or celluloid. Now, almost all campaign buttons are made of celluloid, and are printed in bright colors, though a small proportion are transfer designs on metal.

The first change in construction was the use of long pins instead of shanks, suggesting that the buttons might be worn on the lapel or as a tiepin. Each election time found the pin shorter. At the same time the button became larger. Although all sizes are collectible, the smaller ones are most in demand.

Campaign buttons. Ferrotypes, photographic prints, celluloids—1860–1925. All have pins.

Campaign buttons. From 1840 to 1916. Among the various materials represented are brass, horn, vegetable ivory, and tintypes. All have metal loop shanks.

Presidential campaign buttons are the most sought after, but those depicting the successful candidates are by no means the most popular. Collectors are especially interested in buttons made for the second and third parties, dark horses, the losers, the running mates, and in buttons with pictures, mottoes, names. A collection of campaign buttons can become very large. Jugates, as the buttons with faces of both the presidential candidate and his running mate are called, are considered by many collectors as the choicest items of every election.

Button-like studs for the lapel were made very early. These have pictures, mottoes, or symbols like those on buttons with shanks and pins. They were mostly made of metal, porcelain, and composition. Many of them were thrown away by election night, and research shows that very few, perhaps none, were made for some candidates. There are none known from before Andrew Jackson's campaign.

CANE TRIM. Thin rods of glass (canes) were used to trim glass buttons. Sometimes pieces of the rods were placed in the overlay; sometimes a piece of the glass cane was twisted and laid on the top of a glass button. A cane might be either a single color of glass drawn out to any desired dimension, or several colors of glass fused together as one rod before being drawn thin enough to trim buttons. Cane was also used in making paperweight buttons. Usually, this cane was made up of more than one color. For paperweight buttons, the cane was broken off into pieces a quarter inch in length or shorter, and stood on end on the glass base of the button to form a design before the clear glass top was applied.

CARAMEL GLASS. A term used for the opaque glass that resembles brown-sugar caramel candy. Many buttons were made of this colored glass in the nineteenth and twentieth centuries, and all were molded with metal shanks or self-shanks. The designs were molded as the buttons were being made; some were then painted. A few glass buttons of this color were made in the twentieth century.

CARE OF BUTTONS. *See* Cleaning Buttons; *also* Storage.

CARNELIAN. A red stone that appeared in buttons, chiefly during the nineteenth century. Carnelians were set in jewel-type buttons or were cut to have a pinhead shank. In the twentieth century, lapidaries made some buttons of carnelian, mostly for the collector trade.

CARNIVAL GLASS. A recent term for the luster-trimmed black glass buttons made in the nineteenth century. "Carnival glass" is still a controversial term among button collectors because the buttons were made earlier than the glassware known as "carnival," and because there is a difference between the way the luster was used on buttons and on glassware. Most collectors of nineteenth-century buttons are reluctant to accept the term.

CARTLEDGE, CHARLES, & CO. *See* Calico Buttons.

CARTWHEEL. *See* Dorset Buttons.

CARVING. A method for decorating buttons by cutting into them with hand or machine tools. Carved designs are done in all degrees of depth, and are raised, gouged out, or finely outlined.

Carving can be found on some eighteenth-century buttons, mostly those made of pearl shell. In the nineteenth and twentieth centuries, it has been the means of decorating buttons of such materials as bone, coconut shell, horn, ivory, jet, pearl shell, stone, tortoiseshell, vegetable ivory, and a few plastics. Deep-sea shells lend themselves best for carving of colorful beauty because of their many layers of different shades, even contrasting colors. Carved designs appear on all types of buttons—those for men's and women's regular wear, sporting buttons, presidential commemoratives, and on others.

The idea of carved designs originated early, and they are found in many countries; but the art is seldom used today, though some intricate and beautiful pearl-shell buttons are still being carved by hand in Bethlehem.

Molded designs in glass, processed horn, compositions, and plastics—even though the edges are as sharp as though cut—should not be confused with carving.

CASED. A term borrowed from the glass industry and used by collectors to designate glass buttons that have an overlay of one glass on another. The "core" may be clear or opaque glass; the "casing" over it may also be either clear or opaque, and may be colored. Sometimes the finished button had a mold pressed against it while it was still warm, to produce a design. At other times the "casing" consisted of twisted threads of glass.

CASEIN. A substance derived from milk to which chemists added alkalis and formaldehyde to make a hard material; it was an early plastic. Frequently buttons molded of this plastic will be found with "casein" on the back. Though casein buttons are a 1900 product, they are still being produced in small quantities. They were made in black, white, and various colors.

CASH, J. & J., COMPANY. *See* J. J. Cash & Company.

CASSIDY, ETHEL B. American author. She wrote *Little Buttons*, 1943, and *Button Mounting Hand Book*, 1951, and co-authored *The Old Button Box*, 1951.

CAST, CASTING. Terms loosely applied to the process of molding metal buttons.

CATLINITE. A fine-grain clay, sometimes called "pipestone," from quarries near the present town of Pipestone, Minnesota. When freshly quarried it is very soft, but it hardens when dried. Its colors include gray, pink, yellowish red, red, deep red, and mottled shades. Buttons of this material frequently have Indian symbols painted on them; some have shallow carving done when the clay was soft. Probably all the buttons were made in the 1900's.

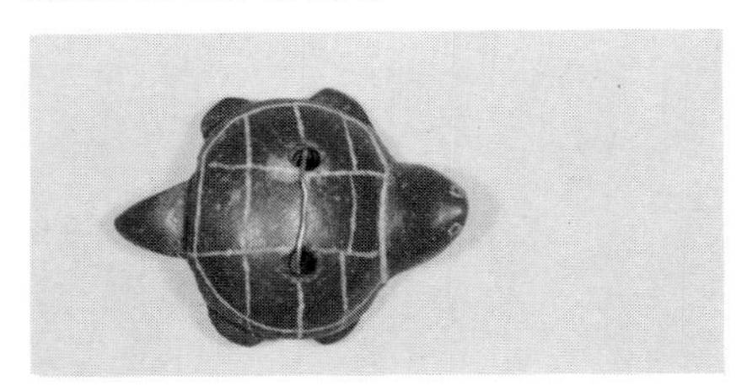

Catlinite (pipestone) button. Twentieth century.

CAT'S-EYE. A term applied to any gemstone or piece of deep-sea pearl having a sharp, well-defined light band or streak of light across the surface that moves as the material is turned about. The band resembles in shape the slit pupil of the cat.

CELLULOID. A material used in a variety of ways to make buttons. Some buttons are made entirely of celluloid; others have a thin covering of celluloid over metal molds, and in some cases it is used in combination with other materials.

Celluloid was discovered by John Wesley Hyatt in 1869. Its first use was to imitate tusk ivory, and buttons made at this early date are sometimes confused with those made of real ivory. To test this material, apply a low degree of heat, and the celluloid will produce a carbolic acid odor; this odor can sometimes be induced by rubbing the buttons until they are warm. A more definite test can be made by gently applying a hot needle.

Celluloid. One-piece molded celluloid buttons, twentieth century.

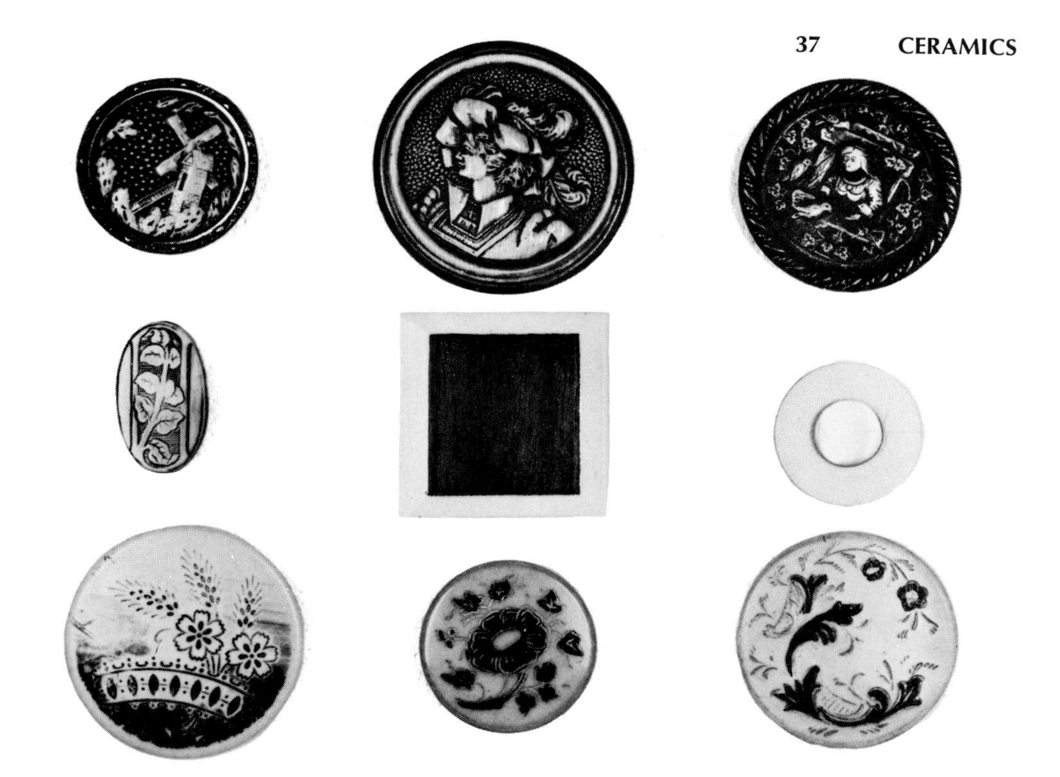

Celluloid. The nineteenth-century buttons in the top row have the design pressed into thin disks of celluloid, and are mounted in brass rims; backgrounds are tinted in black or brown. Row 2—twentieth-century solid celluloid buttons, the second with a wood center, the third with pearl. Row 3—nineteenth-century buttons made by covering metal molds with a thin sheet of celluloid; the designs are finely pressed, with color added.

Some solid celluloid buttons have a stamped design, incised or raised. Others have centers of pearl, wood, metal escutcheons, or jewel-like glass. The thin covering over metal fronts with metal backs usually has a stamped design, often with color added.

Buttons with thin celluloid centers and stamped raised designs are often erroneously called "Ivoroid." The designs for this type are always pictures stamped on thin disks. "Ivoroid" is a trade name for a celluloid made by one firm; it was never used to make buttons.

A type made since 1900 is a two-piece button with a front of thin celluloid through which a design on paper, pearl, or other material is visible.

Dyed celluloid has been used to imitate other materials when making buttons, such as tortoiseshell and colored glass, and celluloid was used instead of glass on some lithograph buttons.

"CENTURY OF CAMPAIGN BUTTONS, 1789–1889." A book compiled and published by J. Doyle DeWitt in 1959. It contains a descriptive list of buttons, medalets, tokens, ferrotypes, and lapel buttons relating to national political campaigns in the United States.

CERAMICS. Ceramic buttons have been found in the excavations of prehistoric tombs. This fact gives the collector an idea of the early date button making began, and the variety of materials and designs. It would seem that every potter in every country produced at least a few buttons, some crudely made and others made with skill and dexterity.

The same difficulty in identifying makers exists for ceramic buttons as for buttons of other materials. Potters' lists often did not specify buttons, though an item added at the end, "small articles," did include buttons. Hence, it is not always known when, or by whom, the early buttons were made, unless they have trade names or marks. Button designs, though, and/or the glaze, are often typical of famous potters, so that their names have become attached to certain buttons even without proof.

For more about the techniques that have been used in making particular ceramic buttons, and illustrations of buttons, *see* Coalport Works; Jasperware; "Norwalk" Pottery Buttons; Pewabic Pottery Company; Porcelain Buttons; Pottery Buttons; Prehistoric Buttons; Ruskin Pottery Buttons; Satsuma Ware; Sèvres Porcelain Buttons.

CHAMPLEVÉ. A type of enameling. *See* Enamels, Enameling.

CHARLES YALE. American manufacturer, 1830's.

CHARM STRINGS. Most of these long strings of buttons, sometimes called "memory strings," were made up by young ladies. The fad of making buttons strings started in the 1860's, according to the dates accompanying strings that have been found. It remained popular until 1900.

Varied and fanciful stories have come down with the charm string. One story is that each friend and member of the family had to add a button to the string, the very loveliest button he or she could find. There had to be a thousand buttons on the string before Prince Charming would come to claim his Lady Love. Unfortunately, very few of the strings reached the goal of one thousand. Many incomplete strings of buttons have been found, wrapped carefully in tissue, with the needle still there, as if the maker had gone on hoping to add another and then another button. It is unfortunate also for button collectors that these strings were not completed.

To start, a young woman would first tie a string to a large button, which has been called the "touch" button (although the term was never fully explained). Usually the strings contained only the very finest small glass and jewel buttons of their day. An original charm string of the late nineteenth century would have a quantity of very small and dainty glass buttons, sometimes including early paperweights, along with small metals of the same period. Many buttons have been taken off unfinished strings by collectors, and grouped with their other buttons of the same material and type. Charm strings with a thousand buttons (or even fewer) are seldom found today. Recently, button strings have been made to resemble the old ones.

CHASING. The extra handwork that was done with a burnishing tool after the design was struck. The "rework," as it has sometimes been called, added highlights and brilliancy to the design. It is not uncommon to find buttons with the same design, one having the stamped design only, and the other, additional chasing. The finest chasing on buttons was done on coined or struck "gilt" and "golden age" buttons made between 1820 and 1850. Chasing is sometimes found on uniform buttons, especially for the Armed Forces, and it is reasonable to assume that these were made for the officers. Although chasing was slow and expensive, it added to the beauty of the button.

CHESHIRE MANUFACTURING COMPANY. Manufacturers of buttons and combs, Cheshire, Connecticut, 1850–1901. They made dress and uniform buttons. In 1901, this company combined with the Ball and Socket Fastener Company under the name of Ball & Socket Manufacturing Company. Cheshire Manufacturing Company has sometimes been referred to as the Cheshire Button Company. A very few buttons carry the company's name on the back, although the company manufactured many buttons. *See* Ball & Socket Manufacturing Company for more on this firm.

CHINA. This term is used very little among button collectors except when they refer to Small Chinas; instead, "porcelain" and "pottery" are used to refer to most ceramic buttons. *See also* Small Chinas.

CHINA STENCILS. Collectors place these "stencils" in the Small China group. Their bright patterns resemble stenciling, although it is not known how they were decorated. The pattern of concentric rings could not have been stenciled. The body of these almost flat buttons is either white or cream, with two holes. Most of these so-called "stencils" are round; a few are modified squares. Nearly forty patterns have been found in black, two shades of blue, two shades of green, two shades of brown, lavender, pink, yellow, and metallic lusters. There is one pattern with a baby's face; the two holes for sewing make the eyes in the face. This has been found only on ivory-colored bodies.

Stencils range in size from 3/8" to 3/4". Their source and age are not definitely known, but no doubt all were made in the twentieth century. In the 1930's they were sold at button counters everywhere, in bags or on cards marked "Made in Czecho-Slovakia." For similar stencil patterns on aluminum, *see* Aluminum Stencils.

Small-china stencils. late 1800's.

CHRISTMAS DESIGNS and MOUNTINGS. Many designs pertaining to the Christmas season are found on buttons—manger scenes, the Holy Family, the Three Wise Men, shepherds, and a star, to name a few. Raphael's Sistine Madonna and the Cherubs have been separately copied on buttons. Collectors have added to the Christmas-design group by including Santa Claus, stars, holly, mistletoe, Christmas trees, wreaths, and other such representations.

Christmas wreath. A suggestion for mounting modern realistic buttons.

Special Christmas button arrangements can be made by including seasonal pictures. For example, buttons resembling toys can be mounted with a pasted-up colored picture of a Christmas tree.

CINNABAR. This is the name given to the only important ore of mercury. One of its uses is as a pigment. Lacquer and other materials colored with cinnabar vary from a bright to a brownish red in color. Buttons decorated with a putty-like substance colored with cinnabar are known as cinnabar. They have wood bases with self-shanks or metal bases with metal loop shanks.

The putty-like material is built up on the button base, then carved with fine tools. This soft material hardens as putty does, and when it has hardened, a "cinnabar" lacquer or varnish is applied to the whole button. In the case of recent buttons, this material often softens again, and therefore care should be taken not to place pressure on the buttons.

The carved designs include Oriental flowers, figures, and scenes. Similar buttons can be found with other colors—gray, green, brown, or black. Commercially, these are also known as cinnabar. Most such buttons came into this country after World War I, and bear the word "China" on the back.

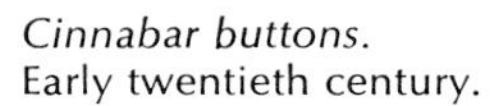

Cinnabar buttons.
Early twentieth century.

CIRCUS DESIGNS. Pictures influenced by old-time circuses appear on many buttons. Two modern sets that came in several colors, and sold six on a card for ten cents, were made for the dress trade about 1940; collectors call them Circus Sets I and II. In one of them, there are a clown, elephant, lion, polar bear, horse and rider, and an animal in a circus wagon, all shown in action. There is still another plastic set that collectors call Circus Act.

Among the nineteenth-century button designs were clowns, lion tamers, and animals that appeared to be in circus surroundings. These buttons, in several sizes, are among the metal pictorials. Original circus mountings have been made into attractive pictures for children's rooms.

CITY BUTTON WORKS. Button manufacturers, 1875–1955, New York and New Jersey. The original business was small and devoted entirely to the manufacturing of fabric-covered buttons. It grew rapidly, and in the eighties the firm started importing fabrics from Lyon, France, to use in making their buttons. In 1885 they began the manufacture of metal buttons, and were one of the first companies to make metal "picture" buttons in this country. They also produced the celluloid buttons with pins that were largely sold to cigar companies for giveaways.

From 1893 to 1895, the City Button Works was out of business. Then a new company was organized in New York, and in 1923 moved to New Jersey, where they remained until they sold out to the Cheshire Manufacturing Company in 1955, a Connecticut firm.

The military buttons made by the company, especially those for World War I, are about the only buttons on which their name appears.

CLEANING BUTTONS. A serious consideration of the many arts, crafts, and materials used in button making is almost imperative if the collector is to know how to clean buttons properly. Some buttons will stand real abuse, but others must be handled with "kid gloves." Therefore, the first step is to make every effort to learn all one can about the makeup of buttons.

More often than not, the real treasures found in old button boxes are buried among an accumulation of utilitarian buttons, garter pieces, thimbles, pins, nails, and dust. The dust can make even the most interesting buttons look dull and unappealing, and perhaps is one of the reasons the hobby of collecting buttons did not begin sooner. But this dust and grime has also often been a lifesaver because it acts like a protective coating. The damage is usually done when trying to bring a button back to its original brightness—by the wrong means. No set rule can be made for cleaning all buttons, nor even for cleaning all buttons made of the same material or by the same craft. Consequently, only a guide can be offered here, and caution must always be exercised in following the guide until experience confirms its recommendations.

Incidentally, collectors find it handy to keep most of their cleaning materials readily accessible in a small box. The contents should include such items as two toothbrushes, one with soft bristles, one with stiff bristles; a cloth moistened with furniture oil and wrapped in foil; a silver cloth; a can of metal polish; toothpicks; a piece or two of turkish toweling; a small glass jar, etc.

All-Metal Buttons. Paint was added to many metal buttons. Picture buttons frequently had paint (often brown) sprayed over them to harmonize with fabrics. Some uniform buttons were also sprayed with paint.

To clean such all-metal buttons, wipe them with a dry cloth; then rub them hard on a fabric like turkish toweling. This treatment will probably be enough for buttons covered with paint or lacquer.

Brass, copper, silver, or tombac buttons that appear to be only tarnished can be cleaned with a good metal polish. Dusty steel buttons will usually shine if rubbed with a soft cloth. Rust can be removed from steel buttons with a light abrasive such as an ink eraser, and kerosene can also be used, but the rust will return. Steel buttons must be continually guarded against it, and should be wiped occasionally to remove any moisture that may have gathered from the atmosphere or from the fingers.

If the original beauty of any metal button is not restored by the suggested treatment, ten to one it cannot be. If the specimen is a rare one, be satisfied to let it remain as found. More common specimens, particularly those in plentiful supply, can be used for further experimentation in cleaning and gaining experience.

Celluloid Buttons. The cleaning of this material depends greatly on how the button was made. If the button is solid celluloid, wipe it with a damp cloth, and the dirt will come off easily. Most of the stains or paints used on celluloid buttons are not permanent; they will take almost no moisture, if any. Celluloid used over metal molds will show any rust that collects under it, and therefore these buttons will have to be wiped off with very little moisture. The brown "facing" on celluloid buttons is from rust under the celluloid; it will often continue to spread.

Ceramic Buttons. Most ceramic buttons have baked or fused surfaces, and can be washed like other china or pottery. If there is any doubt, start with a moist cloth on the fingertip and gently rub the most inconspicuous spot on the button. If the design does not lift, it no doubt has been fired or baked. If the design can be lifted, then it is best to give up on the cleaning.

Enameled Buttons. The enameling on metal buttons is easily cleaned with a damp cloth. Any metal that shows will brighten with a light rub of silver polish. Wipe the whole button thoroughly dry after cleaning. Be careful not to confuse painted metal buttons with enameled ones; very often, the paint is brittle and will flake off easily. In fact, it is difficult to find painted buttons in good condition.

Fabric Buttons. Probably the dingiest buttons found are those covered with fabric. Included among them are buttons covered with threads of any sort. The very nature of the material causes them to gather dust and dirt. In most cases, fabric is not difficult to clean. However, never brush or rub fabric buttons even when the material seems strong; usually the threads are brittle and will break easily.

Pour some cleaning fluid into a glass jar, choosing the size of the jar and the amount of fluid according to the number of buttons to be cleaned. Put the buttons into the fluid and gently stir them around for a minute or two. Take them out, lay them on a soft, absorbent towel, and allow to dry—outdoors, if possible, since air hastens evaporation and dissipates the odor. Usually, other materials used as trim on fabric-covered buttons will not be harmed with this treatment, provided that trim like beads and metal pieces is attached by something other than cement. Buttons with the trim cemented on should merely be wiped with the cleaning fluid.

Glass Buttons. Buttons entirely of glass are probably among the easiest to clean. Warm, sudsy water will remove dust from them just as it does from other glass objects, though dirt in the deep cut and molded designs may need a little brushing. Glass buttons with cemented trim or unfired paint must not go into water. They sometimes can be wiped with a damp cloth, but the paint on most of them is very brittle and may wipe off. Glass designs fused to glass buttons become part of the whole, and buttons made by this technique can be treated the same as all-glass buttons.

Buttons with glass centers must be treated according to their mounting, but the glass center can always be safely wiped off with a damp cloth. There is one type of glass button that has to have special care—the kind with foil under the glass. On some of these, the overlay of clear glass is porous. Wipe the button carefully with an almost dry cloth, for water will damage the foil-like material.

Horn Buttons. Molded horn buttons with fine designs are often as full of dust as fabric buttons are. Rubbing them with a thin furniture oil on a heavy towel brightens them. Plain, polished natural-horn buttons need only wiping—any scratches on them are permanent. Carved natural-horn buttons may need only a good brushing.

Rubber Buttons. Clean these with a cloth dampened with water. A very soft brush can be used on the deeper designs without causing damage.

Shell Buttons. Many of the handsome shell buttons found in button boxes have been "tubbed to death"—abused with soapsuds. It is almost impossible to bring back the natural sheen and luster of this material, whether it is deep-sea or freshwater shell. Rubbing shell buttons back and forth across the heavy nap of a clean towel will remove the dust and a little of the chalky residue left by the soap. Occasionally, rubbing with the thumb will bring back the luster. Care must be taken of shell inserts when cleaning buttons of other materials.

Wood Buttons. Although wood buttons can usually be cleaned like furniture, special care must be given to any trim of other materials, and to cemented parts. It may be impossible to polish the metal trim on wooden buttons without spoiling the finish of the wood, and the trim can seldom be removed for cleaning. Trimmings such as inlaid materials may not take kindly to the use of wood polishes. Here, again, when a combination of materials is used, the several materials must be considered.

CLOISONNÉ. A type of enameling. *See* Enamels, Enameling.

COAL BUTTONS. Buttons made of anthracite coal in Pennsylvania have been produced

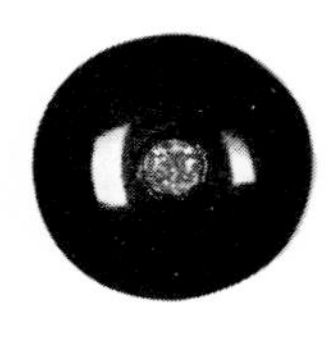

Coal buttons.
Made in the twentieth century.

in small quantities since the early 1950's. Coal takes a high polish, and the buttons are very attractive. Some have holes for sewing, but others have metal shanks.

COALPORT WORKS. A pottery in England, 1750 to date, founded by John Rose. Mr. Rose, who was apprenticed at the Caughley China Works, and then started a small business at Jackfield before moving to Coalport, made many improvements in the ceramic art. He purchased a number of potteries, including the Caughley China Works. The Coalport Works received medals for glazing, coloring, and flower painting. A few buttons have been found with Coalport markings on the backs. The marked ones found so far are believed to have been made since 1891.

Coalport porcelain button. It has bright flowers and a gold border. Nineteenth century.

COATS OF ARMS. *See* Livery Buttons.

COBB, J. HAROLD. American author who wrote and privately published (in 1963) *George Washington Inaugural Buttons and Medalets, 1789–1793.*

COCONUT SHELL. The hard shell of a palm-tree nut, which takes a very high polish, used in the making of buttons. After the fibrous coating of the nut has been removed, the fine cream-color spots left in the dark brown shell add to the natural beauty of the material. Buttons of this material are cut into round, oval, square, and realistic shapes, and then polished. A few are carved. Recently made coconut shell buttons often bear crudely painted designs; most of these were made for the tourist trade.

Carved coconut-shell button. Nineteenth century.

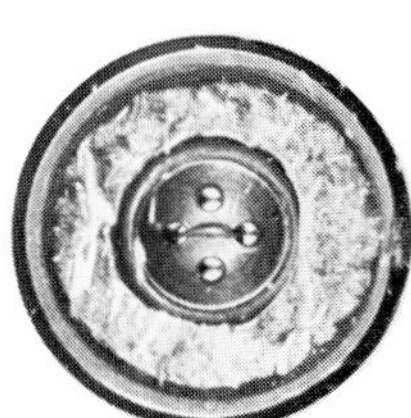

Carved coconut-shell buttons. These date from about 1900.

COIN BUTTONS. There were two types of coin buttons, those made of coins and those made with coin designs.

Many coins were made into buttons. The practice started very early, if the dates and the shanks are any criteria. The dates on some of the coins go back to the seventeenth century. The obverse (face) side of the large coins was not defaced; the heavy silver shank was soldered onto the reverse side. Coin buttons like this have been found with links and bar, a toggle arrangement. It is not possible to know how many had their links removed when link-type buttons went out of fashion, or if the links were removed so the button would have more appeal to collectors. Collectors find large coins with and without links and toggles.

The earliest of the coins used for buttons were foreign. Later in the nineteenth century, small silver United States coins were made into buttons for use on men's vests. On these, very often the obverse side was defaced and initials or monograms engraved. Some, it is said, were called "Freedom Buttons"—the buttons given to young men on their twenty-first birthday. In most cases, the dates on the coins have been removed, but records indicate they were made and worn in the first half of the nineteenth century.

Buttons with coin designs were made of several materials, including twentieth-century plastics. Most coin designs depict Roman and Greek coins. Some designs were molded in black glass and had bronze luster paint baked onto them, but most such designs on buttons were stamped or molded in metal.

Some American-made buttons had designs very closely resembling early United States gold coins. Although the front of these buttons was made of low-grade brass, the back of a cheaper white metal, and a loose shank was attached, the Connecticut manufacturer was forced to discontinue the pattern. Collectors have called them "forbidden money." These buttons were made in the nineteenth century, and are fairly rare.

From 1910 to 1915, the C. M. R. Manufacturing Company made buttons and jewelry from coins ranging from one cent to one-dollar pieces. They got into difficulty with the United States Government for defacing coins. Dies forced the heads through one side, and the shank or jewelry piece was applied to the other side. After striking, they were plated and sometimes filigree was added. The firm's trouble with the government was settled by a ruling that they were beautifying the coins, not mutilating them. However, the business was not successful and it closed about 1915. These buttons are extremely rare.

In 1939 and 1940, some coin-design buttons sold at button counters looked very similar to those made out of coins (described above). Actually, the heads were pressed through the front, but the back revealed that they were made of blanks with shanks added.

Coin buttons. Eighteenth century.

COINED. Coining is the method used in mints of striking designs in the coinage of money. No doubt this is the source of the term "coined" for buttons made by stamping the front and back at the same time, before the shank was attached. It is doubtful this technique was used for buttons before 1830. The entire design was first engraved on a tool or die. To strike in this way required a rather thick disk. One-piece "Early Gilt" and "Golden Age" buttons were stamped in this way.

COLD WATER ARMY. A temperance organization for juniors. To date, several pledge cards have been found, and two or three different buttons. The one-piece buttons are vest size. The date when the organization was formed is not definitely known, or when it was discontinued, but the dates on the pledge cards indicate it was active in the 1840's.

Cold Water Army buttons. They were worn on vests by the young boys belonging to this temperance organization.

Some collectors of campaign buttons include these buttons as representing the beginning of the Temperance Political Party. No data have been found to substantiate this belief.

COLE, LEONA STELLA. Ceramist, Illinois, 1940's–60's. Made porcelain buttons in several sizes, with transfer designs of scenes and heads. They frequently had gold numbers on the back.

Porcelain buttons: Leona Cole made these transfer-decorated buttons in the present century.

COLLECTORS OF HISTORICAL BUTTONS. Since 1954, collectors emphasizing historical buttons in their collections have been invited to meet at Just Buttons Museum, Southington, Connecticut, the last Saturday in April and the last Saturday in September. This group has published five brochures on unlisted uniform buttons. The first brochure, put out in 1954, contained revised prices on buttons listed in *Uniform Buttons* by David F. Johnson. The brochure is out of print. Then a series of brochures, "Unlisted Buttons" (Nos. I, II, and III), illustrated and numbered the buttons *not* in Mr. Johnson's book. The fifth brochure, "Backs of Military Buttons," was compiled by Mrs. Dorothy Lovell. The organization has a moderator and secretary-treasurer. Programs are arranged by the secretary. All collectors are invited to attend the meetings and to show, swap, and sell their historical buttons.

COLONIALS. A term used in the early days of button collecting for metal buttons made in the eighteenth century that were worn by men. Collectors usually referred only to buttons made of copper when using the term, which is seldom employed now.

COMMEMORATIVES. A term used for any button issued in commemoration of important persons or events. Since there are many of these buttons, a sizable collection could be made. Perhaps the earliest and most important commemorative is the one issued in 1889 commemorating George Washington's first inauguration.

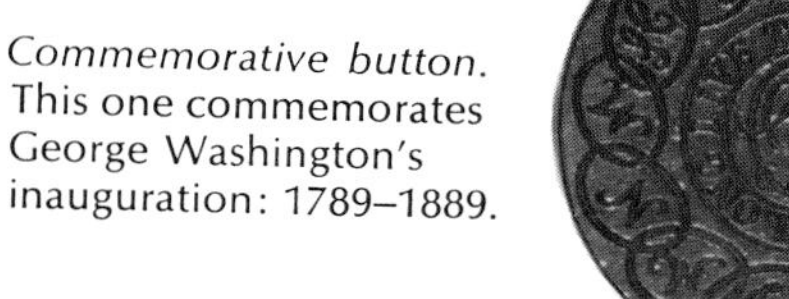

Commemorative button. This one commemorates George Washington's inauguration: 1789–1889.

COMPASS BUTTONS. *See* Locket Buttons.

"COMPLETE BUTTON BOOK." Co-authors Lillian Smith Albert and Kathryn Kent, 1949. It is out of print.

COMPOSITION. Any material made up of a mixture of substances. Many such mixtures have been used to make buttons, and the buttons themselves are often referred to as "compositions," regardless of the contents of the mixture. Composition buttons may be solid colors or a mixture of colors, even with metallic spots. Those containing metallic bits were called "flecks" in the early days of collecting. Composition buttons usually are molded, with holes or self-shanks.

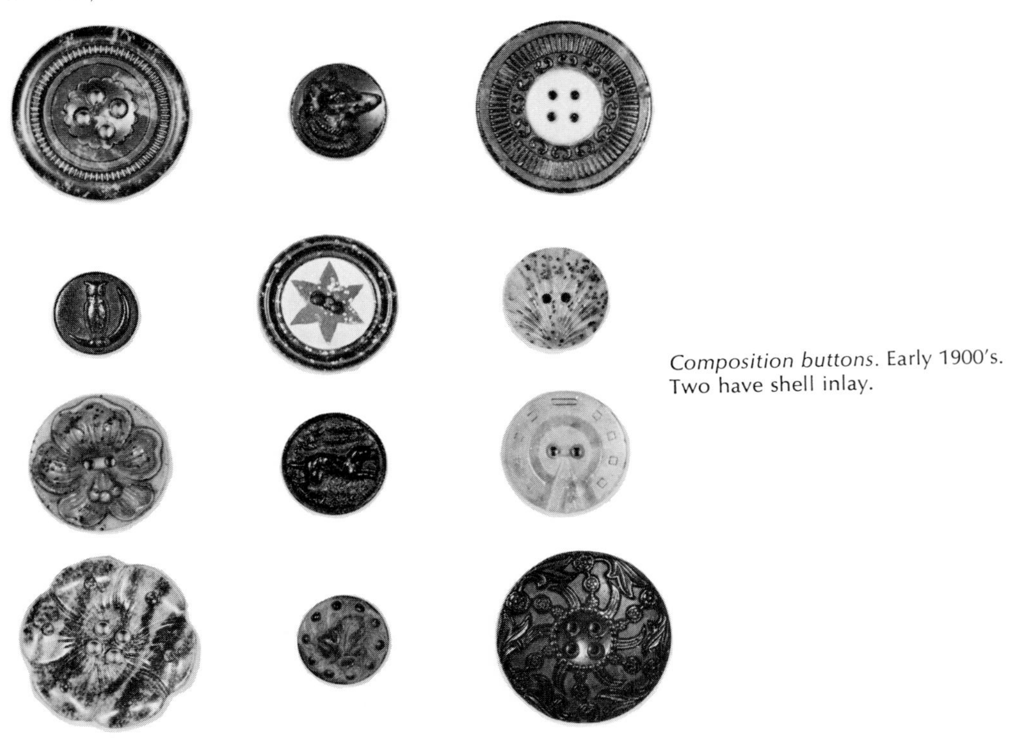

Composition buttons. Early 1900's. Two have shell inlay.

CONE SHANK. Some loop shanks have a buildup of metal, resembling a cone, around the base where the two ends have been inserted in the button. Cone shanks are commonly found on buttons made of tombac *(which see)*.

Cone shank.
Used in the eighteenth and nineteenth centuries.

CONFEDERATE BUTTONS. The uniform buttons worn by the troops of the Confederacy, 1861–65. Included are buttons worn by the General Staff, the Army of General Service, Artillery, Cavalry, Engineers, Infantry, Riflemen, Navy and Marine Corps, and the buttons worn by the men in the companies formed within the Confederate States. Some collectors include in this group buttons worn at southern military schools and by veterans' organizations.

Confederate buttons were made both by southern button manufacturers and by firms in Europe. After 1865, some buttons were copied for the use of veterans, and recently buttons have been struck from the old dies for the dress trade. Back marks are helpful in separating the originals from copies. The back mark "Superior Quality" may be the most confusing, since that mark was put on buttons made by a Connecticut manufacturer both at the time of the Civil War and, by the same firm, on buttons made with the same design since 1960.

Although the following list of back marks is not complete (a complete list would be impossible to make), it does include those most commonly found on Confederate buttons:

Southern:

Courtney & Tennent, Charleston, S.C.
Halfman & Taylor, Montgomery, Ala.
Hyde & Goodrich, New Orleans
E. M. Lewis & Co., Richmond
Mitchell & Tyler, Richmond
H. A. Myers, Richmond
C. Wendlinger, Richmond
Wildt & Son, Richmond

European:

S. Buckley & Co., Birmingham
C. & J., London
S. Isaacs Campbell & Company, London
W. Dowler, Birmingham
Firmin & Sons, London
P. & S. Firmin, London
G. & Company, Paris
J. R. Gaunt & Son, London
Hammond Turner & Bates, Manchester, England
S. & K., London
Smith Kemp & Wright, Birmingham
Smith & Wright, Birmingham, England
P. Tait & Company, Limerick, Ireland
Van Wart Son & Company, London

Confederate buttons. The top row contains General Service buttons. The first four buttons in the second row are Navy buttons. In the third through the fifth rows, the "A" stands for Artillery, the "R" for Riflemen, the "C" for Cavalry, the "E" for Engineers, and the "I" for Infantry.

There are also some crudely constructed Confederate buttons without back marks, coppery in color, which are considered handmade. Confederate uniform buttons were made with the initials I, C, E, or A in the center, mostly with plain fields. The eagle on the Confederate General Service buttons is quite different from the eagle on the United States buttons.

All the Confederate buttons are very rare, even in the southern states. In southern museums, Confederate uniforms can be seen with buttons made for the northern troops. Possibly these were taken from northern prisoners for use as replacements, and were sewed on during the war.

Confederate States buttons.
These were worn during the Civil War.

CONVENTIONALS. A term sometimes used for buttons with nonpictorial designs.

COPPER. A reddish metal used to make buttons for at least three centuries. In the eighteenth century, copper buttons had designs of hand-stamped dots and fine lines. Some had silver plating, some gilt plating; occasionally other materials were added for decoration, such as pearl, enamel, glass, or various metals. Since the eighteenth century, copper in the manufacture of buttons has been used mostly for making alloys, except in studios where handwrought metal buttons were made. When the copper content is very high, the button has the appearance of an all-copper button.

CORAL. A hard formation built up from the calcareous skeletons of tiny sea creatures, which has a distinctive pink shade all its own. Very few buttons were made of this material. The few that collectors find were made in the nineteenth and twentieth centuries, and were primarily sold in European shops set up for the tourist trade. Coral has more often been used to decorate buttons of other materials; for example, flowers made of coral and leaves of jade will be found set in ivory or tortoiseshell buttons.

CORALENE. *See* Glass Buttons.

CORK. The spongy outer layer of bark on a tree known as the cork oak. The bark is carefully removed and seasoned for a few days; then the cork sheets are boiled, and finally pressed. After reaching the factories, these slabs are softened by steaming before being sliced into strips. The manufacture of articles such as buttons involves waste. Cork "waste" is still valuable, however, and when ground has many uses. The better grades of ground cork are also used to make buttons.

Cork is found in three or more shades of brown. The warmth of tone, together with its delicately mottled and veined appearance, gives cork a distinctive charm.

Most cork buttons have been made in this century. Many of the buttons have metal or colored plastics added; and some metal and plastic buttons have been trimmed with cork. Cork buttons are not plentiful, even though they are only a few years old. *See* Linoleum for the further use of cork in button making.

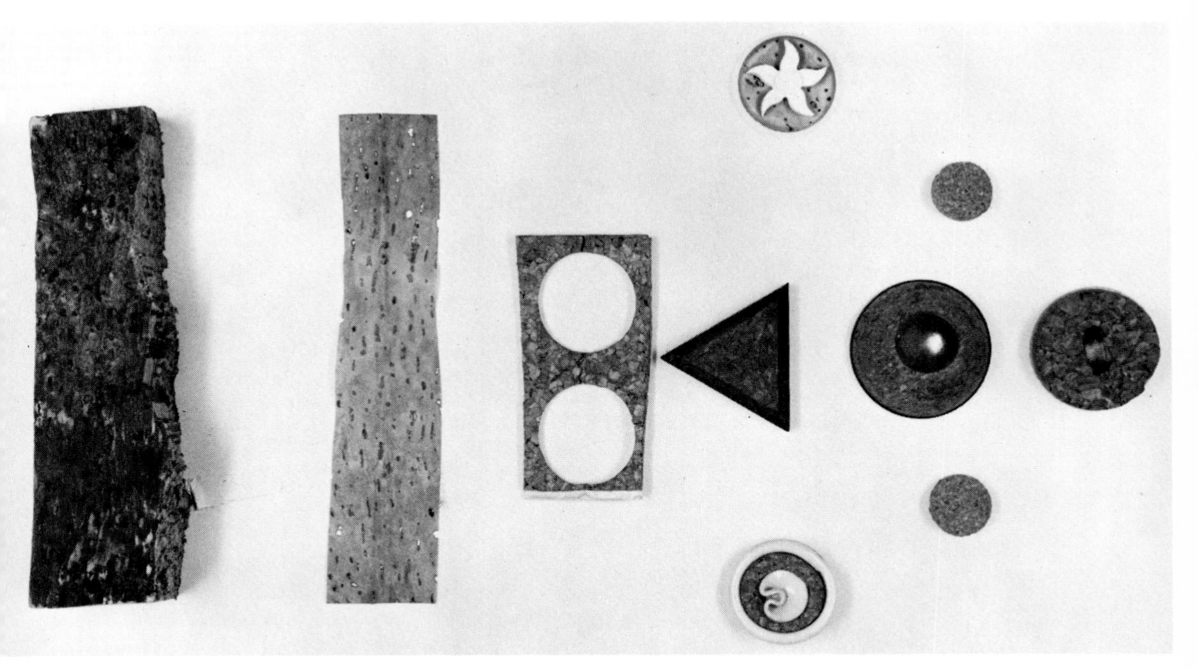

Cork. The material, and buttons made from it.

CORONETS. *See* Glass Buttons: Mechanical Makeup.

COROZO NUT. Used to make the buttons that are known to button manufacturers and collectors as Vegetable Ivory buttons. *See* Vegetable Ivory Buttons.

COUSE, L. ERWINA. Co-author of *Button Classics,* 1942—now out of print. Co-author of *Button Heritage,* 1967.

COVERED TYPE. A term applied primarily to those buttons having a metal cover over a cup-shaped wooden or bone mold. A shank was made by crisscrossing catgut on the outside of the mold and carrying the ends through the four holes in the mold. The ends of the catgut were securely tied in the hollow of the mold. Often the gut was reinforced with embroidery thread.

Another covered-type construction was called "faced type." This had a flat wood, bone, or ivory back with the catgut shank crisscrossed or in a square design. Faced-type buttons can also have a wire loop shank. Some faced types were made for American Revolutionary officers' uniforms; some were made with French and English military insignia. The thin metal covering, which usually had a stamped design, was rolled over the edge of the mold. These buttons were mostly made in the eighteenth century.

Collectors have gradually included, among the covered types, buttons made of a mold covered with other materials—metal or fabric. *See* Fabric-covered Buttons.

COWRIE SHELL. A white or cream-colored deep-sea shell, mottled with shades of brown. From among the 200 varieties of cowrie, the tiger cowrie is the one generally used for buttons. There are four layers to this shell, the outer one mottled, the next one a creamy white, then one in a raspberry color, and finally a pure white layer almost like opaque glass. Carvers have used all three inner layers for backgrounds of cameo designs. Disks cut from cowrie shell have been made into buttons with shanks, buttons with holes, or have been mounted in metal, like jewels. The cowrie shell disks in jewel-type buttons are sometimes as small as a half-inch, and have figures carved on them. Large cowrie shell buttons are, as a rule, not mounted.

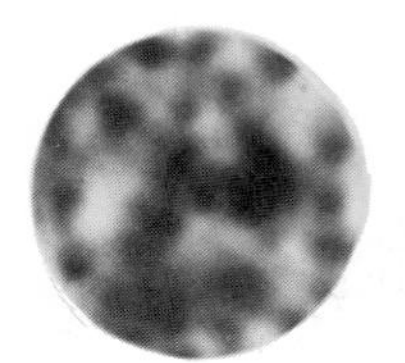

Cowrie shell buttons. (1) Metal-shank button shows outside layer only; (2) button carved through all the layers of shell; (3) the white inner layer makes the background of this shell disk mounted in metal; (4) the creamy layer makes the background of this sew-thru button; the much-mottled outside layer is used in the design; (5) a metal-shank button with the deep raspberry shade for background, the creamy-white layer for the face, and the mottled layer for the helmet.

CRACKLED GLASS. *See* Glass Buttons.

CRAPE STONE. (Sometimes spelled "Crepe.") A trade name for a kind of glass that was used in making buttons. This glass imitated crapestone, usually onyx, which was cut and grooved to imitate crepe fabric. The material, whether stone or glass, was used for mourning buttons and jewelry; both white and black glass were used. This design in glass first appeared in the 1880's. The buttons had metal shanks or metal shanks plates. They were not pretty, and few are found today.

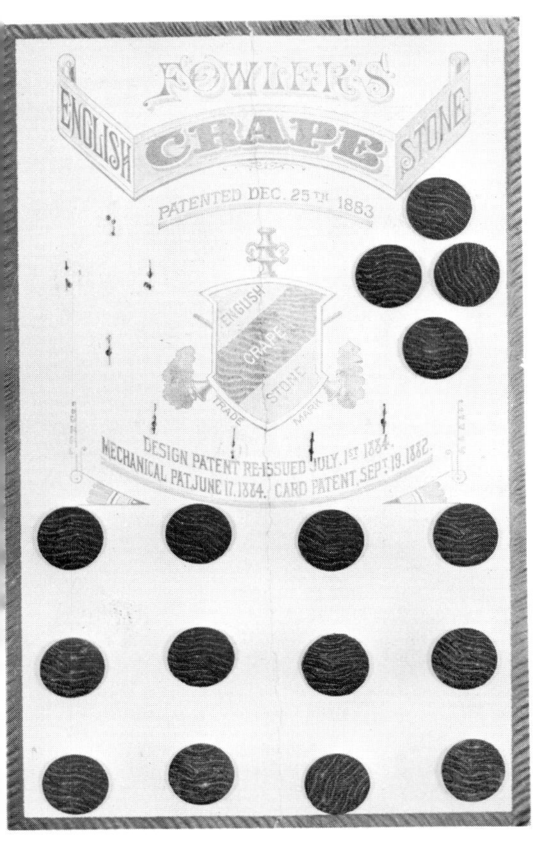

Crape Stone. A sales card of Crape Stone buttons from the 1880's.

CRESTS. *See* Livery Buttons.

CROCHET. A type of needlework made with a hook, sometimes used to cover buttons. At first it was made by hand, later by machine. "Caps" were crocheted, then placed over wooden molds that had first been covered with fine silk threads. The caps were sewed on the back to hold them in place. Black and white crocheted buttons are quite easily found today, but these buttons were also made in pastel and deeper colors. Crocheted buttons first became fashionable in the 1880's. Sometimes beads were put on the thread as the cap was being crocheted, the beads usually being the same color as the thread.

Crocheted covered buttons again became popular in the early 1900's. The caps of this period often were patterned, and made of cotton and linen threads for women's cotton and linen dresses and suits. These buttons are found with cardboard molds, or in the case of ball-shaped buttons, stuffed with cotton.

Crocheted buttons. Crocheted "caps" on wooden molds, late 1800's.

CROSSES. About forty different cross designs have been used on buttons made in a variety of materials and decorated by many methods. Since 1950, twenty-four different cross designs have been carved into mother-of-pearl shell in Bethlehem, and exported to this country. Buttons with crosses are sometimes arranged in Easter mountings.

CRUMPTON, WILLIAM. Maker of military buttons in New Jersey and Philadelphia, 1830's to the 1880's. One of the back marks found on Crumpton's buttons is "W.C.Phila."

CRYSTALLIZED TIN. The metal was treated so that the surface had a crystallized appearance, an effect similar to that on galvanized iron pails, tubs, and pipes. Buttons of this material were made by the Lane Manufacturing Company of Connecticut in the late nineteenth century. Sometimes the crystallized metal was used to make up the complete face of the button; at other times it was used only as the center of a brass button. All buttons of this material were two-piece. Thin clear lacquers in various shades of gray, brown, blue, red, or silver were sprayed onto the buttons. To some degree, the lacquers protected the treated tin, helping it to resist rust. However, many of these buttons have been found with the "crystal" finish gone, and there is no way to bring it back.

Crystallized tin buttons.

CUT STEEL. A small piece of steel cut with many little facets and used to trim steel and brass buttons, as well as buttons of other materials, such as horn, tortoiseshell, bone, ivory, and pearl shell. The term "cut steel" has been used to refer to a metal button completely covered with these little faceted pieces. Cut-steel pieces have been riveted onto metal disks since the early eighteenth century, when the invention of faceting steel was credited to Matthew Boulton. The brilliance of eighteenth-century cut-steel buttons inspired many cartoons in early magazines. Men then wore all the large, handsome buttons; and, it is said, when these buttons reflected the sun, they were dazzling. Their popularity, along with that of other large buttons, went out about 1800. Not until 1850 did buttons trimmed with cut steel come into style again; it was then that cut steel was applied to brass buttons, along with other materials, for women's wear. Also, at this time, steel was struck to imitate cut steel, but close examination shows that the whole disk was struck and that separate pieces were not riveted onto it. In some cases, the "rivet" was only a thin wire on the faceted piece, put through a hole in the button and bent over on the back to secure the piece. Cut steel was sometimes dyed red, blue, or green, and often pieces in several colors were used to decorate one button.

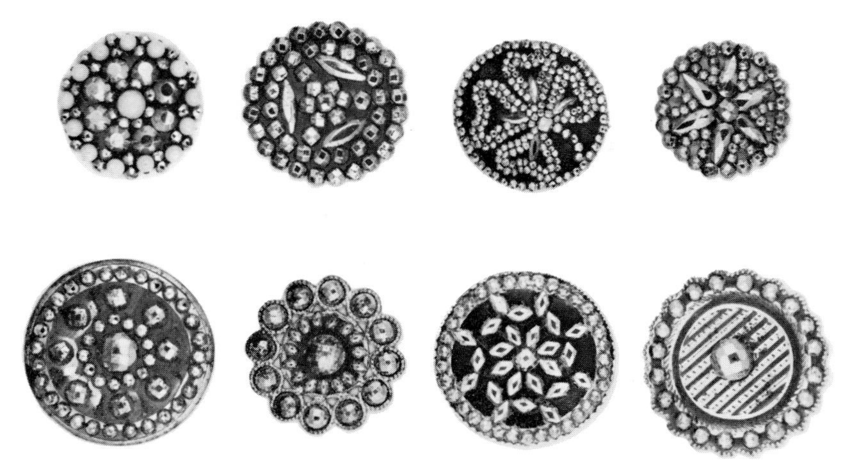

Cut steel. Top row shows nineteenth-century buttons trimmed with cut steel. Those in the bottom row date from a century earlier.

CUTOUT SHANK. To make a cutout shank, the metal back of a button has two parallel slits cut in it, which are raised to form the shank. This type of shank is found only on twentieth-century buttons.

Cutout shank.
One type of self-shank.
Twentieth century.

D

D. EVANS & CO. Button manufacturers in Attleboro, Massachusetts, 1848–1942. They made brass buttons for uniforms and dress wear. Although they were in business during the Civil War period, their buttons are usually not considered acceptable at competitive displays of buttons of the Civil War period. In fact, it is very difficult to authenticate many of the northern uniform buttons as being made solely for the Civil War. Evans' manufacture of gilt buttons for the dress trade did not begin until the quality of this type of button had begun to deteriorate everywhere—at the end of the period known as the "golden age" of buttons. Some Evans brass buttons were plated with white metal and had pearl centers. The company name appears on the back of many of their buttons.

DAGUERREOTYPE. An early process of photography invented by Louis Daguerre, about 1837. The picture was made on a thin sheet of copper coated with a light-sensitive chemical. Daguerreotypes, which were mostly portraits, are occasionally found on a button. They fade easily, and it may be for this reason that few such buttons were made. From the construction of these buttons, a collector can easily assume they were made and worn about the time of the Civil War, between 1860 and 1865. *See* Ferrotypes for buttons sometimes mistakenly called daguerreotypes.

DAMASCENE. An early art for decorating metal, having its origin in the pre-Christian Era in Damascus, Syria. The technique was taken to Japan from central Asia and China around A.D. 700. The design was gouged out on the metal piece being ornamented, the hollows filled with silver and gold, then hammered until the surface was flat. Very few early buttons decorated in this manner are found.

Buttons decorated by this technique have been made for the past twenty years in Japan. Numerous fine lines are chiseled into a steel foundation to form the design; gold and silver threadlike wires are pounded into the lines; after this, the background of the design is first corroded with nitric acid, then rusted with ammonium chloride. When the rust is deep enough, the process is stopped by boiling in green tea. Several layers of black lacquer are baked into the entire surface of the button. A subsequent step is to polish with charcoal until the design is brought out from the lacquer, and the final step is engraving, and perhaps some touching up. Although these modern buttons are not more than twenty-five or so years old, they are not plentiful. They were made in numerous sizes and shapes, one-piece and two-piece. Designs include flowers, fruits, heads, scenes, animals, dragons, and vegetables.

Damascene. Twentieth-century damascene work.

DAMASK. A type of fabric woven on Jacquard looms. The most common colors of damask for covering buttons are white, dark brown, and black. When made for buttons, the design in the damask was often spaced while it was being woven, leaving enough material for sewing onto the mold without cutting into another design. The silky-like designs are usually flowers; some designs have borders that perfectly fit the size of the button.

Damask-covered buttons. These are enlarged to show the woven designs. Nineteenth century.

DANDELION WATER. *See* Gilt.

DECAL, DECALCOMANIA. A printed design on paper that can be transferred to an object for decoration. The art originated in France about 1860. Decal transfers are found on many porcelain buttons, and on a few buttons of other materials, such as bone, pearl, and vegetable ivory. The designs were made in black and white, or multicolor. When decals were transferred to china, they were fired, and sometimes hand painting was then added. On other materials, the decal designs were often coated with clear lacquer. Since these designs were fragile, many buttons decorated with transfers are found in poor condition. This frailty should be considered when they are included in a collection.

DECCAN. A name found on the backs of silver-colored buttons that came into this country about 1950 for the first time. Added to "Made in Deccan" on the backs of the buttons were various factory names, such as Blarath Button Factory, Garath Button Factory, Chonsia Factory, Prakash Button Factory. Sometimes there were also trademarks, such as a swastika in a rayed sun, or crossed flags with star and crescent over them. All these buttons were decorated on the front with molded designs and bright paint or very thin enamel. The designs usually depicted flowers or famous men. The buttons were about the size of a nickel, and were round, square, or realistic in shape. They had long shanks, similar to those made for waistcoats or vests. Deccan is a group of seven states in the central portion of India, which in 1947 officially formed the United Deccan State.

Deccan buttons. Made in Deccan in the 1950's.

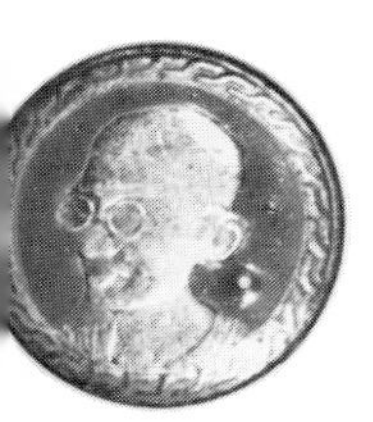

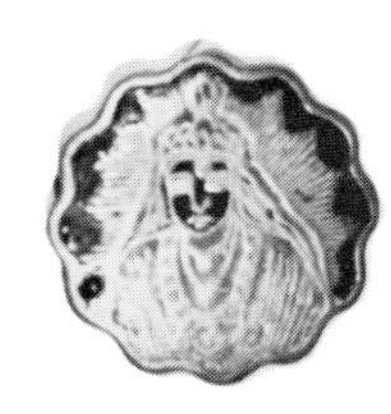

DÉCOUPAGE. The art of using cutout paper designs for decoration. Découpage was derived from the French word *couper,* meaning "to cut." The art of découpage originated in Venice, Italy, in the mid-1700's. For use in decorating furniture, mirrors, and boxes, the designs were usually large, well glued to the object, and covered with many coats of clear lacquer.

Buttons decorated by découpage, most of which are from the eighteenth century, have very fine designs. The small cutouts were mounted on colored backgrounds, which were placed on metal button bases, and covered with glass fronts. Collectors often group these buttons with eighteenth-century "under-glass" buttons. They are extremely rare. When découpage buttons are found in sets, each button may have a different design, a common practice in sets of this period.

Some collections boast a few découpage buttons with colored backgrounds, made in the nineteenth century. These are smaller than the buttons made a century earlier. In the middle of the twentieth century a few découpage buttons were made in studios. The designs are usually pictures cut out from various printed matter, and made up with "watch crystal" fronts.

Découpage. Eighteenth-century button with découpage decoration under the glass.

DESIGN METHODS. Nearly all arts and crafts have been used to make designs on buttons, from the ancient crafts to modern arts. The methods used depended much on the natural materials available to the craftsmen. The individual methods are explained and illustrated under separate materials headings. *See also* Carving; Damascene; Enamels, Enameling; Engraving; Etching; Inlay; Japanning; Lithograph Buttons; Marquetry; Needlework Buttons; Pewter Button Molds; Pyrography; Stenciling; Transfer Buttons, etc.

DESIGNS. The word used for all patterns found on buttons, including anything from a chance pattern to an actual copy of a painting or piece of sculpture. The collector divides button designs mostly into two large basic groupings, conventional and pictorial. For example, pictorial designs on buttons range from a single flower or insect to a scene from a nursery rhyme or a Shakespearean play. Transportation, sports, games, scenes, people, inanimate objects, to name a few subjects, have been pictured on buttons. The kind of designs found is almost limitless.

DEWDROPS. A term used for molded glass buttons having small round humps on the underside that reflect through the front, reminding one of real dewdrops. On some buttons, the humps cover the back; on others, the dewdrops are placed between raised stars or flower petals. When the top is molded with a dome shape, the dewdrops are magnified and seem even more like real dewdrops. The term has sometimes been used incorrectly for the larger hump on the top of some of these buttons. Dewdrops were made in all the clear glass colors—amethyst, red, pink, shades of blue, green, and yellow. These buttons always had a thin wire shank. It is thought that they were made between 1860 and 1880. They are not at all plentiful.

DeWITT, J. DOYLE. American author. DeWitt wrote and published *A Century of Campaign Buttons, 1789-1889,* in 1959.

DICKINSON HARD RUBBER COMPANY. This company, incorporated in Springfield,

Massachusetts, in 1878, advertised their hard rubber buttons with the claim: "Great beauty and design, this button resembles horn." These buttons very often had "D.H.R. Co." as a back mark. Although the company used the phrase "great beauty and design," the designs found are very simple, and of a dull black color. The buttons had two holes or self-shanks.

DIES. Tools used for striking designs on metal buttons. There are two parts to a die: one part with the design raised; the other, precisely cut, with the design in intaglio. The metal button disk to be stamped was placed on the part that had the raised design. The intaglio die was dropped with force onto the disk. In the early days, this dropping was controlled by a foot treadle, but now, of course, it is done by electrically operated machines.

First, master dies were made by men called diesinkers. These were cut by hand with small chisels before the steel was hardened. The diesinker sometimes made the design for a border, sometimes for a center. From these master dies, the two-piece striking dies were made. This is the reason there were so many variations in design. Button buyers for the wholesale trade were able to choose and order buttons with varying borders for a single center design. Or they might order different center designs within the same border. These dies were used for making the fronts of picture buttons, uniform buttons, sporting buttons, and many others. Similar dies were made for stamping the back marks for two-piece buttons.

DISPLAYING BUTTONS. *See* Mountings.

DOMINION BUTTON MANUFACTURERS, Ltd. This concern fonnded in 1870, was the first manufacturer of buttons in Canada. They began by making vegetable ivory buttons. In 1875, they began to manufacture pearl buttons from mother-of-pearl shells and from freshwater shells. In 1935, they developed plastic buttons.

DORSET BUTTONS. Thread buttons made in England from the middle of the eighteenth century to the middle of the nineteenth century. Two kinds were made, one with disks of sheep horn, the other with wire rings. The horn variety, called "high tops," was made by putting a fragment of cloth through the hole in the center of the disk, then building the cloth up into a conical shape, which was held by hand stitches, like a spider web. The wire-ring type, which were flat, were done by lacemakers; the chief pattern of these was the Blanford "cartwheel." A variety of patterns was made, with names such as honeycomb, basket, and crosswheel.

The making of Dorset buttons was called a cottage industry, since both men and women made them at home; even the children twisted the wires and wound the thread to help. Abraham Case of Dorsetshire, England, originated these buttons; hence, the derivation of the name. With his family, he made many of the first thread buttons.

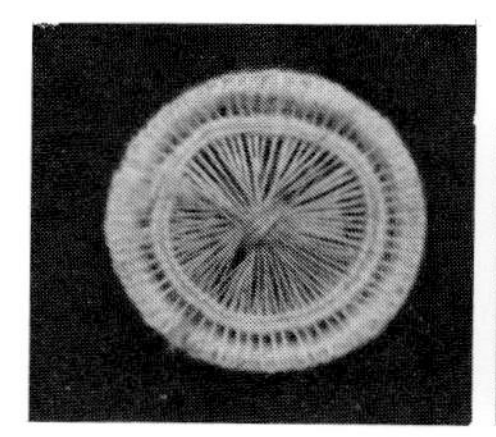
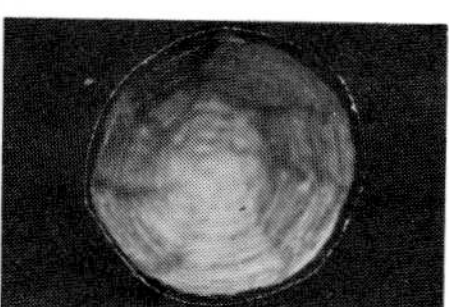

Dorset (thread) buttons.
These date from the nineteenth century: (1) cartwheel; (2) high top.

DRAPER & SANDLAND. Button manufacturers, 1845, Attleboro, Massachusetts. The firm was founded by Albert H. Draper and Thomas Sandland, and is believed to have been in business for about ten years. A very few gilt buttons have shown up with "Draper & Sandland," or "D.&.S. Extra Rich," back marks. The button designs indicate the firm made fine-quality gilt buttons for men's wear.

E

E. E. PRITCHARD. Name found on gilt buttons. *See* Pritchard, Elizur E.

E. FOWLER. Manufacturer of pewter buttons, 1812.

E. M. LEWIS & COMPANY. Makers of uniform buttons in Richmond, Virginia, in the 1860's. The name appears on Confederate buttons.

E. R. YALE. A manufacturer of gilt buttons in the early 1880's. His shop was in Meriden, Connecticut. "E. R. Yale Meriden" can be found on the back of sleeve-size plain gilt buttons. It is not known that he made gilt buttons with designs.

E. RIDLEY & SONS. Merchants in New York City, from the 1880's to 1905. *Ridleys' Fashion Magazine* was published by E. Ridley & Sons in the 1880's. Several pages of dressmakers' items were shown in each quarterly. Among the buttons pictured were crocheted, pearl, steel, and the popular picture buttons, all shown in actual size. The buttons and prices remained the same for at least three years: Pierrot and Pierrette, $1.25 a dozen; Hector, 60¢ a dozen; Lion of Lucerne, 18¢ to 60¢ a dozen. They were listed in several colors.

130 RIDLEYS' FASHION MAGAZINE. [Spring, 1886

"The Warrior" Colored Metal Button, with heavy raised figure in center.

No. 2. Same size as cut, 25c per dozen.

No. 3. Same size as cut, 45c per dozen.

No. 4. Same size as cut, 60c per dozen.
Clasp to match large button, 18c each, in single box.

"The Castle" The center is carved wood with colored metal rim.

No. 5. Same size as cut, 38c per dozen.

No. 6. Same size as cut, 50c per dozen.

No. 7. Same size as cut, 75c per dozen.

"Over the Garden Wall" Colored Metal Button, with oxidized rim.

No. 8. Same size as cut, 25c per dozen.

No. 9. Same size as cut, 38c per dozen.

No. 10. Same size as cut, 50c per dozen.
Clasp to match large buttons, 16c each, in single box.

"The Mikado" Colored Metal Button.

No. 11. Same size as cut, 18c per dozen.

No. 12. Same size as cut, 38c per dozen.

No. 13. Same size as cut, 48c per dozen.
Clasp to match large buttons, 12c each, in single box.

"The Stag" Solid Steel Button, the center ornamented in oxidized or bronze.

No. 14. Same size as cut, 29c per dozen.

No. 209. "The Armored Knight" Colored Metal Clasp, the center of cut steel, size of cut, 25c each, in single box.
Large buttons to match, 85c per dozen.

"Pure Love" Heavy Fine Made Colored Metal Button, with raised figures in center.

No. 23. Same size as cut, 38c per dozen.

No. 15. Same size as cut, 75c per dozen.

No. 16. Same size as cut, $1.00 per dozen.

"The Bugler" Colored Metal Button, with bright polished rim.

No. 17. Same size as cut, 18c per dozen.

No. 18. Same size as cut, 35c per dozen.

No. 19. Same size as cut, 45c per dozen.
Clasp to match large buttons, 14c each, in single box.

"The Lioness" Colored Metal Button, with engraved edge.

No. 20. Same size as cut, 25c per dozen.

No. 21. Same size as cut, 45c per dozen.

No. 22. Same size as cut, 60c per dozen.
Clasp to match large buttons, 18c each, in single box.

No. 24. Same size as cut, 85c per dozen.

No. 25. Same size as cut, $1.25 per dozen.
Clasp to match large buttons, 20c each, in single box.

DRESS AND CLOAK BUTTONS.

Exact size of cuts in colors as quoted only.

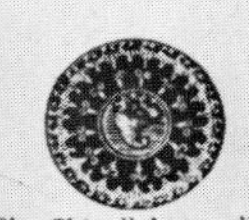

Size 7½; light, medium, and seal ..., garnet, blue, and green, 8c doz.

No. 494. Size, 7½ line, 15c doz.; size, 16 line, 40c doz.; in medium brown, plum, navy, seal, drab, and black.

No. 2894. Black only; size, 7 line, 8c doz.

No. 548. In brown and black; size 7½ line, 10c doz.

Size 12; light, medium, and seal ..., garnet, blue, and green, 10c doz.

No. 585. Cloak size, 20c doz., drab and brown; dress size, drab and brown, 10c doz.

No. 2894. Black only; size, 12 line, 10c doz.

No. 548. In brown and black; size, 12 line, 15c doz.

Size 16; in garnet, blue, green, and seal brown, 10c doz.

No. 516. Size 16; only light and medium brown, olive, seal, navy, and black, 10c doz.

No. 2894. Black only; size, 16 line, 10c doz.

No. 548. In brown and black; size, 16 line, 20c doz.

Size 7½; in seal brown, 10c doz.; also, 12 line size, 10c doz.

No. 496. In light, medium, and dark brown, navy, green, drab, copper, and black; 7½ line, 8c doz.

No. 2893. In bronze, brown, navy, green, and black; size, 7½ line, 8c doz.

No. 520. In light brown, dark brown, blue, black, and tan; 7½ line, 10c doz.

...4. Size 16; in seal brown, 10c doz.

No. 496. In light, medium, and dark brown, navy, green, drab, copper, and black; size, 16 line, 10c doz.

No. 2893. Brown, garnet, blue, green, and black and bronze; size, 12 line, 10c doz.; same colors, in 16 line, 10c doz.

No. 520. In light brown, dark brown, blue, black, and tan; 16 line, 10c doz.

... In light and medium brown and black, 7½ line, 10c doz.

No. 589. Size, 8 line; lt. tan, garnet, navy, green, plum, lt. and dk. brown and black, 8c doz.

No. 1500. Size, 7 line; light, dark, and medium brown, garnet, dark blue, olive, dark beige, 8c doz.

No. 564. In drab, navy, garnet, steel, and brown; 7½ line, 10c doz.

... In light and medium brown ...black, in 15 line, 15c doz.

No. 589. Size, 12 line; light tan, garnet, navy, green, plum, light and dark brown and black, 10c doz.

No. 493. Inlaid with steel; light and dark brown and tan color, 70c doz.

No. 1500. Size, 16 line; light, dark, and medium brown, garnet, dark blue, olive, dark beige, 10c doz.

No. 564. In drab, navy, garnet, steel, and brown; 15 line, 15c doz.

E. SCOTT (or SCOTT & CO.). Connecticut button manufacturers, early 1800's. Both names are found on buttons.

EASTER DESIGNS. Easter Boat Ride and Easter Parade were among the designs used to decorate nineteenth-century picture buttons. Other buttons from the same century that are suggestive of Easter had crosses, bunnies, and Easter lilies. Since 1950, pearl-shell disks have been beautifully carved in Bethlehem in the Holy Land for buttons with designs symbolic of Easter. Twenty-four different crosses, the Crucifix, Christ praying at Gethsemane, and Christ carrying the Cross are some of the designs. *See also* Crosses.

EAVES, WILLIAM, & SONS. *See* William Eaves & Sons.

EDITH'S STUDIO. Mrs. Edith Morlock, ceramist, made porcelain buttons and decorated porcelain medallions for metal buttons in the 1950's and 1960's in Fowlersville, Michigan. Her earliest buttons, mostly about $1^{1}/_{2}''$, had transfer designs of flowers; some had state flowers and also included the names of the states. In the 1960's she made a set of metal buttons with porcelain medallions in commemoration of the "Walk-in-Space." One set was given to astronaut Edward White. The transfers were made especially for Mrs. Morlock, in red and blue, and she applied them to white porcelain medallions.

Porcelain buttons. Buttons from Edith's Studio, including those with space-oriented designs.

ÉGLOMISÉ. A type of reverse painting on glass. This art had been known by the Chinese for centuries. It was introduced into France by M. Glomy, and became popular there and in England in the latter part of eighteenth century. In églomisé buttons, gold was first laid on the reverse side of the glass disk, and then the design was cut out of the gold with fine sharp tools. After this, the whole reverse side of the disk was covered with black, which filled in the cut details of the design, as well as formed a background. It is the artistic skill of carving the design in gold that differentiates églomisé from reverse paintings done with a paintbrush, one color at a time. *See also* Reverse Painting.

Églomisé. An eighteenth-century button with a gold design on a black background, in Églomisé, a type of reverse painting on glass.

ELECTROPLATING. A method used for plating buttons made of metal or other suitable materials. The buttons to be plated were placed in containers, sometimes called barrels or tumblers, with chemicals and the metal to be deposited on the button. By means of electrolysis, nickel, silver, or gold was deposited on the buttons. A few plastic buttons have been plated in this manner. Electroplating has been used for coating buttons almost since the time this process was invented; it replaced the "Sheffield" plate method.

ELLIOTT, WILLIAM. An Englishman who took out five patents between 1837 and 1851. One was for an improvement in the manufacture of covered buttons made with flexible

Salesman's sample case. The buttons were covered with silk brocade by an Elliott machine (1830–50).

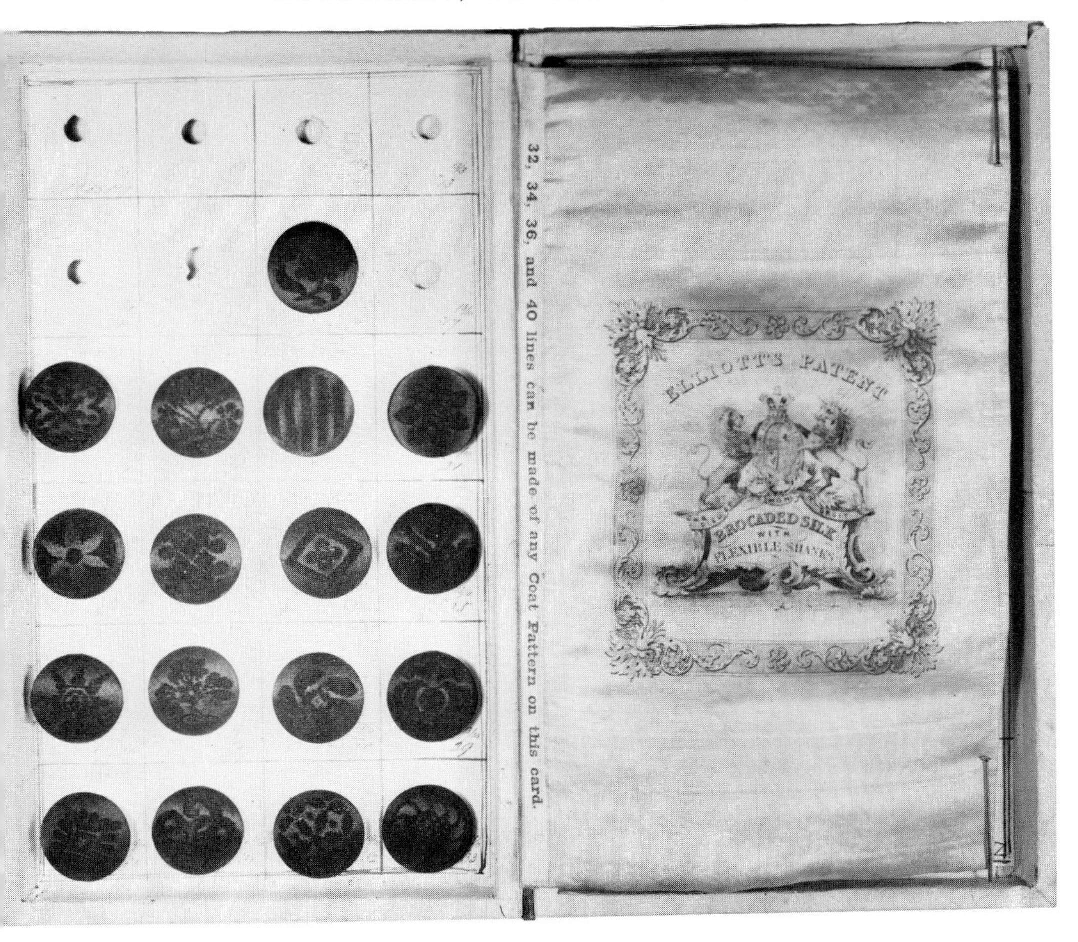

shanks; another was for a machine to cover fabric buttons "with a figure or design in the central position in respect to the face."

ELLIOTT TYPE. A term used for cloth-covered buttons with glass ornaments in the face of the button, which had a metal back. This type was named after the inventor of the machine that made the buttons. The term is seldom used today.

ELLSWORTH MANUFACTURERS. Makers of hats, caps, gloves, and raincoats, 1889–1928. Within the period of the Ellsworth firms, there appeared black, molded composition buttons $1\frac{3}{4}$" in size on which the company names are found. One marking was "Straw & Ellsworth Mfg. Co. Milwaukee, Wis."; the other was "Ellsworth & Thayer Mfg. Co. Milwaukee, Wis." Apparently it was the same Ellsworth in both firms, in business with Straw from 1890 to 1900, and with Thayer from 1890 to 1928. Whether these buttons were made to wear on the black raincoats they made, or to be given away as advertisements, is not known. Probably the Ellsworth firms did not make the buttons.

Ellsworth Manufacturers.
Early 1900's.

EMAUX PEINTS. (Painted enamels.) *See* Enamels, Enameling.

EMBEDDED. This term refers to molded buttons with escutcheons applied by inserting the metal decoration while the molded material was soft. Glass buttons were decorated in this way as early as 1860. *See* Glass Buttons: Mechanical Makeup.

EMBOSSING. A method used to raise designs in leather or other soft materials. An outline of the design was first drawn on paper, then placed on the grain side of the leather, which was set on a hard surface. With the tip of the modeling tool, the outline was slightly traced onto the dampened leather, and then the pattern was removed. The narrow end of the modeling tool was used to go over the traced design; this raised the design above the surface by depressing the surface next to it. The term "embossed" has sometimes been used for the stamped designs in low relief found on wood, vegetable ivory, and other buttons of hard materials.

EMBROIDERY. A needlework art of making raised and ornamental designs on fabrics and other materials. Embroidery was used extensively to decorate buttons for several centuries. In the seventeenth and eighteenth centuries, men's coats and waistcoats were elaborately embroidered. Whether the coat was made of pale-green silk and embroidered in shades of pink, or of deep-purple velvet embellished with gay stitches, the buttons were embroidered to match. Very often sequins, beads, and metal threads were included in the design. It was not until the nineteenth century that women had embroidery on their buttons; this embroidery was often the only decoration on the garment. Embroidery on material for covering buttons was done by hand until nearly the twentieth century; then embroidering machines were introduced.

Embroidered fabric buttons. Two red buttons in the top row are embroidered with ribbon and metal threads. All the others are embroidered with silk threads. Nineteenth century.

EMILIO COLLECTION. The uniform buttons collected by Luis Fenollosa Emilio, New York City, a captain in the United States Volunteers from 1863 to 1865. Mr. Emilio offered his collection to the Essex Institute in Salem, Massachusetts, on November 28, 1908, and it was accepted on December 6, 1908. The Essex Institute, a museum, possesses many relics, arms, uniforms, and equipment pertaining to the wars of this country. At the time the button collection was transferred, it was understood that the donor would arrange, classify and, if possible, publish a catalogue. The museum agreed "that the collection shall always be kept in view." The collection was arranged in large frames, which were hung on hinges so that they could be viewed on both sides, like the pages of a book. The collection consists of American, British, French, and Spanish military buttons, with some buttons of other countries, and a few nonmilitaries. The descriptive catalogue has been reprinted several times in book form, *The Emilio Collection*, and sold to collectors.

ENAMELS, ENAMELING. Enameling is thought to have started in the East, long before the birth of Christ. About the thirteenth century, it is believed, enameling was begun in Europe without any knowledge that it had been practiced years before in China.

There have been few changes in the method of enameling since the sixteenth century. The glass is still ground by hand; the coatings of powdered glass must still be applied to the metal with much care. The main difference is in the heating—from kilns heated by wood to those heated by electricity.

The disk for the button must be cleaned by acid and heat-treated. After the glass particles have been pulverized and washed, they are laid on the metal disk with a sharp spatula. The disk is then heated in the kiln, and the glass melted and fused to the metal.

The artistry is in the interplay of the opaque and translucent colors, the depth of pure tones achieved through many firings. As one artist said, "It is like working with colored sand." This "colored sand," which is to be the enamel, has been used to produce different types of enameled buttons—Basse-Taille, Champlevé, Cloisonné, Emaux Peints, En Grisaille, Encrusted, Limoges, Paillons, and Plique-à-Jour.

Basse-Taille. A pattern was stamped on the metal disk in low relief. This was a symmetrical, engine-turning sort of decoration. It was covered with a transparent enamel of a single color. Sometimes a foil with a stamped design was laid on a plain metal disk, or paint was added before the ground glass was put on for firing. These buttons were made in the nineteenth and twentieth centuries in small numbers.

Basse-taille. (1) Color under transparent enamel; (2 and 3) colored transparent enamel.

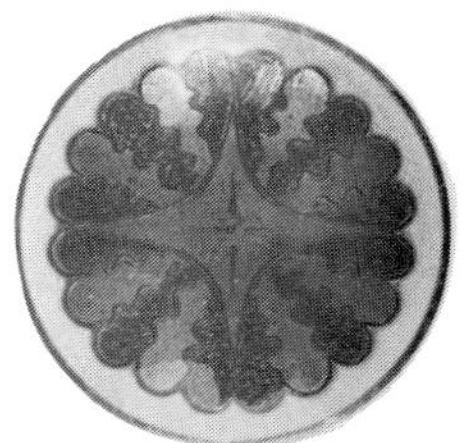

Champlevé. The disks were stamped or hand-tooled with the design, thereby creating wells for the enamel (ground glass). Sometimes this stamping can be seen on the back. The wells were filled, one color at a time, and fired. If the wells were not completely filled after one firing, more glass was added and the disks were fired again. The process was repeated until all spaces were filled, each with its own color. Each button had to be hand-polished after the last firing. Sometimes the champlevé technique was used for the border of the button. These borders were dainty in design and color. Champlevé buttons are probably the easiest of enamel buttons to acquire.

Champlevé buttons. Nineteenth-century enameled buttons with polychrome designs.

Cloisonné. One of the oldest methods of decorating with enamel. Fine wires were soldered to the button disk to form the pattern. The wells, or cloisons, were usually deeper than those stamped for champlevé buttons, but the process of filling the wells and polishing was the same. Although many small cloisonné items were made, such buttons are extremely scarce; except for the poorer grades made for the tourist trade in this century, there are almost none to be found. The colors in the early ones were dark; in the more recent ones, lighter.

Cloisonné buttons. Twentieth century. Made in Japan.

Cloisonné: Note the twisted wires and polychrome design of the first button (early nineteenth century). The second is a twentieth-century specimen with polychrome design.

Emaux Peints. (Painted Enamel.) The button disk was first built up with repeated coats of ground opaque glass, each one fired and polished. Then little paintings of men, women, cupids, animals, buildings, flowers, birds, even miniature scenes, were added by using bright paint mixed with different amounts of ground glass. These designs were laid flat on the background or raised according to the amount of ground glass in the paint. Enamel picture buttons are probably the most popular with collectors.

This method of enameling was also used on glass and porcelain buttons. The glass in the paint caused the design to fuse and produce a raised effect on either glass or porcelain. On glass buttons, the enameling was mostly done with white opaque glass; these buttons are sometimes called Mary Gregory buttons, after the well-known painter of glassware.

Emaux peints. Three nineteenth-century buttons with polychrome designs.

En Grisaille. The art of applying white enamel on a black enamel background, creating a design in tones of gray. En Grisaille enameling was introduced sometime during the sixteenth century. Early records indicate that it was used to decorate buttons in the eighteenth century. The black background was made by firing coat after coat of black ground glass onto the metal disk. After the black background had been built up and polished to a smooth surface, a design was created on it in varying densities. A thin first layer of white was applied, creating a darkish gray tone; the number of applications of white determined the shading of gray, with some built up to create white. Each layer of white was fired separately. *See* Grisaille for a similar art of black and white decorations on other materials.

Encrusted. A term used to describe the beadlike enamel dots that were made to imitate jewel trimmings on buttons. The artist placed the ground opaque glass directly on the brass base in dotted rows; after firing, the dots resembled tiny cabochon-shaped jewels. Turquoise blue and ruby red were the colors most frequently used, though other gems were imitated. These imitation stones were used mostly to form a border around enamel buttons, but they also have been found around small picture buttons. More broadly, the term "encrusted" refers to any built-up enameling on any material.

Encrusted decoration. Nineteenth-century buttons showing the beadlike enameling called "encrusted."

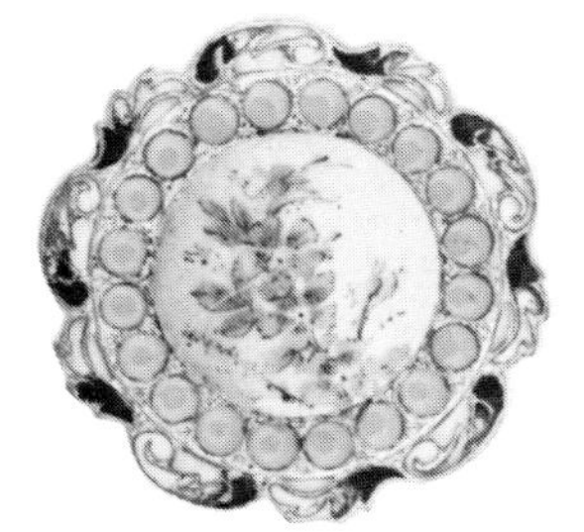

Limoges. This term is now used broadly by collectors to describe a button having an overall covering of enamel, instead of recessed colors as in champlevé, or colors separated by thin wires as in cloisonné. Léonard (Nardon) Pénicaud first used enamel in this way in Limoges, France, at the end of the fifteenth century. His method was to fuse a layer of opaque white over the entire surface; then, with fine enamel, he drew the outline of his design. This was covered with transparent enamel, and fired. Next, he built up his design with opaque enamels. After the design was fused, transparent layers were added for covering. Painting on enamels with finely ground colors was a further development of the Limoges type. Enamel buttons decorated in this manner are not known to have been made in the Limoges factories. Nearly all buttons with decoration of this kind were made in the nineteenth century. A few less beautiful ones made in the twentieth century have been sold to tourists in Europe.

Enamel.
Nineteenth-century
Limoges-type.

Paillons. Designs cut out or stamped out of gold or silver foil and used to decorate enamel buttons. Since it is not always known whether the Limoges techniques were carried out, many collectors refer to the designs simply as foil designs.

The metal disk for the button was prepared for its first coat of enamel, sometimes with an engine-turning type of design. After the disk had been sufficiently covered with enamel, possibly two or three firings, the foil design was laid on the enameled surface with an adhesive substance, and fired. Over this, transparent enamel was applied and fired to protect the foil. Do not mistake embedded wire for foil that has been used around jewel-like bits of enamel or paste jewels in enamel buttons. That this wire was *not* covered with enamel, can be determined with a sharp tool.

Plique-à-Jour. In these buttons, wires formed the designs. The wires were soldered to each other, and there was no base. The filigree pattern was then filled with ground glass, and fired. The finished effect resembled a stained-glass window. Very few of these buttons are found, perhaps because they were so fragile.

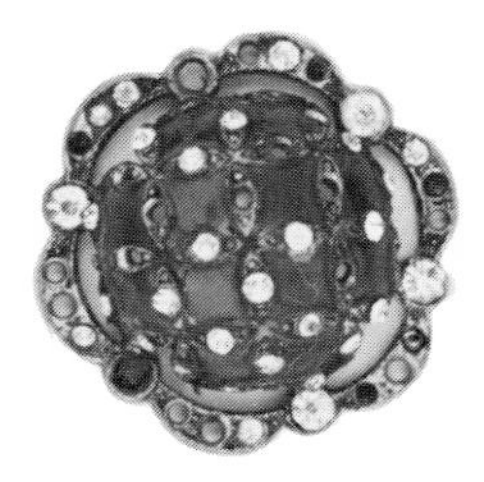

Plique-à-jour. The border of this nineteenth-century button is silver set with paste; solid center is amethyst enamel.

ENCRUSTED. *See* Enamels, Enameling.

ENGINE TURNING. A term used for the process or method of finely engraving lines into metals with a cutting tool held in an "engine," or machine (now more frequently called a lathe). In the same lathe, there was a "chuck" (holder) to hold the button disk on which the design was to be made. Engine-turned designs were sometimes cut on dies so that the pattern could be repeated many times. However, it is believed that buttons with these designs were not made in large quantities and that most of the buttons were decorated by hand. Once the tool was placed, it remained stationary while the disk moved against it to make the design. Engine-turned patterns were made by changing the position of the tool. The variety of patterns of concentric, zigzag, or curved lines was almost limitless.

The first engine-turned buttons were probably made in Europe around the middle of the eighteenth century. Just how early this method of decorating buttons was used in America is not known, though 1800 is a reasonable date if buttons were decorated by engine turning as early watchcases were.

Not only were metal buttons decorated with finely engraved patterns by means of the engine-turning method; the metal disks for basse-taille enamel buttons were also prepared in this way. *See also* Enamels: Basse-Taille.

Tombac buttons. Engine-turned designs; eighteenth century.

ENGRAVING. A method used to cut patterns into button disks (and for decorating many other objects as well). The outstanding difference between carving and engraving is the depth of the cutting. Engraved designs are made up largely of finely cut lines. To carve a design, the artist began with a plain piece of material, such as a shell or a piece of wood; then, with a cutting tool, he deeply gouged out a cameo or intaglio. Engraving was often used to add fine lines to designs already carved. A wholly engraved design is made entirely with fine lines. Black in the engraved lines of a pearl button or white in the lines of a dyed vegetable-ivory button made the design stand out. Engraving was used to make very intricate designs on buttons of many materials. The fine designs on some buttons that appear to be engraved were actually stamped or molded. In those cases, a die was first engraved with the design, then used to decorate quantities of buttons. Examples of designs with fine lines made by molding are those found on glass buttons that have paint added.

ERICKSON, THURA. A glassblower and maker of paperweight buttons, Brockton, Massachusetts, 1945–63. Though Erickson was not a glassblower by trade, he took up the making of glass articles when paperweight buttons were being made by four other American glassblowers. The buttons created by these five men were made mostly for the button-collector trade in the second quarter of the twentieth century. Since Erickson's buttons were first sold by Miss Eleanor Colangelo, they were called "Colangelo buttons"; it was some time before the maker's name was known. His flower designs excelled in their depth, complete with stamens and leaves, and had delicate colors. Sometimes he made a flower on a colored base; at others, the flowers appeared separated from the base, as if they were floating in the middle of the button. He also made the more customary designs with preformed canes. Erickson did not make many buttons; they are scarce today.

ESCUTCHEON. A metal ornament applied to the center of a button. Buttons of several materials—including glass, vegetable ivory, horn, fabric, and wood—were decorated with escutcheons. The escutcheons were usually stamped out in realistic shapes such as heads, animals, flowers, or insects. Some escutcheons were round or square with conventional designs. Often an escutcheon had two pins on the back, long enough to go through holes in the button and be bent down on the back. Other escutcheons were made with one pin long enough to go through a hole in the center of the button and form the shank. Sometimes these are referred to as pinhead shanks. If the ornament was held by the material—as in glass—collectors called the decoration "embedded."

Escutcheons. Trim was applied in the form of escutcheons to buttons of fabric, metal, leather, pearl, vegetable ivory, and wood.

ETCHING. A process of engraving by means of acid. In etching buttons, the surface to be decorated was covered with an etching wax, and the design was traced through the wax with a sharp-pointed tool. The button was then dipped in an acid solution. The acid cut into the material where the wax had been "tooled" to form the design. Some people think that buttons were never actually decorated by etching and that the term has been incorrectly applied to some finely carved or molded designs.

ETRUSCAN ART. The Etruscans were skilled metalworkers, and were particularly noted for their work with gold; their jewelry and buttons are museum treasures today. Their beautiful handiwork dates from 600 to 400 B.C. The outstanding characteristic of their buttons is a trim of minute balls of gold. These tiny balls were made by melting specks of metal of a selected size, so that the metal would flow into identical spheroids, which cooled with a flattened base. Each tiny piece used was graded, and so accurately applied that no trace of solder showed. The Etruscans kept this art so secret, it is said, that others could never copy it. It has never been recorded what material was used to solder the gold balls to the buttons and jewelry.

EVANS, D., & CO. *See* D. Evans & Co.

F

FABRIC-COVERED BUTTONS. Buttons covered with materials made of threads that have been woven, knitted, crocheted, or joined by some other process of needlework. Records show that "fabrics" (as they will be referred to here) were made as early as the seventeenth century, but descriptions are scarce until the early eighteenth century. Therefore, it can be presumed that the earliest fabric buttons were not decorated. By the early 1700's, fabric buttons were elaborately embroidered and worn on men's coats and waistcoats.

Fabric buttons had to have a hard mold to maintain their shape. The early molds were disks of bone, ivory, or wood, or were metal rings. The fabric was cut in circles larger than the area of the mold, allowing enough material to be stretched over the mold and stitched on the back to hold the fabric tight. The needlework on trimmed fabric buttons was done before the mold was covered with the fabric. Many of the eighteenth-century buttons were decorated to match the embroidery on garments. However, garments of plain materials might also have buttons that were richly embroidered or decorated with gold braid and spangles.

Toward the last quarter of the eighteenth century and into the nineteenth century, fabric buttons became very elaborate. Gold foil, carved pearl disks, and bright metallic threads were sewed onto them. Most buttons of this period were imported, many from France and Germany. There were few tailors in America at this time, and those that there were had learned the trade in Europe. The kinds of cloth used for these buttons were as numerous as those used for the garments; they included silk, wool, linen, and several others.

Fabric-covered buttons.
Here they are being manufactured.

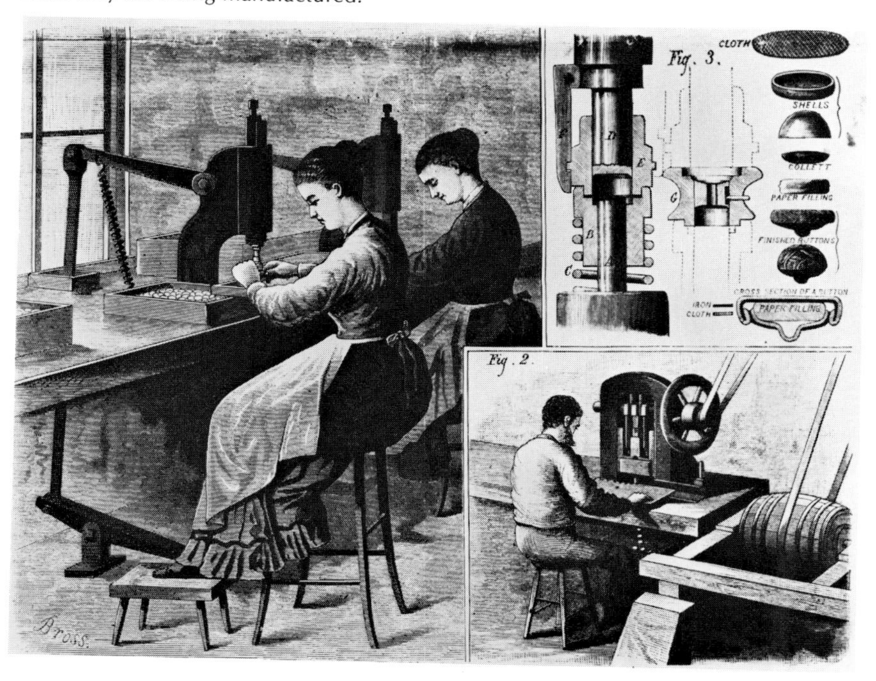

Early in the nineteenth century, machinery began to be used for making fabric-covered buttons. With this change, iron shells took the place of wooden molds. B. Saunders (sometimes spelled Sanders) established a small factory in Birmingham, England, where he introduced a fabric-covered button with a metal shank. A few years later, in 1825, his son invented the canvas, or flexible, shank for covered buttons. About this same time, the Willistons in America were beginning to manufacture fabric buttons in Easthampton, Massachusetts.

Late in the nineteenth century, clerks in fabric shops began to use small hand machines to cover buttons for customers. In fact, shops were set up for the sole purpose of covering buttons. Other machines were invented for including raised self-covered decorations, metal or glass centers, while the buttons were being covered. Machine-covered fabric buttons are still made today.

All sorts of fabrics have been especially woven just for covering buttons, including tapestry, damask, and brocade. They were made with medallion-like designs, large enough so that each medallion could be cut out and used to cover a single button mold.

Caplike covers for buttons were also crocheted or knit in delicate patterns, using silk, cotton, or linen thread. Sometimes the button mold was first covered with material of a contrasting color, which would show through the open design of the needlework cap.

Never have fabric buttons ceased to be made by hand. Those of the eighteenth century were frequently called needlework buttons, and those of the mid-nineteenth century were often referred to as dressmaker's buttons. Whether the dressmaker was hired or a member of the family, she made fabric buttons for the ladies' garments. Among these were beaded, embroidered, crocheted, and handpainted buttons, and also those made of soutache braid or laces.

Hand machine. Used in department stores in the 1880's and 1890's for covering buttons with fabric.

FACED TYPE. *See* Covered Type.

FACETED BACK AND/OR FRONT. Buttons of many materials were designed with facets, usually molded or cast, on the front. The term "faceted" is used most frequently in reference to molded glass buttons decorated in this way. Black glass buttons were made with large facets, small facets, or a combination of sizes in one pattern. Faceted buttons of black glass must have been very popular, as many are found in old button boxes today.

The facets in glass buttons might be square, oblong, triangular, or diamond-shaped. Most of the early colored transparent and opaque glass buttons with facet designs had plain backs and self- or metal shanks. Glass was also faceted to imitate jewels, and used for the centers in buttons made of other materials.

In the early twentieth century, glass buttons with designs on the back as well as the front came from Europe. These buttons, which have been called "faceted back" glass buttons, were either transparent or opaque, clear or colored. Some had inserts of mottled glass or pearl in the center of the faceted fronts. They were made in several sizes, ranging from 1/2" to over an inch, and were round or oblong. They were made either with self-shanks or four-way metal shanks.

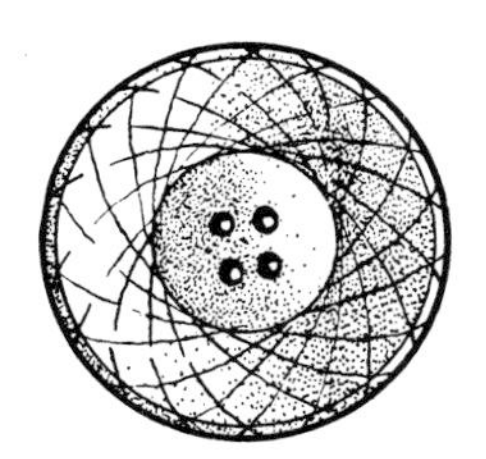
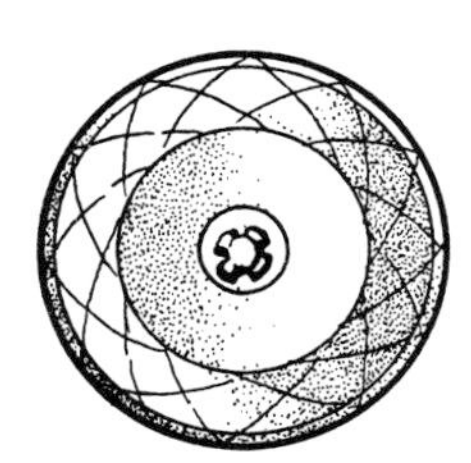

Faceted-back buttons. At the left is the front view of a faceted-back glass button (1898–1910); back view is at the right.

FEATHERS. Bird feathers were used to decorate buttons, and feathers were also popular as designs on buttons. Some buttons had small feathers arranged under glass against backgrounds of different materials. For example, blue and green foils were put under glass to simulate the "eye" in a peacock feather. Feather designs appeared on ivory-under-glass buttons in the eighteenth century, and in the last two centuries feather designs have been molded or stamped into buttons of almost every other material.

FERROTYPES. (Also called tintypes.) Ferrotyping was a process introduced by Robert Hunt of England in 1844. Just when the term "tintype" was first used is not known, but in some places it is more common than "ferrotype." The negative for a ferrotype (a thin iron plate) was developed in a saturated solution of protosulfate of iron with mucilage of gum arabic; the image was fixed by soaking in water to which a small quantity of ammonia or hyposulfate of soda had been added.

Ferrotypes. 1860's to 1900's.

After the discovery of collodion in 1846 by Louis Nicolas Ménard and, independently, in 1848 by Dr. J. Parker Maynard of Boston, Scott Archer invented the wet collodion process of making ferrotypes, which displaced Hunt's method. This process was not patented, and many ferrotypes were made during the next forty years.

For use on buttons, the same ferrotype image was reproduced many times, close together, on one sheet. The pictures were cut out with a circular chisel to make button disks. The disks were rimmed. Some buttons had backs with shanks; others had backs with pins or studs.

The earliest ferrotype buttons appeared about 1860. It is said that men going to war wore small-size buttons on their vests with pictures of their mothers, wives, or sweethearts. Except for the buttons with pictures of politicians, most ferrotypes were

Ferrotypes. Buttons and plates, 1855–80.

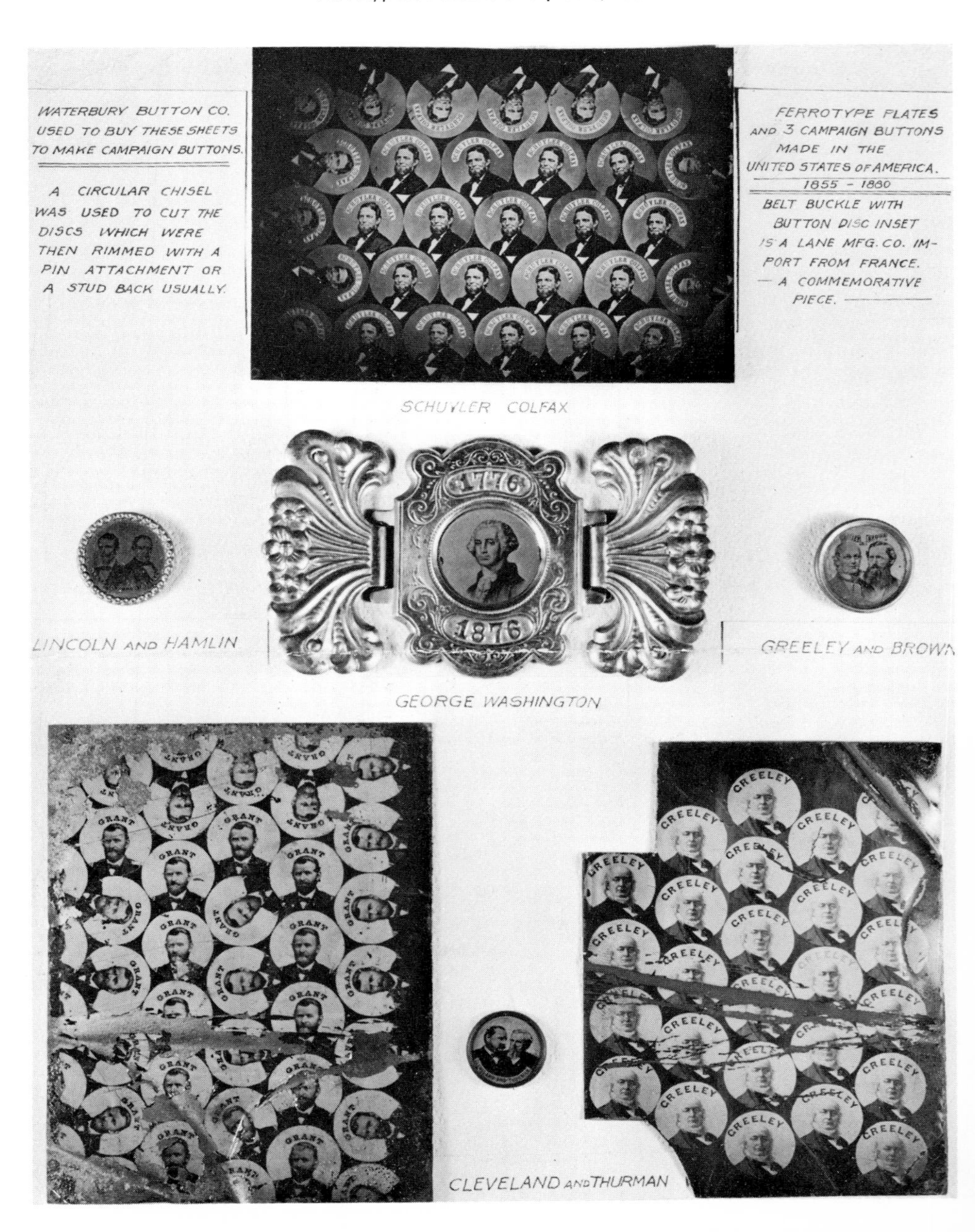

pictures of pretty women. About 1900, men with cameras and developing equipment went from door to door to take pictures of customers. These pictures, if put into button frames, were larger. Ferrotypes taken and developed at resorts at that time were also sometimes put into larger button frames.

FIELD. A term used in connection with uniform buttons. It refers to the background of the design on the face of a uniform button, exclusive of the border. Terms such as "plain field," "lined field," "stippled field," accurately described this surface. The eagle design, for example, is sometimes found on a lined field and at other times on a plain field.

FILIGREE. An ornamental button of silver or gold wires. Some filigrees were delicate and lacy; others were made of heavier wires. Those most commonly found were made of silver wire in the eighteenth or early nineteenth centuries, though the first known reference to these buttons indicates that they were made as early as the sixteenth century. Hungary, Russia, Italy, and the Scandinavian countries excelled in filigree work, and many filigree buttons were made in those countries in the eighteenth and nineteenth centuries. These buttons usually have hallmarks or other marks. Some filigrees were made in the United States, but they had no identification marks.

Most filigree buttons were ball-shaped, and originally pairs of them were sometimes connected with links. More often, there was a bar on one end of the link and a button on the other.

The term "filigree" has, on occasion, been mistakenly applied to stamped buttons with a cutout lacy design.

FINDINGS. The unassembled parts of metal buttons were often referred to as "findings." These included fronts, backs, rims, shanks, separate designs for application, and background pieces.

FIREMEN'S BUTTONS. The earliest firemen's buttons were made for insurance organizations, which gave the first active support to fire fighting in this country and in Europe. Benjamin Franklin is believed to have organized the first fire company in this country—in Philadelphia in the 1730's. In less than twenty years there were six or more companies. As fire-fighting equipment grew more elaborate in decoration, so did the uniforms worn by the men. Old firemen's buttons have not been accurately dated, but the companies for whom the special buttons were made date back as early as 1805. Buttons made for insurance-company fire fighters were one-piece and of brass, and ranged in size from 1" to 1¼". They were worn on bright red "blouses" (actually, short loose coats). *See also* Uniform Buttons for more about the buttons made for town and state fire departments.

Firemen's buttons.

FIRMIN & SONS, LTD. English manufacturers of buttons, mostly uniform buttons for the Armed Forces and for family liveries. The Firmin concern is one of the earliest button manufacturers. The names found on the backs of their buttons are as follows: Samuel Firmin (1771–96); Firmin and Westlake (1797–99); Firmin and Company (1800–11); Philip Firmin (1812–14); Firmin and Longdale (1815–23); Firmin and Son (1824–25); Robert Firmin (1826–37); Philip and King (1838–40); Philip and Samuel Firmin (1841–52); Firmin and Sons, Ltd. (1875–to date). Few concerns have a history of nearly three hundred years of ownership and operation by members of the same family. Firmins made a very high grade of button, producing uniform buttons for several countries, including the United States. The names found on the backs of their buttons help to date them.

FLECKS. A term used for composition buttons described as having an "ornamental coating for the exterior of the button, composed of tinsel, foil, goldsand, or other finely subdivided material combined with shellac." A patent was issued for this coating on June 29, 1880. The buttons were made in bright colors as well as subdued tones. The flecks were only on the surface coating; underneath, the buttons were solid colors. Wolf and turtle designs were molded in high relief. Such designs as snowflakes and conventionals were molded in low relief. Many of the buttons were of the sew-thru type, though some have self-shanks.

"*Flecks.*" Late-nineteenth-century composition buttons with a coating containing tiny pieces of pearl, tinsel, or other material.

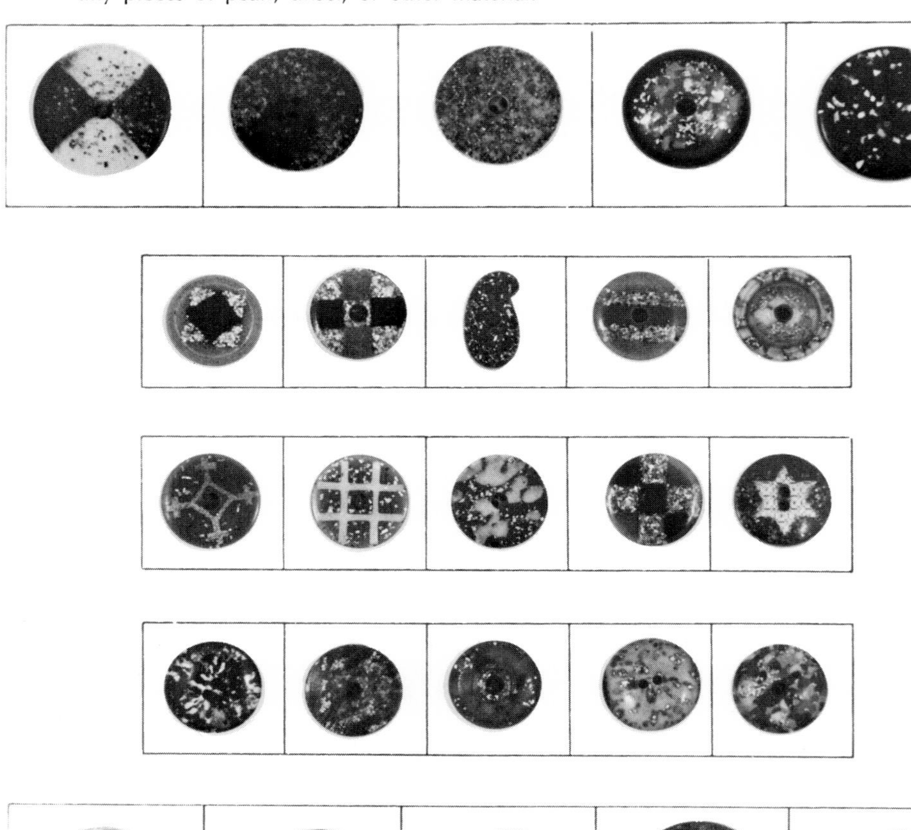

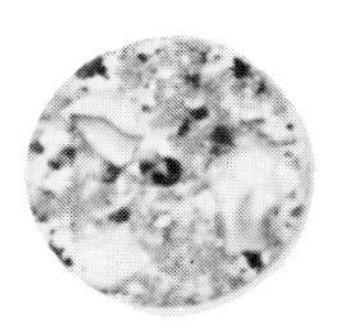 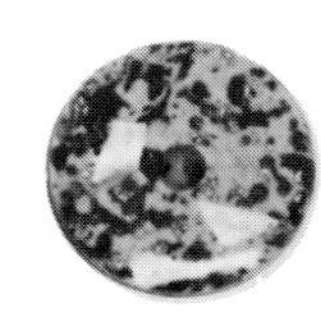  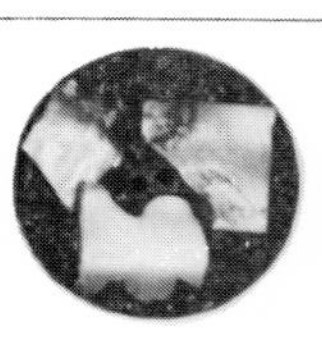 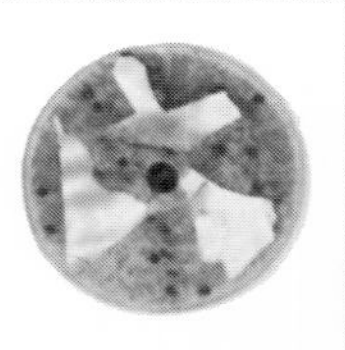

Flexible shank.
Sometimes called a pad back.

FLEXIBLE SHANKS. *See also* Shanks; B. Sanders.

FLOWERS. *See* Plant-Life Designs.

FOIL TRIM. Foil has been used to trim buttons in various ways for over two hundred years. It is often called tinfoil because it was first made of thin layers of tin. Some of the foil used in making buttons was colored, at least on one side. In the eighteenth century or earlier, foil was used as background for cutout designs under glass. At other times, it was laid on covered buttons between the fabric and the applied decorations.

In the nineteenth and twentieth centuries, foil was used for decorating glass buttons. Cutout designs of foil were placed on layers of glass as the glassblower built up paperweight buttons. In the nineteenth century, both clear and opaque buttons had foil designs laid on top of the glass core before the thin overlay of clear glass. These designs were frequently stars of silver color, but animal and flower designs were also cut out of colored foil. Foil was used in decorating Tingue buttons (*which see*), usually shades of gold foil, although a few had silver-colored foil. *See* Enamels: Paillons.

Foil trim. Silver- and gold-foil trim on enamel buttons; nineteenth century.

FORBIDDEN MONEY. *See* Coin Buttons.

FORD, GRACE HORNEY. American author who wrote *The Button Collector's History,* 1943. It was privately published, and is now out of print.

FOUR-WAY SHANK. *See* Box Shank.

FOWLER, DE GRASSE. Manufacturer of wood and bone buttons during the 1830's in New Brandford, Connecticut.

FOWLER, E. Manufacturer of pewter buttons, 1812.

FOWLER, MALTBY. Manufacturer of pewter buttons in Northford, Connecticut. The back mark "M. FOWLER NORTHFORD" may be found on pewter buttons made between 1800 and 1820.

FOX PATENT. Accurate data on this patent has not been found. The date "Aug. 3, 86" sometimes appears on the back of the buttons with "Fox Pat." These marks were on uniform buttons of the staff shell type, equipped with a sliding plate for closing over civilian buttons when the suit was worn as a uniform.

Fox patent. Shell- or cap-type uniform buttons.

FOXED. Term used for the discoloration found on celluloid buttons. Such discoloration begins with very small spots, and continues to spread. It is found on lithograph buttons with celluloid fronts and on celluloid campaign buttons.

FREEDOM BUTTONS. *See* Coin Buttons.

FREEMANS. Button manufacturers: Freeman & Bro., 1847–55 and 1858–79; Freeman Bro. & Co., 1855–58; B. S. Freeman & Co., 1879–96.

FUR. Buttons for fur coats were often covered with fur, though it was rarely used to trim buttons of other materials. Possibly, when fur-trimmed buttons of other materials were made, they were intended only for use on fur coats.

G

G. SMITH. Pewterer, Connecticut, 1815. Name found on pewter buttons.

GAITER BUTTONS. Most frequently, this term is used for a type of Small Chinas similar in construction to the buttons worn on gaiters. Hearsay and memory are mostly responsible for the term. The buttons have been found on women's and children's dresses, and from the gay colors, lusters, shapes, and sizes, it is easier to believe they were made for garments than for gaiters.

Gaiter buttons have a flat or slightly rounded back with a white metal shank plate and loop shank. They were shaped in domes, cones, flat pills (sometimes called "aspirins"), or were slightly rounded with hobnail humps, with or without self-rims. Most had a white body, but some were made with colored bodies, especially black and brown. They range in size from 3/8" to 3/4", and were made in the middle of the nineteenth century.

Those decorated with colored concentric designs over white are called Bull's-Eyes (*which see*). Others do not have as many variations in decoration. Those decorated with lusters sometimes have two colors, and are daintier than other gaiter buttons. The plain buttons with no decoration are the most commonly found, and they may have reached a gaiter now and then. All others are fairly scarce.

GALALITH. A plastic of German invention, which was made of milk. It is one of the early plastics mentioned, but one of those impossible to identify in buttons.

GALENA. A brilliant gray ore used for decorating buttons, mostly in the nineteenth century. First, a stiff paper or lightweight cardboard was covered with an adhesive material, and on this, ground galena was heavily sprinkled. In most cases, the prepared paper was used as background for metal or glass ornaments in the center of metal buttons. Buttons have often been found with only a slight trace of the glittering galena remaining, and these look shabby. Those found in fine condition are attractive.

Galena. Nineteenth-century picture buttons with galena used as the background.

GARTER BUTTONS. These buttons were made especially for fancy garters worn on the outside of stockings, below the knees, from about 1910–20. The garters were trimmed with silk, lace, feathers, and buttons. The buttons were covered with cotton or silk, and each had a painted face on it. The faces were painted mostly on white, but sometimes on pastel colors. The buttons were about 3/4" in size.

Garter button. The face is painted on fabric; twentieth century.

GATES, THEODORE. A button maker in Pennsylvania in the 1960's. The first Gates buttons were made with parts of Watch Crystal buttons. Later, Mr. Gates obtained thin glass disks and made the complete buttons. They resemble Watch Crystal buttons in construction, but the designs are découpage-style, being cutout paper pictures, under glass. In most cases, Mr. Gates put his initials and the date on the back of his buttons.

Watch crystal buttons. These were made by Theodore Gates in the 1960's.

GAUNT, J. R., & SON. *See* J. R. Gaunt & Son.

GENTLEMEN'S BUTTONS. A term used mostly for fancy buttons that seem as much like ladies' buttons as gentlemen's. In most cases, the term is used to refer to black glass buttons, two-hole sew-thru type, with metal backs. Some have been found on store cards labeled "Gentlemen's Buttons." They were often decorated with overlay trim in color and goldstone or with luster designs; they were made in several sizes. The holes were deeply molded, larger on the front to allow for heavy sewing thread. These buttons have also been found on women's dresses. The term does not apply to pants buttons, work-clothes buttons, or those made for breeches and vests.

Gentlemen's buttons. Late 1800's.

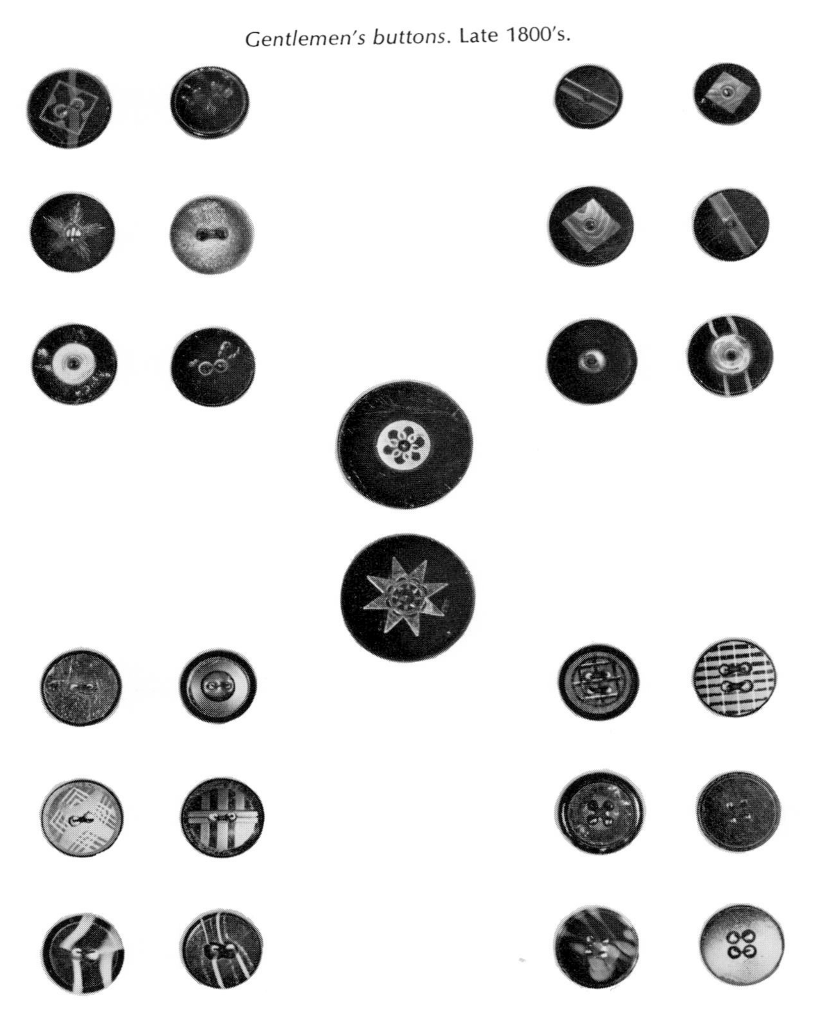

GERMAN SILVER. This metal was rarely used in button making. *See also* Nickel Silver.

GILT. A term used for a type of brass buttons made between 1800 and 1865, mostly those made before 1850. Many gilt buttons had a coating of gold, often so thin that the coating was referred to as "Dandelion Water." The gold coating usually wore off quickly, and then the brass buttons needed frequent polishing.

With the introduction of machinery to the manufacture of buttons around 1800, a new type of gilt button resulted, and a new fashion in buttons began. This new type was called the Omega Type gilt button, smaller and thicker than the aristocratic Alpha Type of the eighteenth century. It represents the last improvement in this kind of button and the best quality ever made.

Probably because of the lack of proper dies, or for some other reason, only plain gilt buttons were manufactured for the first thirty years. These small buttons continued to be standard for men's coats. The absence of ornamentation focused attention on their fashionable "orange tint." Vest buttons, however, were permitted a modest design and an added extra rim ("Rimmed Omega Type"). Similar rimmed gilt buttons occurred nowhere else in the history of button making.

Since these buttons had neither decoration nor unusual shape to intrigue prospective users, manufacturers played up the color of their product with back-mark designations such as "Rich Color," "Double Gilt," "Rich Orange," etc. It is believed most of these phrases were purely promotional, as collectors do not see any differentiation.

In the two decades that followed (1830–50), manufacturing circumstances permitted more elaborate buttons and, fittingly, this period came to be called the Golden Age of button making. Gilt buttons made in this period were referred to as "Golden Age" buttons both because of their golden color and their manufacture at the zenith of button qualities. (*See* Golden Age Buttons.) The gilt buttons that followed 1850 lacked the quality of material and workmanship of those produced in the first fifty years of the century. Most of them were smaller, and had cheaper brass fronts, less gilt, and thin metal backs. Many of these buttons were worn on women's dresses well beyond the time when it was the fashion for men to wear fancy buttons.

Gilt buttons. One- and two-piece gilts dating between 1810 and 1850.

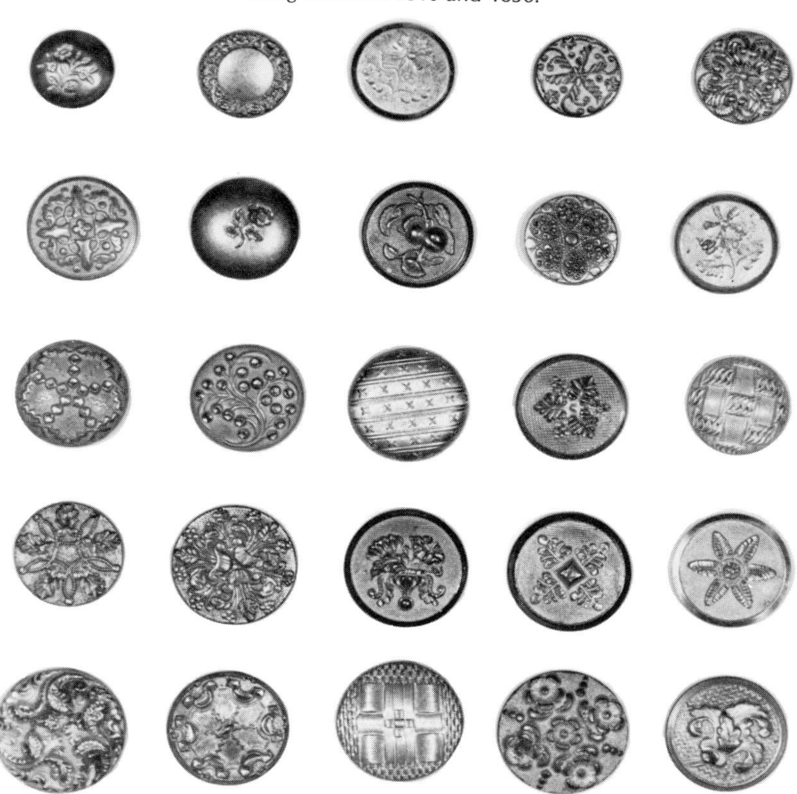

Gilts. A dark-blue coat from a dress suit of the 1820's. The buttons are two-piece gilts.

GLASS BUTTONS. Despite its fragility, glass was used to make a great many buttons. It is believed that the manufacture of glass buttons flourished from the 1840's, although a few earlier ones have been found.

Glass buttons are broadly grouped into two classes: (1) Clear and Colored Glass, and (2) Black Glass. This rough division is made to facilitate classifying the large quantity of glass buttons, although often the identical design and construction are found in both classes. Many more black glass than colored glass buttons have been found from the nineteenth century. Many of the designs, especially those found on the black glass buttons, were continued into the twentieth century. Exact dating of glass buttons is difficult; popular types and decorations were called "stock patterns," and were made as long as they were considered "good sellers." It is also known that World War I interrupted the making and exporting of glass buttons in Europe, and probably many buttons made prior to the war were not sent to markets until after 1920.

"Clear" is the term for transparent glass with no color; many buttons were made of clear glass. Colored glass includes transparent, translucent, and opaque, each with colors, from almost colorless to deep shades of blue, brown, green, orange, purple, red, clambroth, camphor, and imitation tortoiseshell. The colors found in twentieth-century buttons are usually more brilliant and sometimes gaudy—no doubt produced to harmonize with the fabrics for which the buttons were made.

CLEAR AND COLORED GLASS

Construction. Buttons have been made of one piece of glass, of glass fused to glass, and of blown glass or molded glass. They were made with various metal shanks, shank plates and other metal reinforcements, self-shanks, or holes. The metal backs were solid, open, or of screen. The shanks were metal box, key, loop, pigtail (the term used for an unfinished loop shank), pin, rosette, staple (also, frequently called antiquarian); and occasionally they were made of fabric or threads.

Mechanical Makeup. It is very difficult to draw a distinction between the mechanical makeup and the decorating of glass buttons, since so much of the decorating was done during the makeup. Whether the front of the button had a metal piece embedded, crushed glass added to the surface, or a complete overlay of glass applied, these decorations were done while the body of the button was still warm enough to be soft and adhesive. Because of the confusion caused by separating methods of making and decorating buttons, only those methods used during the makeup will be discussed below. Decorations and designs applied to cold buttons will be treated under a separate heading.

Blown Glass. These buttons were actually blown and were hollow. The early ones had clear glass loop shanks; later ones (probably after 1900) had metal shanks on metal plates. Color and sometimes bits of tinsel were blown into some of the hollow buttons. Most common are those that imitate pearl color, but there were a few made in pastel colors as well as in deep red, gray, and black; some have been found with cotton or a waxlike substance inside. Blown glass buttons were usually ball-shaped, but a few have been found faceted or oval. They range in size from 3/8″ to 3/4″.

Coronets. A term used for the glass buttons that had a preformed piece of glass added and fused to their tops. This preformed piece was small, shaped like a berry top, "doughnut," or a conventional blossom, and usually made of a contrasting color. The buttons were made in ball, cone, or dome shape.

Coronets. Front and side views of the nineteenth-century glass buttons known as coronets.

Crackle. A sixteenth-century Venetian technique used to decorate glass buttons in the nineteenth century, and still in use today. While the glass was hot and still in workable state, it was suddenly plunged in and out of cold water, causing the center surface to contract and break into interesting little lines, creating an intricate crackled pattern. Crackle buttons were largely made of clear glass, and in a few delicate colors. Most of them were ball-shaped with thin wire shanks, and were approximately 3/8″ in size.

Embedded Trim. A term used for preformed metal designs embedded into glass buttons. The design was a simple plain ring, a twisted ring, or a pictorial. The buttons with only rings were called, in the early collecting days, "cookies" or "bracelets"; this was before more decorative designs were found. Most of the buttons with embedded trim have swirl backs and wire shanks. The buttons were made in all colors of glass, mostly opaque glass, and were about 3/8" to 3/4".

Frosted Decoration. A term used loosely by button collectors for a dull, frosty finish on glass buttons. Sometimes the dull finish completely covered the surface, but more often it was used for parts of a design. The frosted appearance was achieved by treating the glass with acid, which removed its natural brilliance. This decoration must not be confused with decoration made by rolling the button in finely crushed glass while it was hot. *See* Glass Buttons: Salt or Sanded Trim; *also* Salt Decoration.

Inset Trim. This term has been frequently used for glass buttons having preformed glass decorations that were set into cavities molded for them. The Tingue buttons (*which see*) were made in this way. Insert trims were mostly used for decorating black glass. (*See* Glass Buttons: Black Glass.)

Kaleidoscopes. Glass buttons shaped during construction and decorated when cold. The glass body was molded round, with the front domed, faceted, "dimpled," or flat. After this piece was cold, a transfer design was applied to the flat back, and a metal shank plate covering the entire area was added to protect the design. The design was mostly brightly colored, sometimes consisting of lines in irregular patterns, suggesting the term "kaleidoscope." However, definite concentric, geometric, and pictorial designs were also used to decorate these buttons. Most of the wire shanks did not go through the glass, but a few did with a "pinhead." Those with metal shanks have been called "Tin Backs" and "Metal Backs." A few were made with luster-paint designs on paper for the backs, instead of metal plates. Kaleidoscopes range from 1/2" to 1".

Lacy. A term for glass buttons having a molded lacelike design. Lacy buttons are thin and relatively flat. Sometimes gold or silver luster paint has been put on the molded design. On the back of lacy buttons was applied a transfer or painted design, which showed through the front. Over this, a coat of paint, usually black, was used to protect the design. Lacy glass buttons were usually clear, though occasionally colored glass was used. They were made in two sizes. The small size measures about 3/8", the large size about 1 1/4". It is not easy to find these buttons in good condition; varying degrees of paint and design are often gone.

Lacy glass buttons.
Nineteenth century.

Mirrors. These buttons were constructed like kaleidoscope buttons but had silver only on the back of the glass, to produce a reflection. A metal shank plate with a wire shank covered the back. The fronts were sometimes partially frosty; at ther times, they had a cut design similar to Victorian mirrors. These buttons came ıostly in clear glass, but they were also made with amber, blue, green, and urple glass. They were made in sizes from 3/8″ to nearly an inch; the largest ones re the scarcest.

lolded Designs. Probably this method was used more than any other in creating esigns on glass buttons. Glass of every color was molded with countless designs –concentric, geometric, and pictorial with Victorian, *art nouveau,* political, his-orical, and modernistic influences. The designs were molded with either in-ised or raised patterns, sometimes in shapes to further the face design. Molded esigns were used on glass buttons of all sizes.

)utline Designs. (Also called Incised.) A finely molded outline barely "scratched" ıe surface to form a design, which commonly was filled with paint such as gold, lver, or white.

Glass buttons. Late-nineteenth-century glass buttons with outline designs.

)verlay Trim. This term refers to decorations produced by fusing glass to the front f the button; many types of decorations and designs have been found. Opaque lass sometimes had an overlay of transparent glass, and transparent glass was immed with opaque. The overlay trim might be banded, dotted, swirled, tipped, ıreaded, or a combination of these; or it might completely cover the button sometimes called "sheath overlay"). A trim of crushed glass (fine like salt, or ırger pieces called Spatter or Splatter) is also classed as overlay. The fine trim ometimes was allowed to remain rough, but the larger pieces were reheated and llowed to spread over the surface. There were also preformed overlay designs uch as cane, fruit, and flowers. (*See also* Hylas.)

Glass buttons. These are nineteenth century, with overlay trim (Hylas).

Paper Backs. A term for a type of glass buttons similar in construction to kaleidoscopes. In fact, many collectors include glass buttons with paper backs in a collection of kaleidoscopes. Instead of the design being on a metal back, the back of the glass button was slightly recessed, and into it a paper with a design was cemented. This paper back had no protection, and is often worn when found today. The buttons usually have a wire shank; very few have holes. The top of the button was sometimes molded with a design before the paper was added.

Paperweight Buttons. Collectors have recently adopted this term for buttons resembling glass desk paperweights in makeup. Most collectors use the term only for those glass buttons having high "caps" of clear glass that cover the design and nearly all the base. Others apply the term to all glass buttons having a base with a preformed design and a clear glass cap of any depth.

The materials for these button designs were also preformed: fancy canes were made; glass, including goldstone, was crushed; realistic objects were fashioned of glass, ceramic, or foil. The ceramic designs that appeared silvery when encased were called sulfides (*which see*). After the designs were made, the glassblower placed them on a base of translucent or opaque glass. This he covered with clear glass, sometimes pressing a mold against it to make a fancy top. Some glassblowers would start to built a paperweight button on a wire shank, which they held with tweezers; others would insert the shank while the glass was still hot and soft. All this building of paperweight buttons was done over a flame, so that the parts fused together into one piece of glass. Directly from the flame, a button was placed in a closed receptacle to cool gradually (to prevent shattering).

The earliest paperweight buttons had less variety of design than those made in the twentieth century. Most of the early ones had fancy coil cane, laid crosswise or placed on end, with finely crushed goldstone; the buttons with low caps were made with a larger variety of preformed designs on bases. All the early buttons were probably made in Europe. At the end of the nineteenth century, American glassblowers often demonstrated their skill at carnivals; included among the small articles they made were pieces that resembled paperweight buttons, but it is not known whether they put shanks on any of them.

Soon after World War I, glass buttons again came from European areas famous for their glassblowers. Among them were paperweight buttons on cards labeled "Czecho-Slovakia." These buttons resembled the nineteenth-century buttons with pink roses (twisted cane on end) and goldstone. However, they were smaller than the earlier ones and had small brass shank plates with loop shanks; a few had four-way box shanks. There were also two-piece buttons, sometimes called "two-piece paperweight" buttons. On the base of these was a painted design, usually flowers; the top was then cemented onto the design. The base had a box shank or self-shank.

About 1940, almost one hundred years after the first paperweight buttons, two American glassblowers with 1890–1900 glass-making experience began to make paperweight buttons—one in Boston, Massachusetts, and the other in Millville, New Jersey. Since then, other glassblowers have also made paperweight buttons. The two glassblowers in Boston and Millville followed very closely the simple patterns of nineteenth-century paperweight buttons, but later glassblowers have copied the intricate designs of desk paperweights made in early glassworks—latticinio, millefiori cane, bubbles, sulfides, foil, overlay, and other types of decorating—with a high cap of translucent glass. A few twentieth-century paperweight buttons have been made of colored glass. (*See* Paperweights.)

Although several glassblowers have produced paperweight buttons, and none of the buttons are more than thirty years old, these buttons are scarce.

Radiants. A term used for clear glass buttons with colored glass fused to the back. Sometimes just a very small amount of colored glass was placed around the shank; at other times, dots or lines were added to the molded design on the back. This decorating caused different designs to show through the front, according to the shape of the front. Such terms as "glories" and "reflectors" have been applied to the various uses of the added colored glass.

Salt or Sanded Trim. Two terms used by collectors for the application of finely crushed glass to glass buttons. Almost always the fine saltlike bits of glass were crushed white opaque glass, but occasionally colored glass was used to harmonize with the body of the button. The button was rolled in the crushed glass while it was still hot and soft, giving it a rough surface or a roughened design. These terms were not used by glassblowers.

Salt or sanded trim. Top row: camphor glass buttons with crushed white glass. Second row: dark glass with crushed colored and white glass. Nineteenth century.

Spatter, Splatter, or Splash. All three of these terms were used for the same method of decorating buttons with small chunks or fragments of crushed glass. The buttons, while still hot, were rolled in these prepared fragments of white or brightly colored opaque glass. Then the glassblower warmed the button again, which spread the added glass smoothly over the button in a definite pattern or a haphazard design.

 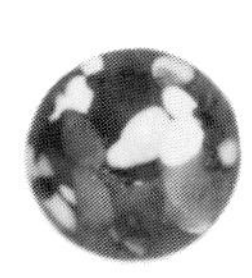  

Glass buttons. Nineteenth-century opaque glass buttons with overlay spatter trim.

Decoration and Design. Many glass buttons had added decorations; these, listed below, were applied after the buttons were cold.

Coralene. A method used for decorating glass buttons with smooth, beadlike pieces of glass. Just how many years this art has existed is not known, but in 1883, Arthur Schierhotz of Plaue, Thuringia, Germany, was given a patent for an improvement in the process for applying coralene decoration.

The area of the button to be decorated was first coated with an enamel compound of "syrupy" consistency, either colored or transparent. While this was still sticky, small solid or hollow beads, colored or not, were strewed over it. Then it was subjected to heat sufficient to melt the enamel coating and cause the beads to become cemented to the surface of the button without losing their shape.

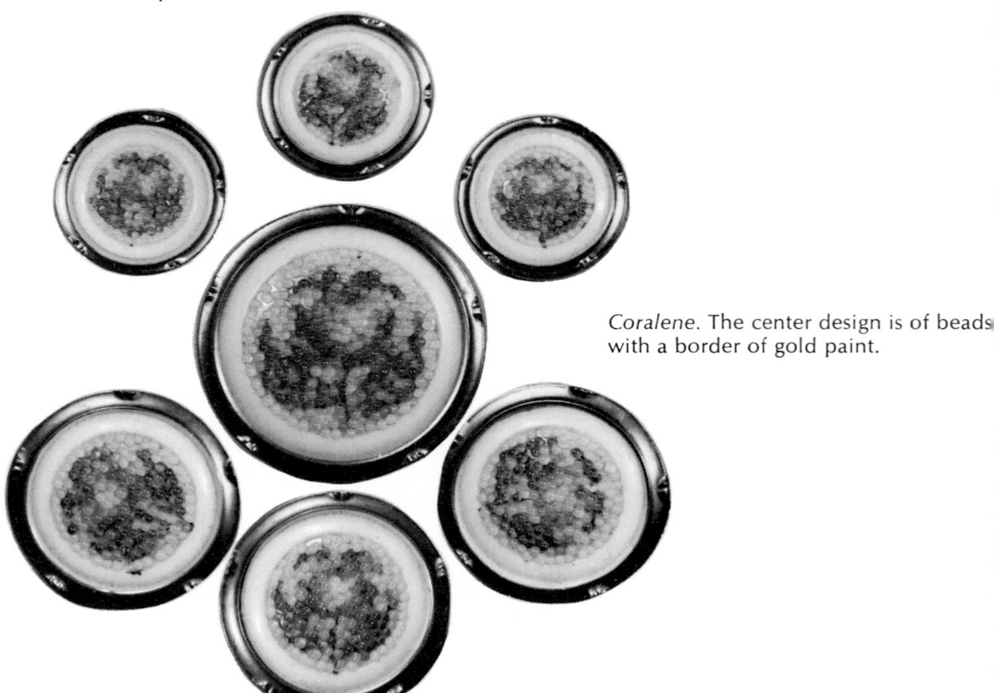

Coralene. The center design is of beads with a border of gold paint.

Enameled and Painted Designs. Many painted designs were used to decorate buttons, the paint being used either with or without ground glass. When the paint was used with finely ground glass, the decoration is called enamel. When paint was used alone, even though it was baked, it would flake or scratch off easily; therefore, many painted buttons are found in poor condition. When a design was made of paint combined with glass, it fused to the button when the button was warmed again. Very few clear or colored glass buttons were painted with the ground-glass mixture. Paint alone was more frequently used to add further decoration on the fronts and backs of molded glass buttons. Painted designs were put on the reverse side of wafer-thin buttons.

Painted Under Glass. The design was hand-painted on a cold, thin black glass button, and dried; then a thin layer of clear glass was laid over the design, and the whole was refired until the top layer of glass became fused to the button. About fifteen designs have been found. The colors of the designs are dark green and brown. The buttons range in size from 1/2" to almost 2". They were made in the late nineteenth century and are extremely rare.

Riveted. A term used for glass buttons having small faceted pieces, each one with a pin, fastened separately to a metal plate in the same manner as cut-steel trim.

There were very few of these made of colored glass. These buttons have sometimes been referred to as "passementerie," which is incorrect. (Passementerie was made of beads, silk braids, and other materials sewed together with needle and thread.)

Thread-Bound Trim. Threads were crisscrossed over the glass button in grooves molded for them. The threads were fastened around the wire shank; then, over the ends of thread and shank, a shank plate was placed. Usually the buttons were made of clear or black glass. The silk threads were white, but have turned cream-colored over the years. The buttons range in size from $^{1}/_{2}$" to $^{3}/_{4}$".

teenth-century glass buttons. ad-bound trim.

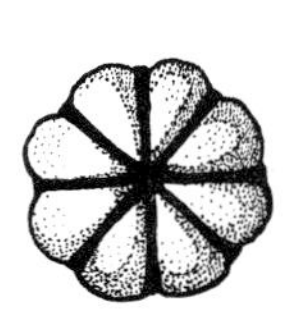   

Wafer Buttons. Wafer-thin buttons were made with flat glass fronts, metal backs, and loop shanks. Between the glass and metal disks there was usually a design. Cutout paper pictures (see Découpage), scattered tinsel, and paper with streaks of silver paint were among the decorations held in place with adhesives. Some buttons have geometric cuttings on the glass face; a very few were made of colored glass. Wafer buttons range in size from $^{1}/_{2}$" to over 1". The adhesives holding the glass and metal wafers together had a tendency to dry, letting the buttons fall apart. In most cases the adhesive was black, though a few buttons with amber-colored adhesive have been found. The latter have tinsel sprinkled under the glass.

Watch Crystal. This button consisted of a thin glass disk, usually slightly convex in the manner of a watch crystal, cemented to a flat metal back having a wire shank. Its construction was similar to that of a wafer button, but the type of decorating was different. There were often black and gold designs on the underside of the thin disks, concentric or pictorial. On the inside of the shank plate, showing through the "crystal," was a putty-like substance in which thin, irregular pieces of pearl shell had been placed. Unfortunately, these buttons have often lost the black "cement" on the back, placed there to hold the back and front together, and so they have come apart and the pieces have been lost. A few of these buttons do not have the common wire loop shank, but were made with holes for sewing.

Watch crystal buttons. Nineteenth century.

BLACK GLASS

Construction. Many buttons made of black glass were constructed in the same manner as all opaque glass buttons. It is true that some nineteenth-century glass buttons called black glass will show a deep blue, green, red, or purple tint when held to a strong light. However, if they appear to be black glass in normal light, they are acceptable in the black glass group. After 1900, black glass was almost always used for these buttons. In the nineteenth and early twentieth centuries, black glass buttons were often advertised as jet because of their color. *See* Glass Buttons: Clear and Colored Glass, Construction.

Mechanical Makeup. Most of the same techniques were used for shaping and trimming black glass as were used in the makeup of clear and colored glass buttons. Regardless of the color of the trim, if the body of the button was made of black glass, the button is included in the black glass group. For example, a black glass button having a large preformed trim of pink glass is still a black glass button; paperweight buttons having a base of black glass are included with black glass. (*See* Clear and Colored Glass: Paperweights.) However, Radiants having black glass trim are not black glass buttons (*see* Clear and Colored Glass: Radiants). Also, for makeup of other black glass buttons, *see* Clear and Colored Glass: Blown Glass, Embedded Trim, Frosted Decoration, Molded and Outline Designs, Overlay Trim, Salt or Sanded Trim, Spatter, Splatter, or Splash.

Black glass buttons. Painted under the glass; late nineteenth century.

Inset Trim. Black glass buttons more often had inset trims than those made of colored glass. Insets consisted of mosaic designs, single pieces of glass, shell, and the Tingue setups (*see* Tingue Buttons). Mosaic designs in glass without metal mountings are very scarce. In these, colored bits of glass were formed into designs of flowers or scenes, which were placed into a molded cavity of the button (*see* Mosaic Buttons). When single pieces of glass were used for insets, they might be wafer-thin pieces of plain glass, mottled glass, or twisted glass cane of more than one color. Sometimes buttons with insets of wafer-thin pieces have been called "Tile." When shell pieces were used, they were frequently cut into shapes such as flowers and stars. We cannot always tell whether insets were cemented or fused.

Sheet-Overlay Trim. This method of decorating is more often found on black glass than on colored glass buttons. The term is descriptive of the "sheets" of white or colored glass that were fused, one by one, to the black glass base; then a design was cut through the layers on the face or on the edge of the button, showing the several layers. Buttons with this trim are very scarce in any color. Sometimes they are found with the layers showing just around the bevel-cut edge, with a fancy head of a pin shank in the middle of the button.

Decoration and Design. More often than in the case of clear and colored glass buttons, buttons made of black glass were decorated after the buttons were made.

Enameled. The material used for this method of decorating consisted of finely ground glass mixed with the colored paint needed for the design. After the designs were painted by hand, the buttons were again heated sufficiently to fuse the decoration to the button, not long enough to injure the shape or surface of the button. These buttons have sometimes been called "Mary Gregory," after her manner of decorating glass. Some black glass buttons have little figures on them, but mostly the designs were birds, butterflies, fruits, and flowers. Occasionally, the buttons were first molded with the shape of the design before the enamel was applied. All enameled decorations were raised slightly above the surface, which differentiates them from painted designs.

Painted. The kinds of paint and the manner of applying them for decorations on black glass buttons were widely varied. Probably the most frequently used paints were the lusters. Luster paint was often applied by dipping or spraying the entire button; the lusters used were silver, gold, bronze, gunmetal, and iridescents of various hues. The lusters used in the nineteenth century were soft and rich in quality; twentieth-century lusters were more harsh and brilliant. The buttons to which luster paint was applied usually had molded designs, which included pictures of all kinds (*see* Picture Buttons), concentric, geometric, and conventional patterns.

Some of the painted designs were applied by the stencil method, one color at a time, such as those that imitated fabrics or wood. Paint was used as additional decoration on incised or finely molded designs. Much of the paint, except the lusters, dried out over the years, and many buttons with painted designs are found in poor condition.

GOLD. This material was seldom used for buttons. One reads about or sees in museums gold specimens called buttons, made prior to 1800, but records do not indicate these items were actually buttons. Because of the fabrics worn in the period of the gold specimens, it is more likely that these so-called "buttons" were pieces of jewelry rather than buttons to fasten or ornament garments. Gold was used to plate metal buttons, and as foil to decorate buttons in several ways.

GOLDEN AGE BUTTONS. A term for fancy gold-plated brass buttons made between 1830 and 1850. During these twenty years, button makers vied with one another both at home and abroad to produce elaborate designs of fine quality, for buttons were still an important part of a man's dress. They were selected with much aesthetic concern for their design and quality.

Handwork was still an important part of the manufacturing process; and the old standards of quality and excellence, combined with the exactness made possible by the use of machines, produced remarkable buttons. All buttons of the Omega and Sanders Type produced in this period are collectors' items. They are very scarce. The same excellent qualities appear in many of the campaign buttons made during the period. (*See* B. Sanders; Omega Type.) The designs were well drawn, and the dies for striking were finely made. Both one-piece buttons (Omega Type) and two-piece buttons (Sanders Type) often had added chasing.

One of the most interesting of the two-piece Golden Age specimens is called a Hunting Case button because in construction and ornamentation it is similar to the hunting case used on watches. A scrolled or floral design was popular. Sometimes part of the design was impressed, but the main design was always raised to the same level throughout.

Golden Age buttons. 1830–50.

GOLDSTONE. *See* Aventurine.

GOLF CLUB BUTTONS. Organized clubs for golfers have been very popular in several countries since the late nineteenth century. During that time and in the early twentieth century, golf clubs had buttons for members to wear on their jackets. This was especially true in England. Golf clubs and balls were popular designs for buttons made for sporting wear.

English golf-club buttons. 1890–1910.

GOODYEAR, AMASA J. *See* Amasa J. Goodyear.

GOODYEAR, CHARLES. American inventor who in 1839, while experimenting with rubber, accidentally dropped a mixture of sulfur and rubber on his stove. The lump became tough, and remained tough but elastic, a result he had tried to obtain for some time. This process—mixing rubber and sulfur and heating them to the necessary temperature—was named "vulcanization," after Vulcan, the Roman god of fire. Goodyear was granted a patent for the process on June 15, 1844. Charles Goodyear should not be confused with his brother Nelson, whose patent dates appear on rubber buttons.

GOODYEAR, NELSON. An American inventor who secured two patents relating to rubber, one in 1849 and the other in 1851. The 1849 patent was for "elastic cords for suspenders." The 1851 patent was for an improvement in the manufacture of India rubber. In this second patent, Nelson Goodyear explained the difference in the materials he used and his improvements in the process. The dates 1849 and 1851 are of particular interest to button collectors because they appear on hard-rubber buttons with the name Goodyear. The date 1849 appears very rarely, always in the combination as "1849–1851." The name and dates on the buttons do not indicate the date of their manufacture. *See also* Rubber Buttons.

GOOFY. This term was used first by Miss Dorothy Foster Brown, in her book *Button Parade,* for twentieth-century buttons. It refers to an odd, humorous, or picture button made from modern plastics, china, wood, nuts, cork, etc. (*See also* Realistics.)

GREEK KEY. A pattern used frequently for decorating buttons. It consists of straight lines bent, or joined, at right angles. The pattern is also called Greek Fret, and Meander. Sometimes it is repeated continuously to form a border; at others, it is used as a band across the button. Occasionally a single Greek key pattern is in the center of the button. Most commonly, the pattern is found on black glass and metal buttons.

Greek key design. The row contains a brass, horn, rubber, and steel button, in that order.

GREENAWAY, KATE. English artist and writer, 1846–1901. Many of Kate Greenaway's illustrations were copied by button designers, and buttons with these decorations are of particular interest to collectors. Several of her illustrations from her children's book *Under the Window* were used; others came from diaries and calendars. The designs appear mostly on nineteenth-century metal buttons, but were used also on buttons of other materials, particularly black glass. Sometimes the entire illustration was used; sometimes only a detail from it. There were other buttons made at the same time with similar (or imitated) designs of children, but these are not considered Kate Greenaway buttons until identified with an illustration. In the twentieth century, Kate Greenaway designs were molded on jasperware in the United States by Marie LaBarre Bennett; and metal buttons were stamped abroad, using nineteenth-century dies, for the American trade.

Picture buttons. Kate Greenaway designs; nineteenth century.

GRIFFIN, J. & G. *See* J. & G. Griffin.

GRILLEY, HENRY, SAMUEL, AND SILAS. Pewterers in Waterbury, Connecticut, 1790. Henry Grilley and his two brothers introduced the wire eye shank about 1800. This was an improvement over solid pewter shanks. Their names can be found on the backs of pewter buttons, but the buttons are very scarce.

GRISAILLE. The art of grisaille painting was introduced in the sixteenth century. It is found on ivory and on enameled and lacquered metal, as well as other materials. (*See* Enamel: En Grisaille, for this work on enameled metal buttons.) Grisaille painting was done in all white on a black background, the white being so applied that its varying thicknesses produced the shading. In fine items such as buttons, the layers of white were often cut into, to bring out the shades of gray produced by the layers of white. Sometimes the white-painted designs on black japanned buttons are referred to as Grisaille because of their gray shading; perhaps they were purposely painted to imitate Grisaille.

GROTESQUE DESIGNS. Two designs of unexplainable origin, found only on black glass buttons, have come to be designated as "grotesque." One is a turkey wing with a nail through it; the other is the foot of a turkey or some similar bird. These designs are always incised, never raised. The incised lines were filled with gold or silver paint.

GUT LOOP SHANK. This type of shank was used on metal-covered buttons with wood or bone backs. It has crossed loops of gut or string. *See also* Covered Type.

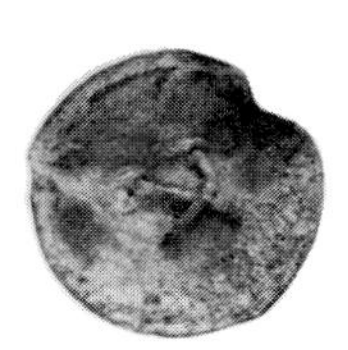
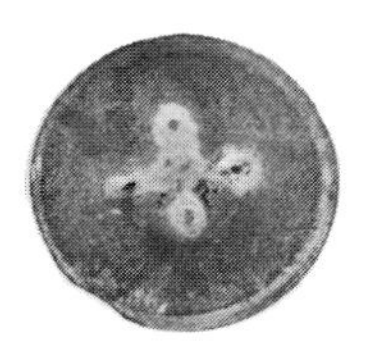

Gut loop shanks. Crossed loops of gut or string are used as the shank on these eighteenth-century face-type buttons.

GUTTA-PERCHA. The many articles, including buttons, which were made of a mixture of gutta-percha latex and rubber were also called "gutta-percha," although gutta-percha latex alone was never used. Buttons that appear to have some gutta-percha in their composition resemble hard-rubber buttons.

H

H. SMITH. Pewterer, Connecticut, 1815. Name found on pewter buttons.

H. T. & B. These initials represent Hammond, Turner & Bates of Manchester, England, probably outfitters, makers of uniforms, during the middle of the nineteenth century. Their initials and names have been found on the backs of Confederate uniform buttons.

H. T. & D. The firm Hammond, Turner & Dickinson, English makers of buttons about 1800. Buttons so marked were used in the War of 1812.

H. V. ALLIEN & CO. Makers of uniform buttons of all kinds, New York City, 1870–1900. Their name is found on the backs of buttons.

H. YOUNG. American button maker before 1833. Name found on buttons.

HABITAT BUTTONS. A group of buttons, probably of French origin, made in the eighteenth or very early nineteenth century, with the decoration placed under glass. It consisted of plant and animal specimens, or parts of them—the reason for the name "Habitat." Usually, these buttons have copper frames, and the glass face is convex. Habitat buttons are extremely rare, and often found in poor condition with the specimens dried and deteriorated.

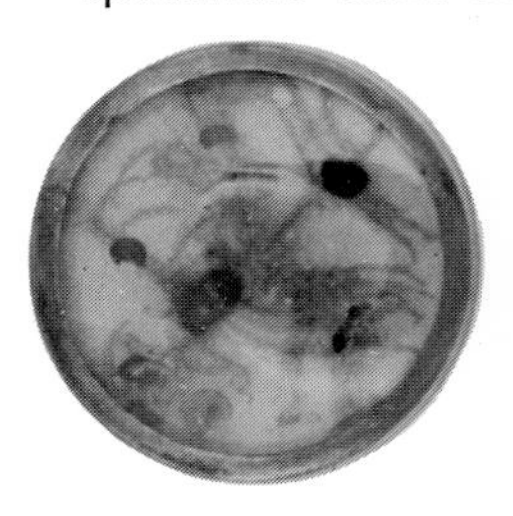
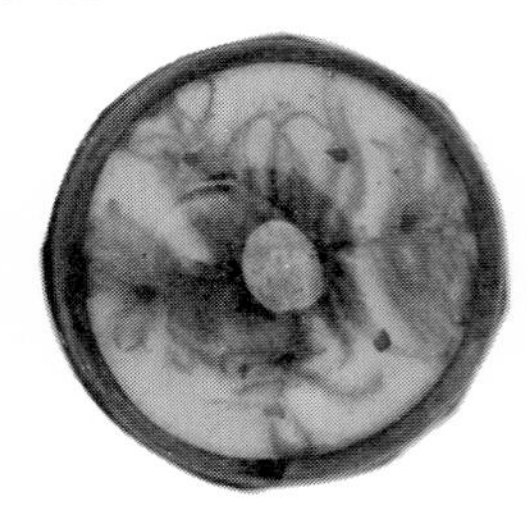

Habitat buttons. Eighteenth century.

HAIR BUTTONS. Very few buttons with locks of hair have been found, though lockets and brooches with hair are frequently found. Preserving locks of hair was a Victorian fancy, but there are no records of precisely when the fad first started. There are records of a "new kind" of hair jewelry that appeared earlier, about 1817—hair was woven into a web or net, and fashioned with gold into brooches, earrings, and buttons. These also are seldom found.

HALLMARK. An official stamp on gold or silver articles impressed at assay offices to attest standard. It is not to be confused with a trademark, maker's mark, or registration mark, which often appear on buttons. The hallmark consists of several symbols: the mark or marks of the town where the silver was assayed, the *lion passant* common to English silver, and the date letter. This letter shows the year in which the silver was assayed, but as the alphabet used was different in each town, it is necessary to consult a handbook on silver to determine the date. After this came the maker's mark, and since 1739 makers have been legally obliged to use the initials of their Christian and surname on their articles, or the initials of their firm. Most English makers' initials are listed in the book *Reference*. A maker's mark was stamped at the place of manufacture, before the article was taken to the assay office. The letter "F" indicates the article was not made in England, but sent to an assay office to ensure that it passed the English standard.

Hallmarks have been placed on the fronts and backs of buttons and on the shanks. In some cases, they were stamped in the design, as a part of it. *See also* Back Marks.

HAMMOND, TURNER & SONS. Button manufacturers of Birmingham, England, in the middle of the nineteenth century. The name has been found on Confederate uniform buttons and sporting buttons of fine quality.

HAND MACHINES. *See* Machines, Hand.

HANDKERCHIEF CORNERS. A name given nineteenth-century metal picture buttons that were cut square and had the corners bent over the front. Sometimes one square piece of metal was placed diagonally on a second square piece so that there were eight corners to bend over the front. Handkerchief Corners are sometimes called "Turned Corners." Frequently the corners have nails or screwheads on them, and usually there is an applied design in the center of the buttons, which are of fine quality.

Handkerchief corners. Nineteenth-century picture buttons with the corners bent over the front.

HAWKEYE PEARL BUTTON COMPANY. This company was an outgrowth of a Muscatine, Iowa, firm, in the button blank business since 1894. The new company, incorporated as the Hawkeye Pearl Button Company in 1903, continued the button blank business, but also installed automatic and hand machinery for making fancy freshwater shell buttons. For many years they headed the freshwater shell button business in this country.

HAYDENS, THE. New England manufacturers of buttons between 1820 and 1850. So far, it has been impossible to unravel the history of the Hayden families in Connecticut and Massachusetts. David and Daniel Hayden were making buttons in Waterbury, Connecticut, when a nephew, Festus Hayden, joined them. It is believed Festus was the son of Henry H. Hayden, who was later one of the organizers of the Waterbury Button Company. The Hayden name appears fairly frequently on gilt and sporting buttons—with these tentative dates: D. Hayden, 1827–29; D & S Hayden, 1850's; J. & J. Hayden, 1820's; Hayden & Son, 1840's; Hayden & Hobson, 1840's.

In Haydenville, Massachusetts, named for the Haydens, the town history gives the following facts: In 1831, Joel and Josiah Hayden started the manufacture of japanned and tin buttons (pants buttons); Joel Hayden (no date) experimented on a machine for lasting buttons, later known as "flexible shank" buttons. Joel Hayden entered partnership with Samuel Williston in 1848, and together they manufactured fabric-covered buttons. In 1844, Josiah Hayden manufactured horn buttons.

HEINZ GREEN GHERKINS. Realistically warted and molded, and bearing the Heinz name and sometimes the number "57," these green gherkins were believed for years to be buttons. Collectors frequently found them, with shanklike loops, in button boxes. They were originally made with pins, which linked to the loop that collectors mistook for a shank. H. J. Heinz Co. was founded almost one hundred years ago by a young man from Germany, who sold horseradish. The green pickle pin came into being as a publicity stunt at the World's Columbian Exposition in 1893. The company has no records of the quantity of pins given away at this exposition or later fairs, but it is estimated there were millions. Here is an example of a discarded souvenir that later became a collectible; pickle pins are scarce, especially the early ones. The first ones were made of plaster of Paris; later ones, of polystyrene plastic. Following are the most commonly found varieties: "Pat. 1895," early and rare, plaster of Paris; "Heinz," plain back, plaster of Paris; "Heinz, 57" on back, plaster of Paris; "St. Louis 1904," souvenir of St. Louis World's Fair; "Heinz Keystone," plain back, believed to have been given away at the sesquicentennial fair at Philadelphia, 1925; small charm-bracelet type, "Heinz 57," dark green polystyrene, New York World's Fair, 1938–39; polystyrene plastic, hollow, pin-back, recently made.

HERALDIC BUTTONS. Heraldic designs were used on many buttons. Most collectors consider these buttons in two groups: those with family coats-of-arms and crests; and dress buttons with designs including parts of heraldic symbols. There could be a third group, uniform buttons bearing imaginary coats-of-arms or crests, the designs being used on stock patterns and offered to concerns like hotels, motels, and restaurants. The first group, with family coats-of-arms and crests, are usually called Livery Buttons (*which see*).

The buttons called "heraldic" among picture buttons were usually made of metal, but in the twentieth century some have been made of plastics in bright pastel colors. Dress buttons of the nineteenth and twentieth centuries often had combinations of parts of coats-of-arms or crests, and pieces of armor such as helmets, knives, axes, or breastplates. This is one of the groups of buttons bearing designs unusual for women's wear, but judging from the number that have been found, the designs must have been fairly popular for this purpose. However, they are not popular collectors' items. One or two heraldic designs have appeared on buttons for men's inexpensive sports coats in the twentieth century. Some of these are almost exact copies of women's nineteenth-century buttons.

Heraldic uniform buttons. Silver-plated, one-piece; early 1800's.

Heraldic designs. These are on metal picture buttons; nineteenth century.

HIGH TOPS. *See* Dorset Buttons.

HISTORICAL. This word is very broadly used among button collectors, almost to the extent that a button with a design that merely causes reminiscence is referred to as a historical. There are, of course, buttons that were purposely designed for particular nonhistoric events that afterward became part of history. The designs on picture buttons were sometimes suggested by current celebrities or events in which the designers and salesmen of buttons saw popular appeal, such as Jenny Lind, world's fairs, centennials, and political caricatures. Gradually, buttons issued for groups that are no longer in existence also were referred to as historicals—those showing railways, steamship lines, school cadets, and so on. All Armed Forces buttons, too, are studied in historical groups. *See also* Armed Forces Buttons; Commemoratives; Picture Buttons; Political Buttons; Souvenir Buttons; Transportation Buttons.

HISTORICAL WOOD BUTTONS. Over the years, buttons have often been made out of woods from early buildings that were undergoing restoration or demolition. These buildings had historic associations—for example, the national Capitol or the birthplace of Henry W. Longfellow. Such a button must be accompanied by authentic data, or it becomes just another wooden button.

HOLLOW TYPE. Most of these buttons were constructed by brazing together two cupped pieces at the edges. In the eighteenth century, they were made of silver. Sometimes the back pieces were cast with an embedded wire shank. The term is more frequently used for buttons made by hand before 1800. Since that time, some have been made of other metals, and at least partially by machine.

HOLMES, BOOTH & HAYDEN COMPANY. Organized by Israel Holmes in Waterbury, Connecticut, in 1853 to roll brass. During the Civil War, they made brass buttons for both military and civil uniforms. They were succeeded by the company Rogers and Hamilton, 1886.

HOOF. Usually, this animal material was ground up with scraps of horn, and mixed with other materials into a plastic composition. The combination of materials was dyed in various dark colors and used for making buttons. It has been learned that more horn scraps were used than hoofs, but it is not possible to know if there is any hoof in the mixture of a particular button. Gradually, collectors have discontinued using the word "hoof." *See also* Horn Buttons.

HORN BUTTONS. The horns of animals were often used to make buttons. Horn lent itself to manufacture by reason of its natural characteristics. It could be split into thin sheets, welded together, or the fragments could be molded into various forms. All these processes required a combination of moisture, heat, and pressure.

Most collectors divide horn buttons into two groups, Natural and Processed. Natural horn buttons are those that were cut from the solid parts of the horn, shaped, and polished; sometimes they had self-shanks, sometimes wire loop shanks or holes. Those in the processed group were made in various ways out of the hollow portion. Horn was used for making buttons in the eighteenth century, but most buttons of this material that are found in old button boxes were made in Europe and in the United States in the nineteenth century.

Some natural horn buttons were cut by hand, others shaped by machinery. Designs were carved, or the buttons decorated with inlay of metal or pearl shell. Because of the natural coloration of the cattle horn, no two buttons were alike. In Europe, especially Austria, staghorn was used for making buttons decorated with carved designs in high relief. Occasionally, it was simply cut into disks, and two holes were bored for sewing.

Processed horn buttons are much more plentiful than those made of natural horn, perhaps because there are larger amounts of the hollow part of the horn. Such terms as "plastic" and "molded" are occasionally used. "Plastic" correctly refers only to those buttons made up of ground horn, which was mixed with adhesive materials. "Molded" is not always correct, since buttons made of the hollow pieces of horn usually had designs stamped by dies. "Processed" seems to be a more accurate term for all horn buttons that were not made of the solid ends of horn. It often seems unbelievable that such exceedingly fine designs could have been stamped into horn. Some processed buttons have fine designs, others designs in high relief; but horn buttons always show fine workmanship.

Horn was processed for buttons in several ways. The hollow ends of the horn were cut open and flattened under steam and pressure. The slabs made in this way could be welded to other slabs for thickness, or sliced for thin layers. The slabs were usually dyed before disks were cut out. Very often a design was stamped several times on one slab, the shanks being inserted before the buttons were cut away. If the dye had not penetrated through the horn, the natural edges were touched up with color to match. Most dyed horn buttons were black; dark colors such as red, green, brown, or imitation tortoiseshell were rare.

Among the variety of designs used on processed horn buttons were pictures, stories, conventionals, concentrics, and geometrics. These buttons had self-shanks, metal shanks, or holes.

Horn buttons. Molded and painted; nineteenth century.

Horn buttons. Processed horn picture buttons, dyed black. Nineteenth century.

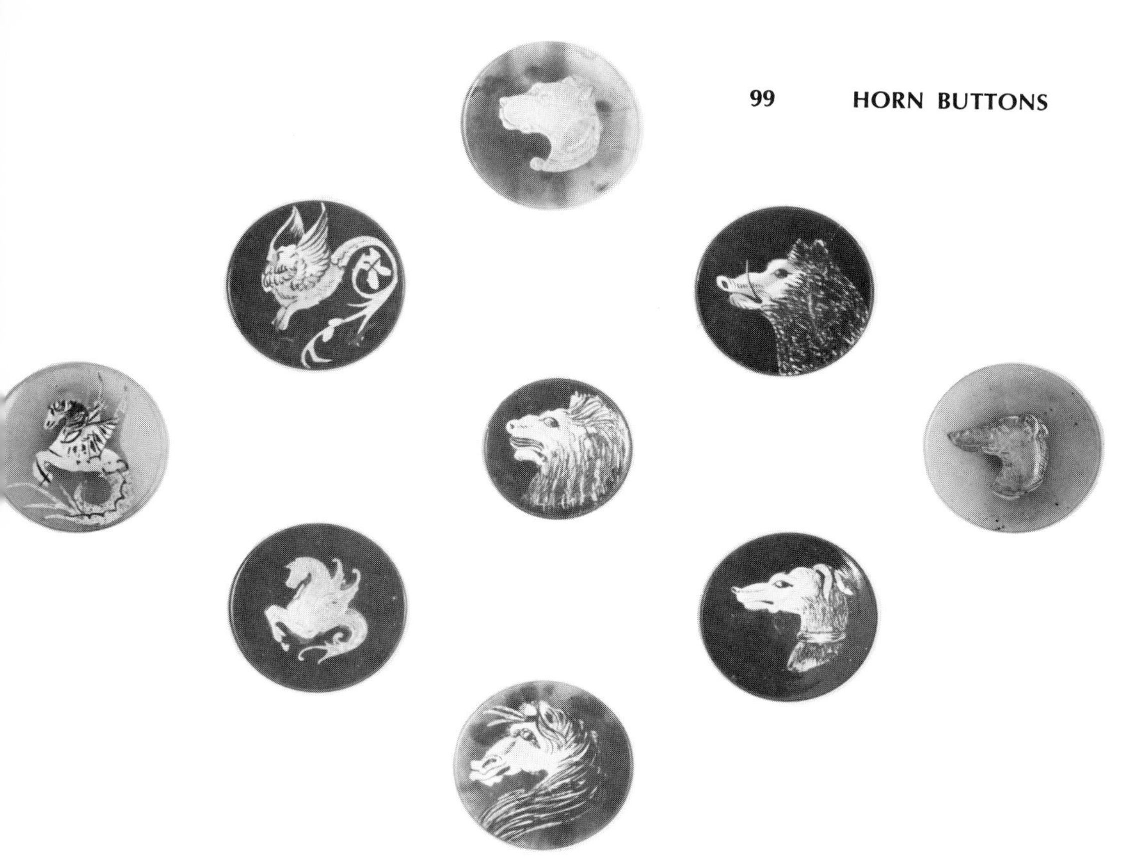

Horn buttons. Inlaid molded horn buttons, with gold and colored paint added. These are from a salesman's sample card (1885).

Horn buttons. Of natural horn with carved sporting designs. Nineteenth century.

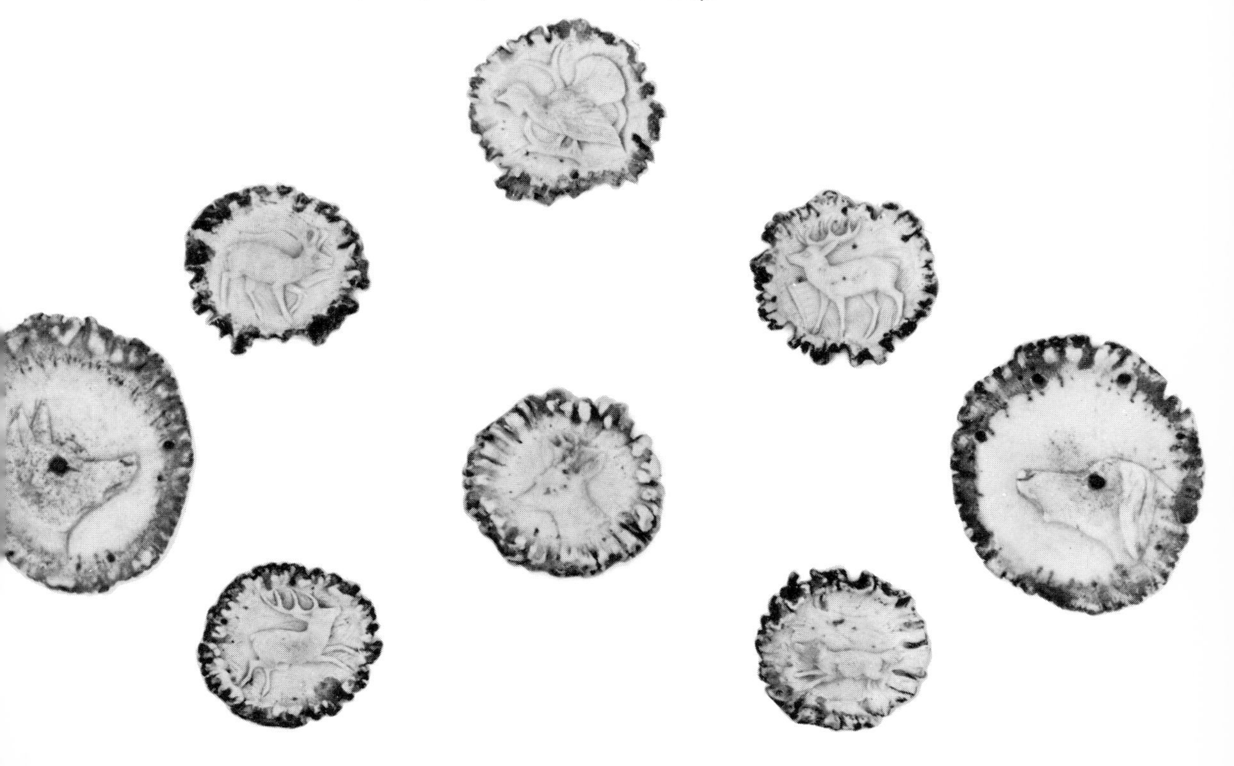

HORSEHAIR. A fabric woven of hair from horses' manes and tails. It was used to upholster furniture in the nineteenth century. Many pieces of furniture had buttons covered in the same material, and occasionally these buttons are found in button boxes. It is believed horsehair was never used to cover buttons for garments.

HORSTMANN. Military outfitters, New York and Philadelphia, 1860's to present. Firm names found on the backs of uniform buttons are: Wm. H. Horstmann, 1829–51; Wm. H. Horstmann & Sons, 1843–59; Horstman Bros. & Co., 1859–63; Wm. H. Horstmann & Co., 1864–66; Horstmann Bros. & Co., 1867–95; Wm. H. Horstmann Company, 1895–1942.

HORSTMANN BROTHERS & ALLIEN. Importers and outfitters, New York, 1850's to 1860's. Name found on backs of uniform buttons.

HUNT CLUB BUTTONS. In America and Europe there have been many hunt clubs, and most of them had specially made outfits, including buttons with club insignia. Sometimes a club had one outfit for riding and another for social events. Some clubs had a different habit for the women members, the color combinations and buttons varying. The buttons were made in silver or gold. There have been more hunt clubs in America than is generally realized, and so it is not too difficult to obtain a collection of American hunt club buttons. There is a Masters of Foxhounds Association of America, which has buttons of its own. There were United States Military Hunts after World War I, approximate dates 1920–39. To date, only fourteen clubs have been definitely confirmed. Some hunt club buttons have become almost obsolete, and are now rare.

British hunt club buttons. Nineteenth century.

HUNTING CASE. A term used for the two-piece Golden Age buttons that resembled, in construction and face stamping, hunting cases for watches. *See* Golden Age Buttons; *also* Watchcase Buttons.

HYDE and GOODRICH. New Orleans, Louisiana, 1850–60's. Name found on southern states' uniform buttons.

HYLAS. A term used for glass buttons decorated with glass dots and/or line trim in contrasting colors. Hylas were made of several colors, usually in dome or cone shapes. Some had a design of several dots; others, one or more dots and a thin line, which were fused to the button. Usually the button had a swirl back and always a wire shank. This term is not used as often as in the early collecting days; these buttons are now more often referred to as Dot Trim or Overlay Trim. *See also* Glass: Mechanical Make-up; Overlay Trim.

I

IGLOO. A type of Small China, so called because the applied piece in the center reminds one of an igloo. This is a two-piece china button ranging in size from 1/2″ to 1″. Some of the buttons have white bodies; others have light-brown mottled bodies. The igloo-shaped mound was fused onto a flat disk with two holes. The mound itself had a tunnel-like hole that was positioned close to the disk. When sewing the button to a garment, the thread was passed through one hole of the disk, then through the tunnel, and back through the second hole in the disk. Some collectors have mistaken the mound for a shank, and when the button has no design, this error is understandable. A few igloos have white mounds on mottled disks; some have black circles on a white disk and a black painted mound. This type is very scarce.

An igloo.
A type of small
china button;
nineteenth century.

INANIMATE. A picture button that has a design using inanimate objects such as nails, screws, hinges, locks, fences. Today, buttons in this group seem more popular as collectors' items than for dress wear.

INAUGURALS. Very few buttons were issued for inaugurals until the celluloid pins and ribbons came into use. Button collectors seldom include the latter in their collections. The origin of some early presidential buttons has not been definitely dated, and whether they were issued for campaigns or inaugurals is not accurately known. These are grouped as Presidentials and Politicals. The inaugurals issued for George Washington's inauguration have been authenticated, and several patterns have been found. For more details, *see* Washington Inaugural Buttons.

INDIA RUBBER COMB CO. (I.R.C. CO.) New York, 1880's–90's. In the directories, this company is listed as having made rubber combs and buttons. The buttons usually have the back marking "I.R.C. CO., Goodyear 1851." Back markings show that the company also made rubber bridle rosettes, and rosettes with designs under glass in brass mountings. To date, dress buttons with glass centers have not been found with I.R.C. Co. back markings.

INDIAN POTTERY BUTTONS. A few pottery buttons were made by the American Indians. These, usually terra-cotta, have light-brown or tan painted surfaces with boldly painted Indian symbols outlined in black and filled in with orange or brownish red. Generally, they were molded with slightly convex fronts and flat backs, with holes, though a few are square or triangular. They are usually large, over $1^{1}/_{4}''$. Most of those available to collectors were bought at Indian reservations in the twentieth century.

Indian pottery buttons. Twentieth century.

INDIAN SILVER BUTTONS (American). There are two classes of Indian Silver buttons available today: pawned buttons and buttons made for the market. Pawned buttons were those worn by the Indian, and at some time used as cash at the trading post. They were often transferred directly from the dress or pouch to the trader, in lieu of cash. The buttons were held by the trader for a certain length of time; then, if not redeemed, they were sold. This was the practice in the eighteenth century, and is still the practice today.

The American Indian has always favored silver, discarding gold along with copper and brass as undesirable material. Indian silver buttons vary widely in size, design, and shape. Some were made with simple patterns; others had elaborate settings and die work.

Many of the earliest buttons were made of silver coins and shaped on wooden blocks with designs scratched or filed on one side, the notched edge of the coin being the edge of the button. Coins with a loop soldered on one side have always been favorite buttons of the Indians; as many as one hundred coins of various sizes might be sewed on one costume. Dies were used to make designs, some of which were fluted, others punched. "Squash blossom," really pomegranate, was a popular pattern. Buttons were also made of wire by pulling silver bars through a draw plate.

Sometimes Indian buttons are ornamental pieces of silver too long and narrow actually to have been used as fasteners; these were used as collar ornaments or to outline the opening of the blouse, or in rows around, up, and down the sleeves, and even on the backs of blouses. The favorite stone used for Indian silver buttons was the turquoise, prized by them for generations.

Buttons made specifically for the market in the past few years are mostly machine-made, though advertised as "Indian made." They were stamped by the thousands, made of much thinner silver disks than the pawn buttons, and usually less deeply struck. Very often the stones in buttons made for the market are a cheaper grade, sometimes dyed stones from Germany. There are still a few fine silversmiths on the reservations today, and their work is done by hand.

Indian silver buttons were made in so many forms and designs that there is no limit to the number that can be collected.

Silver buttons. Of the American Indians (pawned silver, c. 1880).

INLAY. The art of decorating one material by setting pieces of another material into its surface. Inlay was used to ornament buttons of such various materials as shell, ivory, bone, horn, wood, and vegetable ivory. Button disks were cut away for the inlay pieces, which therefore had to be precisely cut, and—very often—were extremely

Inlay. The first button in the top row has an inlay of pearl shell and metal in tortoiseshell. The others in the top row are of dark wood with inlays of colored wood. All the buttons in the bottom row are of tortoiseshell with metal inlays. The first and third of these are commemoratives.

tiny. Assorted woods of various colors were used to decorate a wooden button, perhaps to form such a design as yellow flowers with green leaves. Shell was the material most frequently used for inlay in buttons of shell of another shade, as well as in buttons of other materials. The term "inlay" has sometimes been used for the added decorations found on lacquer-coated buttons, such as the pearl designs on papier-mâché buttons. *See also* Papier-mâché Buttons.

INSECTS. A popular subject with designers of picture buttons, and equally interesting to button collectors. Insects appeared on buttons of nearly all materials—either drawn, carved, molded, stamped, or inlaid.

Insects. The designs are inset in ivory buttons; nineteenth century.

INSETS. When designs were set into button disks and not polished off evenly with the surface, they were frequently spoken of as "insets." The raised design was preformed, sometimes in realistic shape. Several ivory buttons have been found ornamented in this way.

INTAGLIO. The art of cutting a design so that it is depressed below the surface of the material, rather than raised as a cameo is. Most intaglio designs found on buttons were not cut, except for a very few cut into gemstones. The term usually refers to designs that have been molded intaglio-style. Many glass buttons have molded designs of this kind, particularly black glass buttons. Intaglio designs should not be confused with recessed cameo designs, which were molded below the surface of the button.

Insets. Ivory buttons with insets of jade, coral, tortoiseshell, and pearl shell.

IRON. This metal was used for buttons that were to be decorated with lacquer or paint. Iron was used for the backs of buttons, and was usually tinned. Hence, it is seldom recognizable in a button.

ISRAEL, JACQUES. American maker of paperweight buttons since the 1940's. His first buttons were made without shanks—the paperweight was cemented into a metal "cup" that had a metal shank. The first buttons he made with shanks had a heavy wire shank with only one end embedded in the glass. Israel made some paperweight buttons with sulfide designs, but most of his buttons had finely drawn-out glass cane. He also made some masklike glass buttons in brilliant colors. The features of the mask were applied; for example, the green devil had red glass horns. These masks, of course, were made for collectors, with no thought of fastening a garment.

IVES, KENDRICK & CO. American manufacturer, 1830's–47, maker of plain and fancy gilt buttons. *See* Waterville Manufacturing Company.

IVES, L. American pewterer, 1814. Only plain pewter buttons have been found with this name.

IVES, SCOTT & CO. American manufacturer, 1830's. Maker of plain and fancy gilt buttons. *See* Waterville Manufacturing Company.

IVOROID. A term used for two types of metal buttons with celluloid centers. It is really not a correct term, since Ivoroid was a trade name for the celluloid rod made by Landers, Frary and Clark (New Britain, Connecticut), and their rods were never used in the making of buttons. The buttons referred to were made of metal. One type had a very thin stamped design; the other had a cutout design, the disk being a little thicker than in the first type. The stamped centers have scenes, flowers, heads, or stories. The cutout centers were usually flowers. The construction of Ivoroid buttons indicates they were made nearer to 1900 than the Connecticut firm made its Ivoroid rods.

IVORY. The tusks of several animals have been used in the making of buttons, but elephant tusk is considered to be the true ivory. Commercially, the teeth and tusks of the hippopotamus, walrus, narwhal, and sperm whale are included. Ivory shows fine arched or contour lines that form very small lozenge-like areas where they intersect. It is to this structural arrangement that ivory owes its fine grain and the characteristic marking by which many people are guided in distinguishing it from celluloid or other imitations.

The art of working ivory had its origin in India. Beautiful work was also done in Italy, China, and Japan. Probably the most popular method for decorating ivory is carving. The carver took a piece of ivory of suitable size, and with saws and files cut away the material until he formulated the design. More recently, the carver would press the ivory against revolving cutting wheels, varying in size from one eighth of an inch to three inches. These wheels were similar to his hand tools, but cut more rapidly. The last step was polishing, which was done with pumice stone and flannel.

Ivory buttons with inlays of horn, shell, or metals are a handsome type to collect. Ivory has also been used to make inlay designs in buttons of other materials.

Hand painting on ivory reached its height with miniatures. Grisaille was one of the methods used for painting on ivory. When made into buttons, these painted pieces were sometimes given frames and glass faces. Stenciling is another method that was used in decorating ivory buttons.

Eskimos, using mostly walrus-tusk ivory, did much of their decorating with "picture writing." The designs were finely cut and filled with black pigment, a process similar to the scrimshaw work of the New England whalemen.

Ivory. Buttons of Alaskan ivory; twentieth century.

Ivory. The design is carved in ivory, under glass, on a foil background (eighteenth century).

J

J. & G. GRIFFIN. Botsford, Connecticut; manufacturers of horn buttons. The firm was established in 1846. John and George Griffin were father and son. John Griffin invented the first cam machine for turning horn buttons. With the invention of labor-saving machines, the firm grew until in 1890 (it was said) they led all competitors in the making of horn buttons, which they turned out in over one hundred styles from 1/4" to 2 1/2" in diameter. In 1890, the firm was known as Griffin Bros.; George and B. N. Griffin were the owners.

J. & J. CASH COMPANY. This company was organized by John and Joseph Cash in 1864 in Coventry, England. They manufactured cloth-covered buttons, ribbons, and labels with woven designs in contrasting colors. The buttons were made shortly after World War I. There was an American branch in Connecticut, but only ribbons and labels were made in that factory. Most of the button designs were flowers: daisy, buttercup, morning glory, chrysanthemum, rose, and poppy; two bird designs were the swallow and robin. The designs were generally woven in white fabric, although some colored materials were used; sizes were 3/8" to 3/4".

J. R. GAUNT & SON. Button manufacturers from the 1870's to the present, with factories in England, offices in New York and London. J. R. Gaunt's name appears on many metal buttons, mostly uniform buttons, made for the European and American trade.

JACKSONIAN. A term coined (by David F. Johnson in the 1940's) for certain buttons made during the period of Andrew Jackson's fame. Jacksonians are small solid, or one-piece, buttons with a separate plain rim turned over the edge to form a border. All were brass, gilt finish, with a plain disk having a raised design. Typical subjects were squirrels, horses, eagles, baskets, fire equipment, locomotives, flowers, harps, and anchors, but

Jacksonians. 1840 to the 1850's.

there were many more. There are other buttons of the same period and similar construction that are not usually included in this group; some collectors call them "cousins." These cousins sometimes have fancy borders, or disks made of pewter and pearl. The buttons range in size from 1/2" to 3/4". Two-piece buttons in these same sizes, with fronts rolled over the back, and self-borders, must not be confused with Jacksonians, although they were made and worn at the same time. To date, there are one hundred or more different designs known.

JACQUARD LOOMS. Invented by Joseph-Marie Jacquard in Lyons, France, these looms were publicly shown for the first time in 1801. Jacquard was born into a family of weavers, and learned the art early. His invention was an improvement over all previous machines for weaving designs into fabrics. After 1801, other improvements were made, but machines that wove patterns continued to be called Jacquard looms. On these looms, damasks, brocades, and other materials were woven with designs made especially for covering button molds.

JAPANNING. A process developed as a substitute for expensive Oriental lacquering, about 1800, in England, France, and Holland. The "synthetic lacquering" known as japanning was simply a high grade of varnishing—with each coat being dried by heat before the next one was applied. Five or six coats were necessary to give sufficient body to prevent the japan from being rubbed through in polishing. Japanned buttons were further ornamented with gold leaf, transfer printing, stenciling, or other decorations. Japanning has been done on papier-mâché, pewter, wood, brass, and tin buttons. Black japan was the most commonly used, but occasionally colored japan is found.

JASPERWARE. A pottery originated by Josiah Wedgwood of England, in the 1700's. This material was used for button making soon after its invention. Jasperware is a very smooth vitreous pottery, needing no glaze. It was made in black, white, and in several colors, such as blue, green, lavender, and brown. Usually, white figures were applied. The white decorations were formed in molds, then carefully finished by hand. The decorations needed only water to hold them in place on the colored disks, since the disk and the design fused in the firing. Most of Wedgwood's figures were classical subjects.

Jasperware. Medallions mounted in silver buttons; eighteenth century.

From the beginning, Wedgwood had many imitators in almost every country, including England. So well did some potters imitate his jasperware that it is almost impossible to be sure the buttons we find today were made in the Wedgwood potteries, unless they are marked. Jasperware medallions were put into silver and steel button mountings as early as the late 1700's. Josiah Wedgwood's early jasperware buttons are extremely rare. In the 1950's, the Wedgwood firm made a few blue and white buttons for the George Ertells.

Jasperware buttons have been made in America since the early 1950's by Marie La Barre Bennett. Her buttons are marked "MB" on the back, sometimes accompanied by the date. They have been made in all the popular jasperware colors, in modern designs as well as classical.

Wedgwood jasperware buttons. 1950's.

Jasperware buttons. Made by Marie La Barre Bennett in the 1950's and 1960's.

JENNENS & BETTRIDGE. Well-known makers of papier-mâché in the 1800's. *See also* Papier-mâché Buttons.

JENNENS & CO. A London firm. The name is found on Confederate buttons.

JET BUTTONS. Buttons made of jet apparently did not appear until the early nineteenth century. Records indicate jewelry was made of jet as early as the sixteenth century, and the little articles of jet called buttons are more likely to have been small dangling pieces from jewelry. Jet buttons are very scarce— most of them are in museums. It is known that craftsmen in Yorkshire, near jet mines, made beautiful buttons; but only a few buttons were known to have been made in Whitby, where much jewelry was made.

The material that most nearly approaches the appearance of jet is vulcanite, and it was used as a substitute. Black glass buttons were often called "jet," but in this usage the term refers only to the color of the glass. It is doubtful that black glass buttons were made to imitate jet; the glass is very much glossier and heavier.

Jet buttons.

JEWEL BUTTONS. (Jewels.) A term used for metal buttons having one "stone" in the center. Though this center was often referred to as a stone, it was made of molded glass or pieces of glass, less frequently of other materials. The molded glass centers were flat or domed, or had raised designs such as flowers or heads. One of the molded designs most popular among collectors is the head of Jenny Lind. Painted designs were often put on the smooth glass surfaces. Clear and opaque glass of all colors was used. Some centers had pieces of glass arranged in various patterns; others had mosaic designs.

The small jewel buttons with round loop shanks were worn mostly on women's basques in the nineteenth century. Some twentieth-century jewel buttons have self-shanks. The buttons with long loop shanks were worn on men's vests in the nineteenth and twentieth centuries.

Jewel buttons range in size from 1/4" to 1/2". Larger buttons with less dainty centers and with wider metal mountings are frequently called Victorian Jewel Buttons. *See* Victorian Jewels; Mosaic Buttons; Jeweled Buttons; and Waistcoat Buttons.

JEWELED BUTTONS. Stories and records tell us that jeweled buttons became an important part of men's costumes in the 1500's. It is written that Henry VIII of England (c. 1500) had quantities of jeweled buttons, and that Francis I of France had several thousand gold and jeweled buttons on a single costume. It has also been reported that Sir Walter Raleigh wore pearls and rubies on his clothes. King James's favorite, the Duke of Buckingham, could afford diamonds tacked on so loosely that they frequently fell off; and Mary Queen of Scots' inventory mentioned four hundred enameled buttons, each with a ruby in the center. Regardless of these accounts, it is believed by those who have done extensive research that actual buttons set with gems or glass did not come into use until the seventeenth century.

As a class, jeweled buttons might readily include early gemstone buttons with a jewel set in the center, or silver buttons with jewels in the border. Those that the collectors are most likely to find today have glass or paste as imitation jewels. The collector also refers to nineteenth-century metal buttons set with a gemstone or piece of glass as jewel buttons.

JOHNSON, DAVID F. American author who wrote *American Historical Buttons,* and its supplement, 1942, now out of print. He also wrote *Uniform Buttons,* volumes I and II, 1948; published by Century House.

JONES, W. H. American manufacturer of gilt buttons, 1830-32. His name is found on gilt buttons.

JORDAN PEARL BUTTONS. Buttons of hand-carved white mother-of-pearl shell made in Bethlehem in the Holy Land during the twentieth century. There have been over a hundred different patterns. The buttons range in size from 3/4″ to over 1 1/2″.

Jordan pearl buttons. Hand-carved mother-of-pearl buttons from the Holy Land; twentieth century.

JUDDS (JUDD and WOOSTER). These names are found on pewter buttons. Very little is known about the men, except that they were in business in Connecticut. The approximate date of their button making was the 1830's.

JUST BUTTONS MUSEUM. Located in Southington, Connecticut; established in 1950. Founded by Sally and Victor Luscomb, and housed in the historic Sally Lewis home, the Just Buttons Museum has both permanent and changing exhibits of antique and modern buttons. A large gallery room contains framed exhibits of buttons illustrating raw materials and button-making techniques, with fine examples of representative buttons. Also on display are early button-making tools such as dies and molds, and all sorts of button-related items. In all, five rooms have exhibits of buttons. The museum is open by appointment.

Since 1942, the Luscombs have published a monthly magazine, *Just Buttons,* issued on a subscription basis. The magazine includes articles by various button experts and authorities in their fields, and collectors find it useful for up-to-date button data and research.

K

KALEIDOSCOPE. *See* Glass: Mechanical Makeup.

KAZIUN, CHARLES. Massachusetts. He began glassblowing in his high-school days—out of sheer fascination with the subject. He is now well known for his glass paperweights and paperweight buttons, which he began to produce in the 1950's. Mr. Kaziun was the first of the twentieth-century glassblowers to use foil designs in paperweight buttons. His buttons can frequently be identified by a small *K* in one cane.

KENDALL, DOROTHY. American maker of porcelain buttons in the 1950's. Miss Kendall hand-painted her buttons with colors that were fired in her own kilns. Some of her subjects were the Presidents' wives, Iwo-Jima, Fort Sumter, and the Spirit of '76.

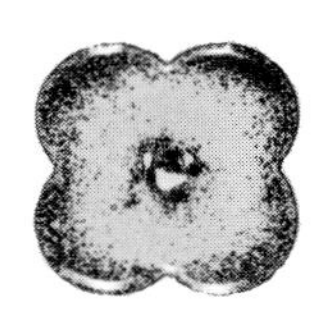

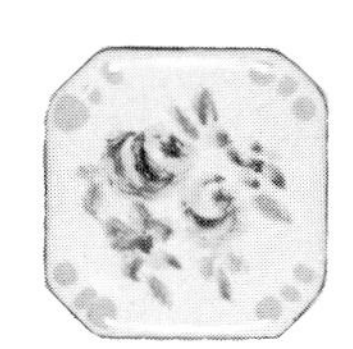

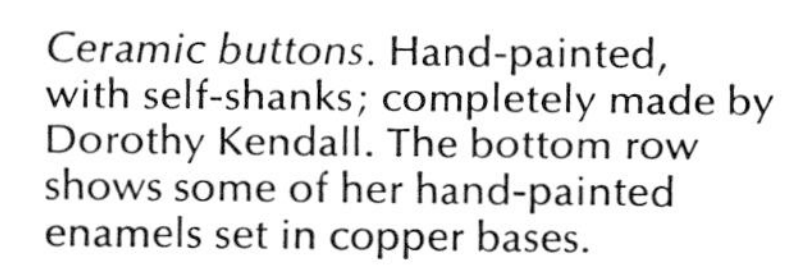

Ceramic buttons. Hand-painted, with self-shanks; completely made by Dorothy Kendall. The bottom row shows some of her hand-painted enamels set in copper bases.

KEY PATTERN. *See* Greek Key.

KEY SHANKS. A term used for a flat metal shank with a hole drilled in it. Key shanks are most frequently found on twentieth-century glass buttons.

The key shank. Usually found on twentieth-century glass buttons.

KNAPP ORIGINALS. A trade name for fabric-covered buttons hand-painted by Blanche Knapp in the 1950's. Most of the buttons were newly covered, but sometimes Mrs. Knapp painted over old fabric buttons. She also painted a few shell buttons. Her subjects were many, including flowers, birds, winter and summer scenes, and famous buildings.

Knapp Originals. Hand-painted, fabric-covered buttons; twentieth century.

KNITTED BUTTONS. Some buttons were covered with little "caps" knit with fine thread. Apparently not many were made, as few are found. All the knitting was probably done by machine. *See also* Fabric-covered Buttons.

L

L. IVES. American pewterer, 1814. Only plain pewter buttons have been found with this name.

L. MERRIAM. American pewterer, 1815.

L. PRITCHARD. Name found on gilt buttons. *See* Pritchard, Leonard.

LA MODE. A trade name found on buttons and cards of buttons. *See* B. Blumenthal & Sons.

LA RUCHE COLLECTION. A collection discovered by Mr. Otto Boschen, the president of Bailey, Green & Elger Company, Inc., New York, button manufacturers and importers.

The circle (beginning with the top center button and reading clockwise): (1) Two-piece copper-rimmed button with head printed on paper, under glass; (2) copper button with reverse painting on the glass center; (3) two-piece copper-rimmed button with the design printed on paper; (4) two-piece copper rimmed button with polychrome painting on ivory under glass; (5) agate button with copper rim and cut-steel pinhead shank; (6) two-piece copper-rimmed button with reverse painting under glass; (7) jasperware disk held to a steel disk by cut-steel pinhead shank; (8) two-piece copper-rimmed button with the design printed on paper, under glass. The center button has a black background painted on ivory, tinsel trim, and the figure outlined in gold.

Row 1: All are eighteenth-century buttons, with the design under glass, and copper rims. (1) Two-piece button with design printed on paper; (2) two-piece button with reverse painting on glass; (3) two-piece button with design painted on ivory; (4) same construction as on (1).

Row 2: (1) Sulfide design with blue background, under glass, set in a copper button; (2) two-piece copper-rimmed button with the design woven in silk and set under the glass; (3) carved pearl shell with paste trim.

On one of Mr. Boschen's trips to France, he found this large collection in an old building near Paris. Mr. Boschen purchased it and brought it to the company's office in New York. After the collection was restored and mounted in display frames of various sizes, collectors were invited to visit. Some of the collection is still on exhibit there.

The La Ruche Collection contained buttons of all kinds, beautiful enamels, stamped metal buttons, some with cut-steel trim, paste, and many others. A great variety and number of specimens were in this collection. Bailey, Green & Elger arranged some of the buttons in large frames for traveling, and for the past fifteen years these have been lent to leading department stores across the country. Quite frequently, announcements are seen in newspapers giving the dates when a portion of this display will be exhibited in a store in a nearby city.

LACE BUTTONS. Handmade and machine-made lace were used to cover buttons. Not many lace buttons have been found, probably because they were not practical.

LACQUERED BUTTONS. "Lacquered" and "japanned" are two words used interchangeably when referring to varnished buttons. However, true lacquer is found mostly on Oriental buttons. In the Orient were certain trees, the resinous juices of which formed the basis of this lacquer, which dried very hard without artificial heat. Often, as many as fifteen coats of lacquer were applied, each coat being dried and polished before the application of the next coat. After the final coat and polishing, designs were hand-painted in gold. Oriental lacquered buttons are extremely rare; they have a softer finish than japanned buttons. *See also* Japanning.

Oriental lacquered buttons. These are made of wood; nineteenth century.

LACY GLASS BUTTONS. In the early days of button collecting, these buttons were sometimes incorrectly called Sandwich glass, probably because their patterns resembled some lacy patterns made at the Boston and Sandwich Glass Company. *See* Glass Buttons.

LAFAYETTE BUTTONS. These buttons were issued in honor of the Marquis de Lafayette's second visit to the United States in 1824. A portrait on buttons at a time when coat buttons were plain was a novelty. It is said that the public responded favorably, and the demand continued for several years. These are probably the collector's finest portrait buttons. The initials of the die engraver can be found below the collar: "Wt Ft." The button most commonly seen has only Lafayette's portrait, and was made in two sizes of one-piece gilt. There is another Lafayette button, less often found, which is a little larger, with the words "General Lafayette" around the edge; it is a two-piece button with tinned back. These should not be confused with the Lafayette Presentation buttons.

Lafayette buttons. 1824 to the 1830's.

LAFAYETTE PRESENTATION BUTTONS. The buttons presented to Lafayette on his visit to the United States in 1824 were made of native gold found in North Carolina. They were made by Leavenworth, Hayden and Scovill. The original die was found in an old chest as recently as 1953. Ten of the original buttons are now at La Grange, France, in the Lafayette Museum, with many other treasures related to the life and works of General Lafayette.

The frequently found one-piece gilt buttons with the head of Washington, which are called Lafayette Presentation buttons, were made by the Scovill Manufacturing Company with a new die, and given away to friends of the firm. The buttons vary somewhat in size and stamping. There are four distinct differences in the fronts of the buttons. The ones made to be given away at the Centennial Exhibition in Philadelphia, 1876, are the smallest of these gilt buttons, a little over 1/2" in diameter. There was a special strike of silver buttons with the same front around 1900. The one-piece gilt buttons have a similar inscription on the backs: "Presented to General Lafayette by L. H. SCOVILL BUTTON MANUFACTURERS/WATERBURY CON." In recent years, the letter "R" with the year has been stamped on the back; for example: "R/52" (restrike 1952). Hundreds of restrikes have been made since 1876; they were given as souvenirs, and are fairly easy for collectors to find. See the illustration under Souvenir Buttons.

LAMINATED BUTTONS. A word used by some collectors for marquetry or inlay buttons. Actually, the process has been used very little, if at all, in button making. *See* Marquetry.

LAMSON, Wm. American manufacturer of buttons, 1814. Name rarely found on buttons.

LANE MANUFACTURING COMPANY. American manufacturer of buttons, Waterbury, Connecticut, 1840's–1924. Although the company made some late gilt buttons, they made mostly picture buttons. One of the most popular of their designs among collectors is the Red Riding Hood pattern. Dies from this concern were purchased by the Just Buttons Museum in the 1940's, when the remaining factory stock was being sold. Among these was the die for the Red Riding Hood button. The Lane Company seldom put its name on the backs of buttons; therefore, it is not easy to identify them. *See also* Dies.

LAPEL BUTTONS. Most of these buttons were made with a studlike back. The group includes buttons issued for campaigns and also those for fraternities and lodges. They have been made of china, metal, composition, wood, and celluloid, and trimmed with many materials—throughout both the nineteenth and twentieth centuries. Most button collectors do not include lapel buttons, but collectors of campaign items eagerly seek them along with other campaign buttons. *See also* Studs.

LAPIS LAZULI. A gemstone rarely used for buttons. When buttons with lapis lazuli are found, they usually have plain, jewel-like mountings, often with a long shank, indicating they were probably worn on men's waistcoats in the early nineteenth century.

LE CHIC. A trade name found on the backs of buttons and on cards of buttons. *See* B. Blumenthal & Company.

LEAGUE OF AMERICAN WHEELMEN. *See* Bicycle Buttons.

LEATHER. Except for the woven, knotlike leather buttons, very few buttons have been made of leather. Some leather novelty buttons were made in the twentieth century. Leather was embossed and used for centers in nineteenth-century wood and metal buttons, and there was a coated paper that was stamped with a likeness to leather, which was also used to decorate metal buttons.

Metal and wood buttons. These have embossed leather centers; nineteenth century.

Leather buttons. Twentieth century.

LEAVENWORTH & COMPANY. *See* Scovill Manufacturing Company.

LEAVENWORTH, HAYDEN & SCOVILL. *See* Scovill Manufacturing Company.

LEAVENWORTH & KENDRICK. Mark Leavenworth and his son, B. F. Leavenworth, and Green Kendrick made buttons between 1829 and 1837. Their names appear on gilt buttons. *See* Waterville Manufacturing Company.

LEAVENWORTH, SPENCER & SPERRY. Manufacturers of gilt buttons in the 1830's. Leavenworth was in business with Kendrick in the 1820's. "L. S. & S." is sometimes found on buttons made by this company.

LEEK. Handwrought buttons were made in Leek, England. They were made of silk thread in basket weave patterns, worked with a needle on the actual button mold. Leek was the term used for most of the needlework buttons made in that area during the nineteenth century. They were made for men's clothes, and therefore most of them were black.

Leek buttons. Hand-woven over the mold with a needle.

LEO POPPER & SONS. Manufacturers and importers, New York, 1870's to 1917. Leo Popper came to this country in the 1840's from the Bohemian part of Austria, which was then the world center for small glass articles. It was not until the 1870's that he turned to glass. Just when he started making buttons is not definitely known, since there was little effort to keep records. In the 1880's, his son Caleb joined the business, and he traveled abroad considerably. In addition to the making of buttons, Caleb Popper imported glass buttons and the makings for glass buttons from abroad. At this time, his brothers Emil L. and Edwin S. also joined the firm. The firm's records of making and importing buttons remained scant, and it is not always possible to identify which buttons were made and which imported by them.

Popper buttons were round, cone-shaped, highly domed, slightly convex, and square, oblong, or oval. They were made in sizes ranging from ½" to almost 2". The firm's buttons were always made by iron handpresses, never by machines. One type of glass buttons referred to as "Poppers" has a key shank, although the firm also used other metal shanks. (*See also* Key Shanks.)

Two Popper specialties were Spangled Glass and Marbled Glass buttons. The "spangles," placed inside a button, reflected through, giving an appearance like that of a paperweight button.

Many twentieth-century glassblowers, including those who made paperweight buttons, bought European-made glass rods from the Poppers. The firm had offices in Chicago, Illinois, and Providence, Rhode Island, as well as in New York City.

LEWIS, E. M., & COMPANY. *See* E. M. Lewis and Company.

LEWIS, GRILLEY & LEWIS. American button manufacturers in the 1820's. Name appears on early gilt and uniform buttons.

LEWIS & TOMES. American button manufacturers in the 1820's and 1830's.

LIDZ BROS., INC. A New York firm, 1895 to the present day. Primarily wholesalers and importers of all types of buttons for the dress-manufacturing trade and retail variety chainstore trade. Their retail trade name is Costumakers. They import from Japan, England, France, Holland, Germany, and Italy. Although Costumakers is their principal trade name, they also have carded buttons under such brand names as Stylerite; Style-makers; Fashion-Mates; Fashion-Aire; Couturier by Costumakers. Sometimes the name Lidz is found on the backs of their buttons.

LINCOLN BUTTONS. Many different Lincoln buttons have been made since the campaign days of Abraham Lincoln, the sixteenth president of the United States. Lincoln was a popular subject for all kinds of collectibles, and it has not always been possible to ascertain which items were made for definite events. Just which buttons of the 1860's are actual Lincoln campaign buttons is not definitely known. It can be assumed that ferrotype buttons with copies of Currier and Ives prints were used for campaign pur-

coln buttons. Probably campaign buttons 60's): (1) horn; (2) tintype.

LINCOLN AND WASHINGTON (Apotheosis.

coln buttons. Probably memorial buttons 0's): (1) horn; (2) tintype.

poses. These buttons have the narrow rims and wire shanks typical of the ferrotype buttons in common use at that time. (*See* Ferrotypes.) They are scarce, and are popular with collectors of campaign buttons.

Black horn buttons with Lincoln's profile are others that, in material and construction, might well belong to the campaign period. As in the case of ferrotypes, information about the exact use of these buttons is lacking; it is not known whether they were made for Lincoln's campaigns or inaugurations, or as memorials. The one most likely to have been a memorial is the button made of black horn with busts of both Lincoln and Washington on it. At that same time, many different items appeared with the two busts, and some read "Father and Saviour of our Country." However, it had become a common practice, and still is, for presidential candidates to include Washington's picture with their own.

Since Lincoln's assassination, many buttons have been designed specifically to commemorate such dates as the anniversaries of his birth, election, and death. And, because of his great popularity, Lincoln buttons with no anniversary tie-in whatsoever have been made for purely commercial purposes. Some were made as late as the 1940's, 1950's, and 1960's for the collector trade. Buttons of celluloid or painted metal with pictures of Lincoln were among presidential sets enclosed with tobacco, cereals, and other products. Lincoln has probably been the most popular of all famous persons as a subject for button designs, just as he has been for other collectibles.

LIND, JENNY. This famous singer who visited America several times was a popular subject for button designs. The most plentiful buttons bearing her profile are the small jewel types. The molded glass centers for these were made in almost every color, some of opaque glass, others of clear. Black glass Jenny Linds must have been the most popular of all; they are the easiest to find today. Those with clear red glass and with pink and turquoise-blue opaque centers are the rarest. These "jewels" vary from less than 1/2" to slightly over that diameter, and have plain or fancy metal borders. Even scarcer are Jenny Lind buttons made of horn or metal. The horn buttons were made in at least two sizes, under an inch and over an inch. A few pearl buttons were made with metal escutcheons of Jenny Lind's head. It is believed all the buttons were made during her visits to America.

Jenny Lind buttons. Nineteenth century. The top button is molded horn. The bottom one is pearl with a metal head. The others are jewels (glass centers).

LINE or LIGNE. A scale used to measure buttons. There are approximately forty lines to an inch. Button collectors have not established a standard measuring system; therefore, it is not uncommon for collectors to give measurements in lines, inches, or millimeters. Lines or lignes (only a difference in spelling) have been used most frequently by button manufacturers and wholesalers. Dressmakers seldom knew that such a scale existed. The line scale is a very early scale that originated in Europe.

LINK BUTTONS. Buttons with regulation wire shanks that have links attached. These buttons have an importance because they are rare survivors of what was at one time a standard type of button, but is almost obsolete today. In some parts of Europe where people clung to old traditions, they were handed down from one generation to another and worn by later generations. Unfortunately, sometimes the links have been removed and the button is no longer in its original form.

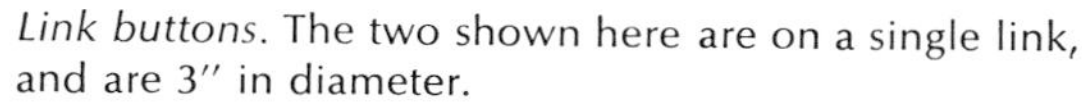
Link buttons. Silver link-type buttons on Dutch breeches.

Link buttons. The two shown here are on a single link, and are 3″ in diameter.

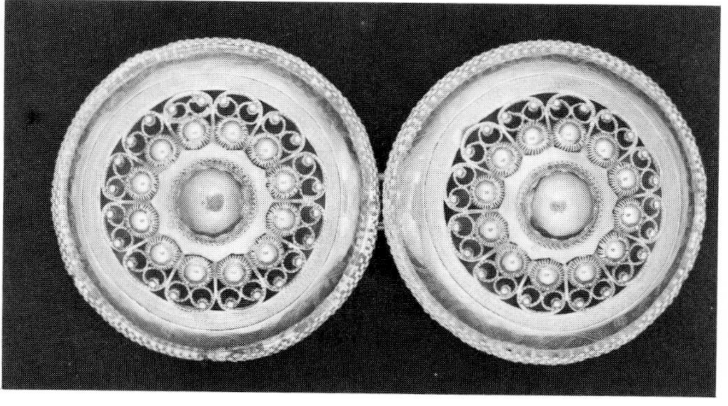

Link buttons were primarily made of silver, and although it is impossible to date most of those found today, it is known they were made as early as the beginning of the 1700's. Except for those that were made of coins with shanks attached, they were all handwrought one-piece or two-piece buttons that were profusely decorated. Some types were made with fancy buttons at each end of the link; others had a plain button at one end, or a bar. These buttons ranged in size from ½″ to over 3″; the links varied in length according to the use. Most links were plain, but a few elaborate ones have been found. Link buttons were worn on men's coats and breeches.

Link buttons. Coins and stamped picture buttons of silver.
Each has a plain smaller button on the other end of the link.

LINOLEUM. This material made from solidified oil, gums, and a cork by-product has been used to make a few buttons in the twentieth century. In Mexico, tourists have found linoleum buttons painted with native scenes in very bright colors. Linoleum was used occasionally to decorate buttons of other materials. It is doubtful that it was used to any extent for making buttons for the dress trade. Buttons made of linoleum are already scarce.

Linoleum buttons. Twentieth century.

LITHOGRAPH BUTTONS. Lithograph buttons make an interesting group because of the technique used to make the pictures. Lithography was developed by Aloys Senfelder. He experimented from 1796 until nearly 1809 before he succeeded. The printing was first done by stone.

Senfelder experimented further, as did other men in several countries, including America. Zinc plates and, later, a specially grained paper replaced the original stone process for commercial use. However, except for these substitutions, there has been very little change from the original process. The success of the art is evidenced by the popularity of the Currier and Ives lithographs in the nineteenth century.

Lithograph buttons. Nineteenth century.

Buttons found to date indicate that lithograph buttons were equally popular. It is believed that some so-called lithographs found in buttons are photoengravings rather than true lithographs, but button collectors call these colored pictures on paper found in metal button frames "lithographs."

These buttons with lithograph pictures range from 1/2" to nearly 2". The small half-inch size has been found on long white kid gloves. Sometimes the pictures were mounted in button frames and fastened only with prongs, having no covering. Very fancy borders sometimes held the pictures in; some borders were set with cut steel, others with paste. Some lithographs were covered with celluloid, others with glass. Those with celluloid are difficult to find in good condition. It is believed that all lithograph buttons were made between 1880 and 1910.

LIVERPOOL TRANSFER BUTTONS. A term used for metal buttons having porcelain centers decorated with transfer designs of black, sepia, or polychrome. Although these buttons were not necessarily made in Liverpool, it is believed that the transfer technique for decorating porcelain was first used there. In view of this fact, and because of the quality of the buttons, the term was readily adopted by button collectors.

Liverpool transfer buttons were made in the last half of the nineteenth century, and are now rare. Most of them have wire shanks; a very few were made with flexible shanks. This same method of transferring designs can also be found on porcelain disks, under glass, in eighteenth-century buttons. Porcelain buttons of the nineteenth century were decorated similarly. However, the term is seldom used except for *metal* buttons with porcelain centers decorated in this manner. The designs were most frequently classic heads; a very few flower and bird designs have been found.

LIVERY BUTTONS. These buttons trace their beginnings to the middle of the eighteenth century, but very few livery buttons found today were made before 1800. Most of these buttons have crests; a very few have coats of arms.

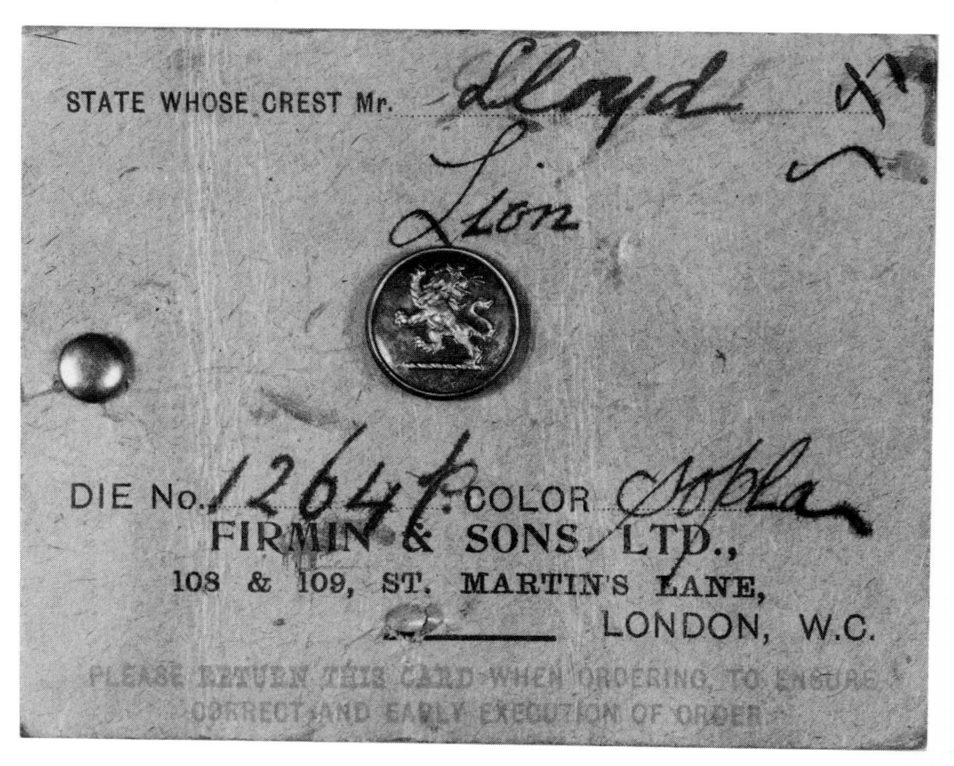

The crest is a most personal possession. To use it on one's household livery was as odd and incorrect as though a man had duplicates of his military decorations struck, and insisted that the household wear them. But this curious unheraldic fashion became popular in England, and even though there were faint cries of protest, it could not be checked.

The collector is grateful for the almost-200-year-old practice—it has cast endless interesting sidelights on the technical side, the historic side, and the heraldic side. He tries to find a series of these buttons used in a single household. One great drawback is that when the head of the household died, mourning buttons were ordered and the old buttons were discarded; then, later, a more modern style of livery button was designed and used.

The first livery buttons were thin shells over wooden or bone molds, and only a few of these have survived; more of the buttons with metal shanks are in collections. The earliest metal livery buttons were flat one-piece disks with no raised rim. The next change was to slightly convex disks with self-rims. The first two-piece, all-metal livery buttons were thin shells over metal backs. These were made as early as 1815.

Many of the first one-piece livery buttons have Sheffield-type silver plating on copper; others were made of brass with gilt plating. Later, when buttons were made of two pieces, some had white-metal and some had "firegilt" finishes. A very few horn livery buttons were made; they were worn during mourning periods.

Rarest among the heraldic buttons are those having two crests, one belonging to each side of the family. In the 1950's, one of the English firms that had made livery buttons for many years cleaned out its stockrooms of huge books with thousands of identified and obsolete livery buttons. They were brought to the United States, and since that time, collectors here have had very little trouble in securing livery buttons for collections.

Livery buttons.

LOCKET BUTTONS. To date, at least two different types of United States uniform buttons, and one picture button, made in locket style have been found. The uniform buttons were undoubtedly worn during World War I and World War II. The one dating from World War I was dark brown, like a government-issued button except that the front and back pieces were fastened together with a hinge. When attached to the garment by its loop shank, this button appeared like any brown, painted G.I. World War I uniform button. When the button was open, there were two places to put pictures, as in a woman's locket. These buttons were sometimes sold in department stores.

There is some secrecy surrounding the buttons that have a compass inside, which are sometimes referred to as Compass Buttons. They seem to have originated during World War II or later. They have a patented hinge and fastener similar to the World War I locket buttons, but they look just like officers' regular gilt uniform buttons when they are on the garment.

There was also another uniform type having a compass. This had threads cut around the edge of the front and back, for closing the button. All the buttons of this style found to date have British insignia on the front.

Until about 1960, button manufacturers were able to use the same eagle design for dress trade buttons as they did for United States Army uniform buttons. Usually the metal for the dress buttons was not so heavy and the stamping was not so sharp; dress trade buttons also had cheaper backs, and the shanks used represented a modification. In 1966, the United States Government prohibited the use of the same eagle; this order came from the United States Army Department of Heraldry. Over the years, frequently, buttons made for the dress trade have been found on uniforms. Whether the uniform maker made the substitutions, or the boys replaced G.I. buttons they had lost, is not known. In any case, the occasional use of locket buttons or compass buttons would not have seemed unusual.

There is only one known locket button with a picture on the face of it. This was constructed like the uniform buttons described above, and may have been made earlier than they were.

All locket buttons are exceedingly rare.

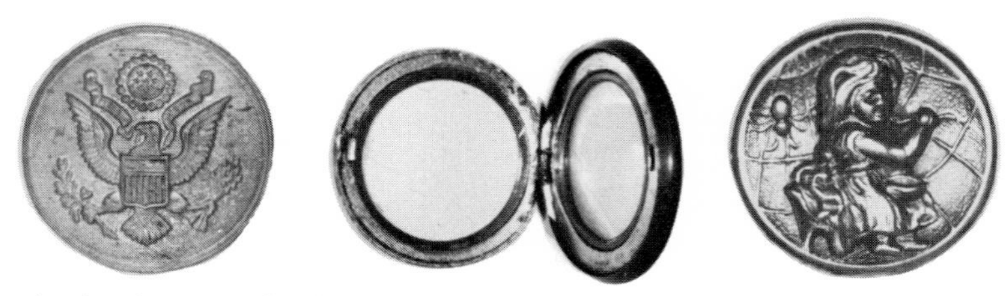

Locket buttons. The first is a United States uniform button; the one at the right has a picture design. The opened button shows the construction.

Locket buttons. Open and closed views of a United States compass button from World War II. The hinged button has a gilt face and a loop shank.

Locket buttons. A British compass button (1900's), with bronze face and a screw loop shank.

LOOP SHANK. To make this type of shank, a round or flat metal wire was bent so that both ends could be inserted in the back of the button. Some loop shanks have flat metal pieces called shank plates close to the button. Loop shanks are found on buttons of almost every material. They are sometimes called wire shanks.

Loop-shank buttons. The one at the right has a shank plate.

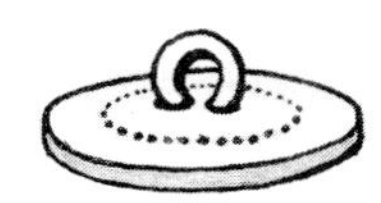

LUCITE. A trade name for a clear plastic. It was used to make buttons in the twentieth century. Although the trade name applies specifically to the clear plastic made by one firm, collectors often use it to refer to all clear plastics. It would be impossible for a collector to differentiate between the clear plastics of various companies. The first clear plastic buttons came on cards with the Lucite trade name; they were molded on the back like glass buttons. Since that time, clear plastic buttons have been decorated in many ways.

LUSCOMB, SALLY C. Editor and publisher of *Just Buttons* magazine since 1942. Co-author with Ethel B. Cassidy of *Old Button Box,* 1951, now out of print. Owner—with her husband, Victor E. Luscomb—and director of Just Buttons Museum in Southington, Connecticut, since 1950.

LUSTER. A metallic finish used to decorate buttons. The colors include iridescent, silver, gold, copper or bronze, and gunmetal. These metallic finishes appear more often on black glass buttons than on buttons of any other material. Sometimes the button fronts are completely covered with luster; sometimes only part of the front has luster trim. Silver luster was used more than the other colors. One iridescent luster is especially silvery, and is sometimes referred to as Tiffany luster.

The use of luster on buttons dates back to the middle of the nineteenth century. Lusters are still being used today, the twentieth-century ones being more brilliant than the soft shades used in the nineteenth century. In the nineteenth century, many of the designs were first molded on the button—pictures of all kinds. These buttons ranged in size from 1/4″ to over an inch. The designs of the twentieth century include fewer pictures; they are mostly geometric and conventional.

The metallic paint used for outline trim and as fill for incised designs differs somewhat from the luster used to cover the face of buttons.

M

M. FOWLER NORTHFORD. Mark found on pewter buttons made between 1800 and 1820 by Maltby Fowler in Northford, Connecticut.

MACHINES, HAND. In the 1880's, small hand machines were used to cover metal molds with fabric. Prior to this, factories had been turning out large quantities of dark fabric buttons for men's wear, as well as some fancy buttons for ladies' wear. But in the 1880's, the fashion in ladies' fabric buttons changed. It became the style for buttons to be covered with the same material the garment was made of, and so dressmakers often covered wooden molds by hand. About this time, small hand machines with metal molds appeared in the department stores, and the clerks would cover buttons for the customer from a piece of the chosen material. A store usually had several hand machines, each one equipped to cover one or two different-size molds. These molds had flexible shanks. The machines were made in the United States and Germany. *See also* Fabric-covered Buttons.

MAPLE, MARGUERITE M. Co-author, with Erwina Couse, of *Button Classics*, 1941.

MARBLE. A stone used to make buttons in the eighteenth and nineteenth centuries. Not many marble buttons are found, so it is reasonable to assume very few were made of this stone.

MARBLED GLASS. *See* Glass Buttons.

MARCASITE. Mineralogists question whether the pyrite used for buttons is actually marcasite or another pyrite. But, since 1845, marcasite and iron pyrites have been used interchangeably, especially in button and jewelry making. The buttons that have been found trimmed with marcasite were made since that date. They were found mostly in European shops, and brought to this country by tourists, either on garments or in sets.

Marcasite was always set in metal, usually silver, and never riveted as cut steel was, nor was it set with prong settings. It is used with jewels (or glass) and set in "cups" to form designs. Its color and faceting sometimes cause it to be confused with faceted steel. Marcasite twinkles; steel has a more dazzling shine. Buttons with marcasite are extremely rare.

Marcasite. Silver buttons with marcasites and jewels.

MARQUETRY. A thin inlay decoration of contrasting materials, placed on a flat button surface, like a veneer. Marquetry designs were frequently used as decorations on buttons of almost every material except metal and glass. Buttons decorated with marquetry are often referred to as inlays or inlaid buttons.

Marquetry buttons. These have inlays of colored wood veneers (1800's).

MASK BUTTONS. These buttons are mostly Oriental. They were made in the twentieth century, but masks themselves are practically as old as the human race. They are known to have been designed and made in almost every part of the world. The designs on some mask buttons represent the masks made for certain of the Japanese Noh dramas.

Mask designs. Twentieth-century buttons with Oriental mask designs.

The stereotyped expressions of Noh masks were never changed. This is probably the reason why so many of the faces on mask buttons seem familiar.

All these buttons are ceramics of one kind or another, painted in bright colors. Some are flat, others realistic, in shape. Mask buttons from Japan were very often sold in shallow wooden boxes.

MATTATUCK MANUFACTURING CO. Waterbury, Connecticut, 1840's–50's.

MATTHEWS, ANSON. Pewterer, Southington, Connecticut, 1806–30. Probably there are more pewter buttons found today with "A. Matthews" on the back than with any other marking. Matthews buttons were all made with wire shanks. A greater variety of his patterns has been found than of any other pewterer. It is not known whether Matthews hired apprentices or made all the buttons himself. Early pewter buttons are scarce; they are of interest to both button and pewter collectors.

MEANDER PATTERN. *See* Greek Key.

MEISSEN PORCELAIN. The making of porcelain in Meissen began in 1715. Prior to that, much pottery such as red ware had been made. Very little is known about button making in Meissen. Only a few buttons had been found with the famous Meissen crossed swords on the back; the style of those found indicates they were made after 1850. Meissen buttons are usually hollow, and have self-shanks with two or four holes. Those found to date have flower designs and are about an inch in size.

MERRIAM, L. American pewterer, 1815.

MEXICAN SILVER BUTTONS. Buttons brought into this country mostly by the tourists who have visited Taxco, Mexico, since 1920. Collectors consider the hollow type, two-piece realistic shapes unique. One- and two-piece silver buttons with gemstones have also been brought back by tourists. Visitors, invited to watch the men at work in the small factories, could choose buttons while they were being made. More jewelry than buttons was brought back, and so the buttons are not easy to find, except in collections.

Mexican silver buttons.
Twentieth century.

MEYERS, H. M. Artist in the 1940's. He hand-painted large porcelain buttons with self-shanks, which were sold in a New Jersey shop.

Porcelain buttons.
Examples of the hand-painted buttons done by H. M. Meyers in the 1940's.

MILITARY BUTTONS. *See* Armed Forces.

MINER, MINERVA. Co-author, with Erwina Couse Chamberlain, of *Button Heritage,* 1967, published by Heritage Press.

MINTON PORCELAIN BUTTONS. Very few porcelain buttons have been found with a Minton identification. Usually, the name Minton is on the back in gold within a border of gold paint. Reports indicate that some buttons were made by early workers in the Minton factory for friends or relatives, but were unmarked. Most of the Minton buttons found have been handsomely decorated with gold encrustation; in all probability, these were made since 1850.

Minton porcelain buttons.
The name is on the back.

MINTZER, W. C. Philadelphia, Pennsylvania, 1850–60's. Makers of uniform buttons.

MIRROR BUTTONS. *See* Glass Buttons: Mirrors.

MITCHELL & TYLER. Makers of Confederate buttons, Richmond, Virginia, 1860's.

MIX MANUFACTURING COMPANY. Records are not too accurate on this Prospect, Connecticut, company. The factory site has been found, and recent excavations have proved that clay buttons were made there. There are two references to the company in local histories. One says: "Captain William Mix and two relatives, John and Titus Mix, organized the Mix Manufacturing Company along the Ten Mile river to carry on the manufacture of Britannia ware." The other: "Several years prior to this organization, when the canal was abandoned in 1846, these men moved back to Rag Hollow and continued manufacturing dress findings, notably clay buttons, under the name of Mix Manufacturing Company." The buttons found at the site were pottery buttons with clay and glaze similar to those of buttons made at the Norwalk, Connecticut, Pottery. *See also* "Norwalk" Pottery Buttons.

MOLDS (FOR PEWTER BUTTONS). *See* Pewter Button Molds.

MOLLUSKS. *See* Shell Buttons, Shells.

MOONGLOW, MOONSTONE. Trade names for two similar types of glass buttons made in the twentieth century. The buttons are so constructed as to create a light that glows and has a slight resemblance to the gem called moonstone. Collectors find it difficult to differentiate between the two varieties after they are removed from the trade cards. Therefore, most collectors are now calling all of them iridescent glass. The buttons were made in light colors, the tops being molded in different patterns. Some have gold or silver decoration.

MORGAN, WILFRED B. Author of *Calico Buttons,* published as small paper-covered booklets in 1939 and 1940. They listed and illustrated nearly 300 different calico patterns found on Small Chinas. Now out of print. *See also* Calico Buttons.

MORLEY MANUFACTURING COMPANY. Portsmouth, New Hampshire, 1890–. One of the first companies to make utilitarian buttons of paper. From a material they called fiber, they first made shoe buttons. Fiber clothing buttons were developed at the turn of the century, and gradually became their largest-selling product. When they are found in good condition, the buttons are bright and colorful, with simple designs and self-rims. Trade names are Milonite and Ebonite.

MORLOCK, EDITH. *See* Edith's Studio.

MOSAIC BUTTONS. Buttons with diminutive mosaic centers became popular for men's vests and for basques in mid-Victorian times. The background for the tesserae (tiny bits of glass or stone) was usually black, colored glass, or goldstone. Many mosaic buttons were made in Venice, Italy, but some late ones were made in China and France. The customary designs on these buttons were buildings and ruins of buildings, but there were some scenes, flowers, and animals. The choicest mosaic centers for buttons were ground flat and polished. Some twentieth-century centers have been left rough on top. Collectors include nineteenth-century mosaic buttons with other jewel-type buttons.

Mosaic buttons range in size from 1/4" to over an inch. Those in good condition are scarce.

Mosaic buttons. Unpolished; twentieth century.

MOTHER-OF-PEARL. *See* Shell Buttons, Shells.

Mosaic buttons and studs. Nineteenth century.

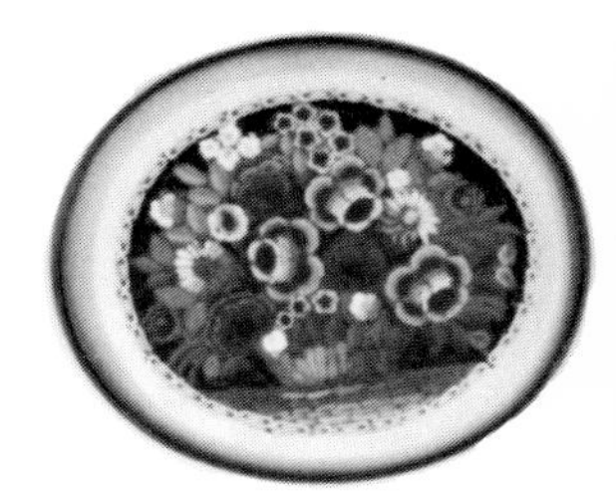

MOUNTING. The mounting of buttons gives the collector an opportunity for originality and self-expression. Certain specific methods have been found efficient and attractive by many collectors, but the individual is always free to create his own arrangements and try out ideas that appeal to him. It is necessary, of course, to consider the number of buttons on hand to be mounted, the types, whether the buttons are to be displayed or not, and—possibly—the available storage space.

Most collectors enjoy displaying buttons in their homes, and today it is the recognized thing to do. For home-display mountings, buttons should be chosen that will harmonize with the decor, thought being given to the color and design of the buttons as well as to the style of mounting. A frame should complete the "picture" if the mounting

Mounting Suggestions.

is for a wall. A few buttons can be arranged on small, easel-like cards to be set on cabinet shelves in the home. Some sets of buttons come in satin-lined boxes, and these look attractive when displayed open—to show the buttons. When planning mountings for the home, it is a good idea to plan replacement arrangements as well, so that the display can be changed from time to time.

Most collections contain more buttons than can possibly be displayed in the average home—sometimes hundreds of them of various kinds and sizes. It is a wise plan to mount all of them, even though temporarily at first. Many collectors like 9″ by 12″ mounting cards in white or cream, which show off the buttons to advantage. For temporary mountings, collectors often use any pieces of cardboard they happen to have

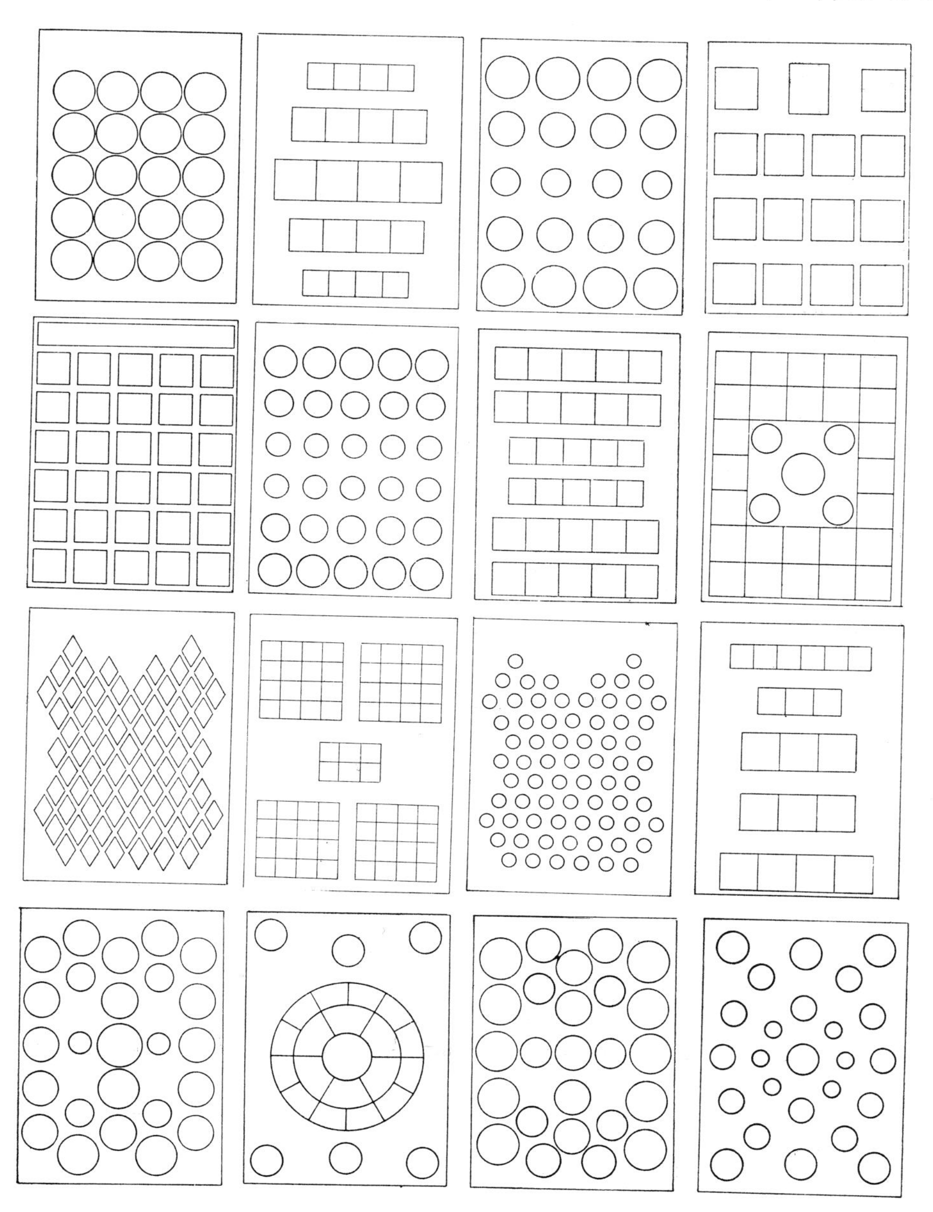

around the house; they refer to these as "work cards." Buttons are tentatively grouped on work cards, perhaps while enough are being gathered for an attractive display card, or while learning more about them.

Buttons can be grouped according to color, design, craft, material, or historic significance. Setting up cards by color or design can easily result in a hodgepodge appearance. On the other hand, buttons mounted by materials supplement each other, and collectors find that this method produces greater harmony and richness. Buttons should be treated as individual items, no matter how small they are or how many are being grouped together. Each button in a group should add to the artistry of the whole mounting, or it should be transferred to another group. For example, lacy glass, horn, lacquered aluminum, and painted brass would not make up an attractive card just because they were all green. However, each is quite rare in its respective material and would be a welcome addition to a mounting of other buttons of the same material.

The number to be put on the card almost has to be determined by the collector. Again, it is wise to remember that each button should be considered individually—not crowded together with others, but spaced far enough apart so that it has its own little "mounting" according to its size. When buttons of several sizes are being grouped together, the largest ones can be put on the bottom row and the others graduated upward, to the smallest at the top. Or they can be placed to radiate out from the center, which can be a large or a small button. When there are only a few buttons for one card, either a smaller card is used or the buttons are arranged together in the center to leave a wider border. It is a good practice to try several arrangements and decide on the most pleasing one before transferring the buttons, one by one, to the permanent card. Today, though cards can be purchased already designed and drawn for the collector, there is an assortment from which to choose, and so here too the collector has a chance for some degree of self-expression.

Pipe cleaners and plastic-covered wires of all sizes are the favorite materials for fastening shanked buttons to cards. Sew-thru buttons can be sewed onto the cards as they are on clothes, but more and more collectors now fasten them on with water-soluble cements. For convenience, many collectors keep all their mounting equipment—fasteners, scissors, a punch (a needlework stiletto or awl), ruler, compass, pencil, pen, needle, and thread—together in a box or drawer.

MOURNING BUTTONS. A term used for black glass buttons with a dull finish.

MYTHOLOGICAL DESIGNS. A popular type of button decoration. Mythological stories and the old gods have been depicted on buttons in the last three centuries, mostly in the nineteenth century on metal buttons. The designs are sometimes referred to as Classics, especially those found on fine ceramic and enamel buttons.

N

N. PARKER & COMPANY. Manufacturers of covered buttons, 1840's to 1850's, Woodbury, Connecticut.

NATIONAL BUTTON COMPANY. Easthampton, Massachusetts. Organized by Joel Hayden, inventor of "flexible" shank buttons in 1834.

NATIONAL BUTTON COMPANY. Waterbury, Connecticut, 1860's.

NATIONAL BUTTON SOCIETY. Organized in 1938 in Chicago, Illinois. It is now the largest organization for button collectors in the country. *See also* Button Collectors' Organizations.

NAVY BUTTONS. *See* Armed Forces Buttons.

NEEDLEWORK BUTTONS. *See* Crochet; Embroidery; Fabric-covered Buttons.

NETSUKE. A toggle attached to the cord of an *inro,* or pouch, to keep it from slipping under the girdle or sash of a Japanese kimono. There were no pockets in the Japanese kimono, and therefore small pouches were used to carry money, pipe, or tobacco. On the cord, between the netsuke and the *inro,* was a sliding bead (*ojime*). The colors of

Netsukes. Those in the left row (starting at the top) are carved ivory, dyed carved ivory, and ivory with inlay of pearl, jade, coral, and tortoiseshell. At the right is a netsuke with its ojime and inro.

the netsuke, bead, and *inro* were related to each other, but the color of the kimono was not considered, since the netsuke was not a part of the costume, and neither fastened nor decorated the kimono itself.

The earliest netsukes (before the fifteenth century) were very plain, simply a necessity for keeping the *inro* from slipping. As the *inro* was elaborated and attained great artistic beauty, there came a demand for the netsuke to be as fine. Although the *inro* is considered incomplete without the netsuke, many are found separate, perhaps because the cords frayed and broke. Today, there are many collectors of netsuke, but the proportion of complete pieces in collections is small.

Netsukes have been made of wood, ivory, stone, horn, metal, ceramics, and lacquer, but the two principal materials were wood and ivory. Sometimes two holes were carved on the back of netsukes, and for this reason some collectors called them buttons. However, many netsukes did not have these two holes. Instead, open spaces in the design were utilized for attaching the cord, the ends of which were always hidden in the netsuke.

Like buttons, netsukes can be collected according to the material or the designs. There were human figures, animals, birds, insects, and many other subjects. The designs were usually realistic, and so beautifully carved that the figures seemed alive. Japanese mythology, literature, history, folklore, and everyday life, as well as natural history, were also the subjects of these minute carvings.

NEW HAVEN AND BALTIMORE BUTTON COMPANY (N. H. & B. Co.). Waterbury, Connecticut, 1808–31.

NEWELL BROTHERS BUTTON COMPANY. Springfield, Massachusetts, 1840's–1900's. Manufactured shell, fabric, and vegetable ivory buttons, at separate times.

NICHOLLS, FLORENCE Z. E. Author of *Button Hand Book*, and three supplements, 1943–49.

NICKEL SILVER. An alloy of copper, nickel, and zinc, sometimes called German silver. This metal has been used to make small articles for about one hundred years, but it was seldom used to make buttons—perhaps, at least partly, because silver-colored buttons have appealed the least to the button trade. It is difficult to distinguish nickel-silver from nickel-plated buttons, or from those made of other metals of similar color. Nickel silver does not tarnish as silver does, but it will react to acids. This characteristic made it a poor material for tableware, for which it was originally invented. The one button known to be of nickel silver is the United States Air Force uniform button. Government orders for these buttons specify nickel silver.

NICOLENE, NICOLITE. Trade names for nickel-plated metal used to trim buttons. The metal was produced in very thin sheets, then cut for the various trims. Small sequin-size circles were used for embedding in buttons of such materials as shell, vegetable ivory, composition, glass, and metal. The nickel-plated metal was also used as the background for window, moon, and water designs in pictorial buttons, and for portions of border. It rusted easily, and therefore is not always recognizable in buttons. Often, embedded pieces of it have fallen out.

NIELLO WORK. A method of ornamentation dating from the Middle Ages. It has also been used to decorate buttons in more recent years. The lines of the design were cut in a disk of silver, which was then completely covered with a black composition consisting of copper, silver, lead, and sulfur. On this was sprinkled a little borax, and the whole was then subjected to heat. When the button was cool, the top surface was scraped and burnished, leaving the black composition in the design lines. Most of the buttons decorated in this manner were made in the nineteenth and twentieth centuries.

Nineteenth-century niello buttons are of fine quality and design, and were probably brought to this country by tourists. A much cheaper grade of niello button with a very thin coating of black was made in the present century.

Niello buttons.
Nineteenth and twentieth centuries.

NOH MASK BUTTONS. *See* Mask Buttons.

"NORWALK" POTTERY BUTTONS. Highly glazed, mottled pottery buttons were made in at least two potteries in Norwalk, Connecticut, and one in Prospect, Connecticut. Earliest reference to the Norwalk potteries was in the newspaper *Gazette,* May, 1825. The buttons made in Norwalk and those made in Prospect are similar in colors and construction. It is believed that Connecticut pottery buttons were made of plastic clay, first molded by hand and later pressed into dies. They were made with pinhead shanks, shank plates with wire loops, or four holes, and in mountings like jewel-type buttons. They range in size from a little over 1/4" to 1 1/2". The colors are mostly a deep reddish brown. Salesmen's sample cards in the Mattatuck Museum at Waterbury, Connecticut, also show pale green, lavender, and cream and blue.

Statistics to date indicate these so-called "Norwalk" pottery buttons were actually made in several places in Connecticut between 1825 and 1853. Properly, all of them should be called Connecticut pottery buttons. Unless they are found with data concerning the potteries, they cannot be accurately identified. Even with the recent excavation of some of these buttons at an old factory site in Prospect, and old factory stock found in an early homestead once owned by the Mix family, they are extremely rare.

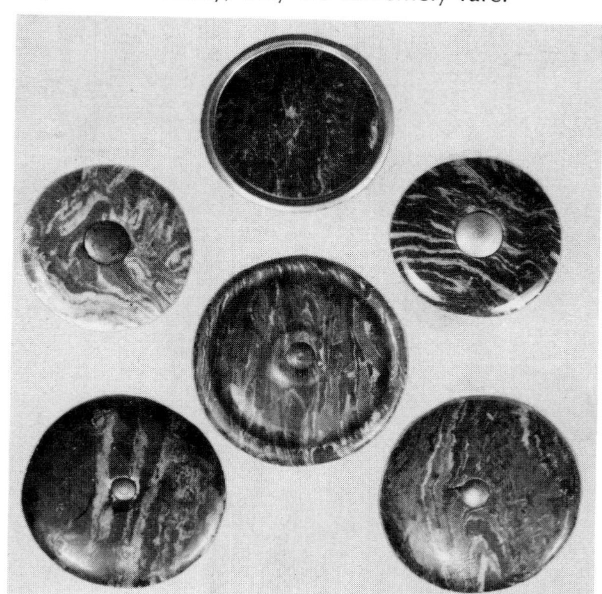

"Norwalk" pottery buttons.
They are of the early 1800's.

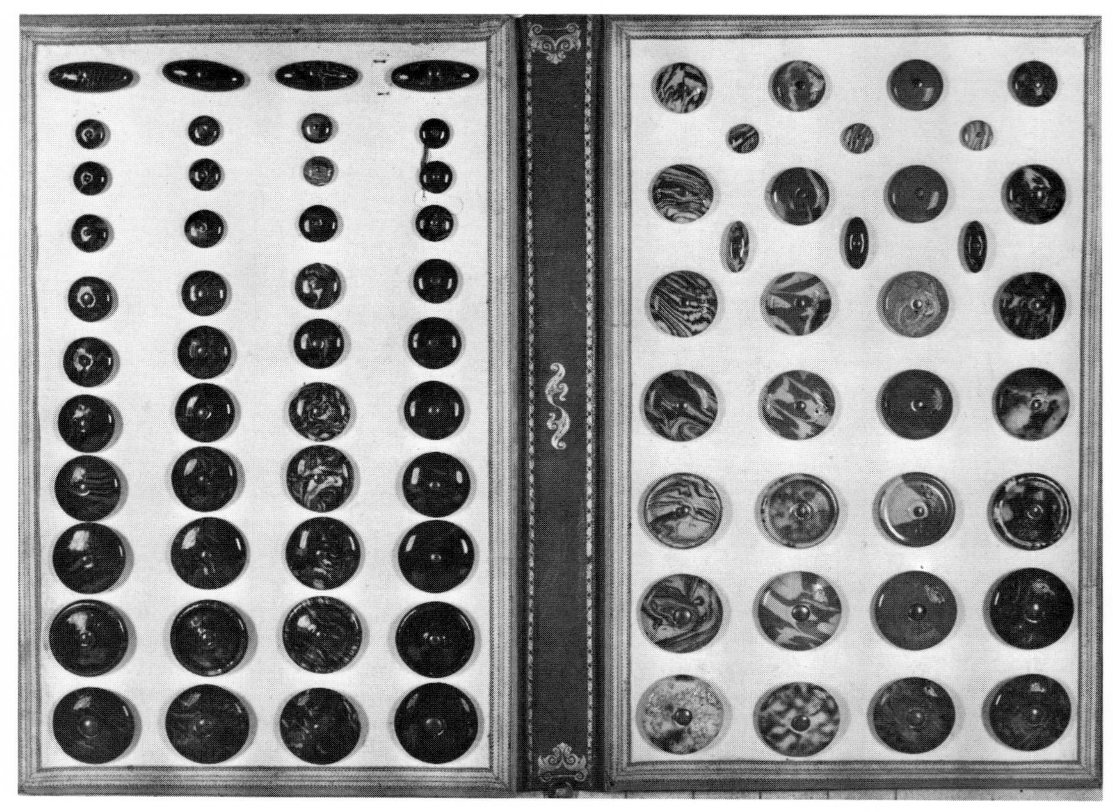

"Norwalk" Pottery. A salesman's sample case of "Norwalk" pottery buttons of the early 1800's.

These pottery buttons were frequently mistakenly called Bennington Pottery Buttons because of the similarity to pottery made in the Vermont factory. It is not known whether the Bennington factory made any buttons, except as workers may have made them as end-of-the-day pieces.

NOVELTY RUBBER COMPANY. New Brunswick, New Jersey, 1855–70. Manufacturers of rubber buttons, on the back of which appears the full name, or "N.R. Co.," along with "Goodyear" and the patent date, 1851. The buttons have metal shanks or holes.

NUT BUTTONS. In the first half of the twentieth century, nuts such as almonds, Brazil nuts, and filberts were made into buttons by adding wire loops. Hazelnut and black-walnut shells were sliced and used as sew-thru buttons. At this same time, plastic buttons were made in realistic shapes to imitate nuts. Earlier—since the mid-nineteenth century, in fact—prisoners-of-war often passed the time by carving fruit pits into buttons, and these handmade pieces have now also found their way into some collections.

NYLON BUTTONS. A translucent button made in recent years of a plastic substance called "nylon." So far, the only buttons found have two holes and a colored circle for decoration. It is difficult to distinguish nylon buttons from other translucent plastic buttons.

Nylon objects are made of a plastic powder that is heated and pressed into molds. When it cools, it keeps the shape of the mold.

O

OAK HALL CLOTHING COMPANY. Uniform outfitters of Boston, Massachusetts, from 1890's–1900's. This company name is occasionally found on the backs of buttons, though most of the buttons they used were made by the Waterbury Button Company.

OBLIQUE DESIGN. A term used for the design of a particular button with the head of Henry Clay. The design was engraved on a die in such a way that when it was stamped on the button disk, it was visible only when it reflected light. The technique for making the design is similar to the one used for making the Opal Design, but today's button makers still do not know how it was done. The engraving was so fine that the surface appears to be perfectly plain. These buttons were made by Scovill & Company. They are considered to be among the very rarest of campaign buttons, as well as of Golden Age buttons.

O'HARA DIAL COMPANY. This Waltham, Massachusetts, company was founded in 1833 and reorganized several times, being finally liquidated in 1958. Its original purpose was to manufacture watch dials, and the basic product always remained dials for clocks, meters, and telephones, all made of vitreous enamel. However, at various times, the firm made other items finished and decorated with enamel, including enamel buttons. The buttons probably were made about 1895. They were beautifully decorated with foil, the "crude" enamel coming from France.

Some of the O'Hara machinery is now in the Clock Museum in Bristol, Connecticut. Porcelain studs made for political campaigns around 1896 have also been found with this firm's name on the back.

O'Hara enamel buttons.

"OLD BUTTON BOX." A book by Ethel B. Cassidy and Sally C. Luscomb. It was privately published in 1951 and is now out of print.

OMEGA RIMMED-TYPE BUTTON. *See* Omega-Type Button.

OMEGA-TYPE BUTTON. The shanks on this type were fashioned in the shape of the Greek letter Omega; hence, the name "Omego type" or "Omegas." These buttons were among the first to be made by machinery, in the early 1800's. Before 1800, all buttons produced in this country were made entirely by hand. Most Omega-type buttons were made between 1800 and 1850, although the manufacturing of this style of shank continued at least 150 years.

The shank was only slightly different from that put on the Alpha-type buttons. The eye of the Omega type was rounder, and the ends of the loop bent over more to permit a larger base for attaching it to the body of the button. The difference between the two types can usually be detected by the separate processes used. Almost all Omegas have trademarks on the backs, the shanks are heavier, the bodies thicker.

Some of the small Omega-type buttons were rimmed with a separate ring, which was crimped over the edge to supply a border. These were called Omega Rimmed Types, also Jacksonians (*which see*).

Omega and Alpha shanks.

OPAL DESIGN. A term used for a design found on Golden Age buttons. The design is very rare, and is known to exist only on buttons made by the R. & W. Robinson firm in Attleboro, Massachusetts. It was produced by a microscopic grooving of the surface that broke up the light as it was reflected. The engraving was done on the die from which the buttons were struck. A die has been found in recent years in the Robinson family's collection. It is engraved with infinitesimally fine lines in a design of hexagons drawn at adjacent angles. Records show that this type of design was known to English button makers in the eighteenth century and that it was produced with hand tools. When an opal-design button is found in perfect condition, it has iridescent colors—hence, the probable origin of the term. Three different buttons have been found with this design in the center—one with a fancy border, one a plain border, and one without border.

OPALESCENT GLASS. *See* Glass Buttons.

OPAQUE GLASS. *See* Glass Buttons.

OVERALL BUTTONS. *See* Work-Clothes Buttons.

OVERLAY SHEATH. *See* Glass Buttons.

OVERLAY SHEET. *See* Glass Buttons.

OVERLAY TRIM. *See* Glass Buttons.

P

PAD SHANKS. *See* Shanks.

PAILLON. A design cut out or stamped out of gold or silver foil and used for decorating enamel buttons. *See* Enamels, Enameling: Paillon.

PANTS BUTTONS. These buttons have been made of bone, wood, metal, vegetable ivory, and plastic. They are the buttons used for fastening suspenders to the pants. Many had the clothier's name on them; some had the button manufacturer's name; comparatively few bore a design. It is possible for the collector who concentrates on this type of button to find hundreds of different ones. The group does not include the work-clothes buttons used on "jumper coats."

PAPER BUTTONS. *See* Morley Manufacturing Company; *also* Papier-Mâché Buttons.

PAPERWEIGHT BUTTONS. *See* Glass Buttons: Clear and Colored, Mechanical Makeup.

Paperweight buttons. Top and side views; twentieth century.

Paperweight buttons. Top and side views; twentieth century.

PAPIER-MÂCHÉ BUTTONS. The making of papier-mâché was an ancient art of the Orient. However, the buttons of this material found by collectors today were no doubt made nearer the middle of the nineteenth century. Papier-mâché—literally, "chewed paper"—was made from paper boiled into pulp or pressed into thin sheets, then mixed with adhesives. The mixture could be molded or pressed into the desired shape.

In 1825, Jennens & Bettridge of England took out a patent for the process of inlaying pearl on papier-mâché. Thin pieces of shell cut into designs or irregular shapes were used. The shell pieces were held to the button disks with a varnish; then the entire surface was covered with a black japan. After the japan dried, it was polished down until the shell showed. Then it was ready for any additional decoration such as painted designs. A few years later, papier-mâché buttons were painted with natural colors and gold, with no shell in the design.

Papier-mâché buttons. With pearl inlay and painted designs; nineteenth century.

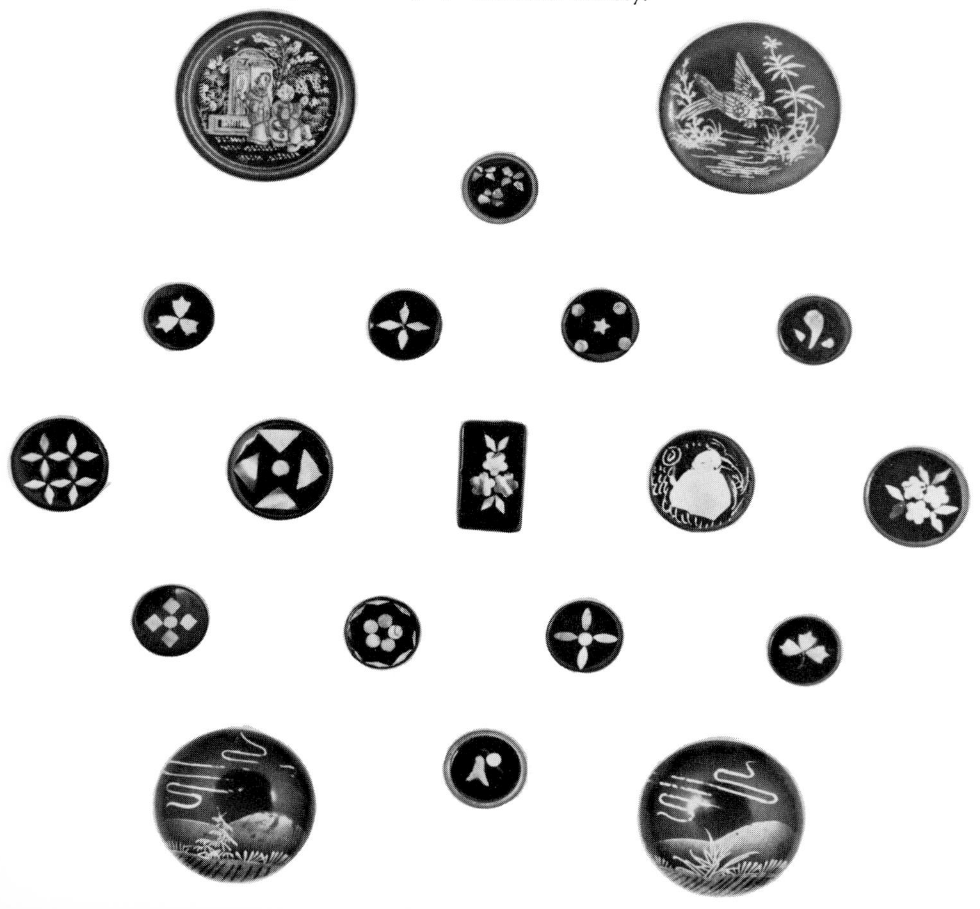

In 1851, a patent was taken out in England for a button "board" of papier-mâché with an indentation for the wire shank. The whole button was covered with the black japan, the loop shank being pressed into the indentation while the japan was soft. Very few papier-mâché buttons were made with holes.

Papier-mâché buttons were made both in one piece and in two pieces (hollow), with and without metal rims. They ranged in size from 1/2" to 1". A commonly found design is a sprig of flowers, but all designs are scarce.

PARIS BACKS (T.W.&W.). A term used for two-piece metal buttons having "Paris" on the backs. At first, the term referred only to a button having "T.W.&.W." as well as "Paris"

"Paris backs." Examples of these nineteenth-century brass buttons.

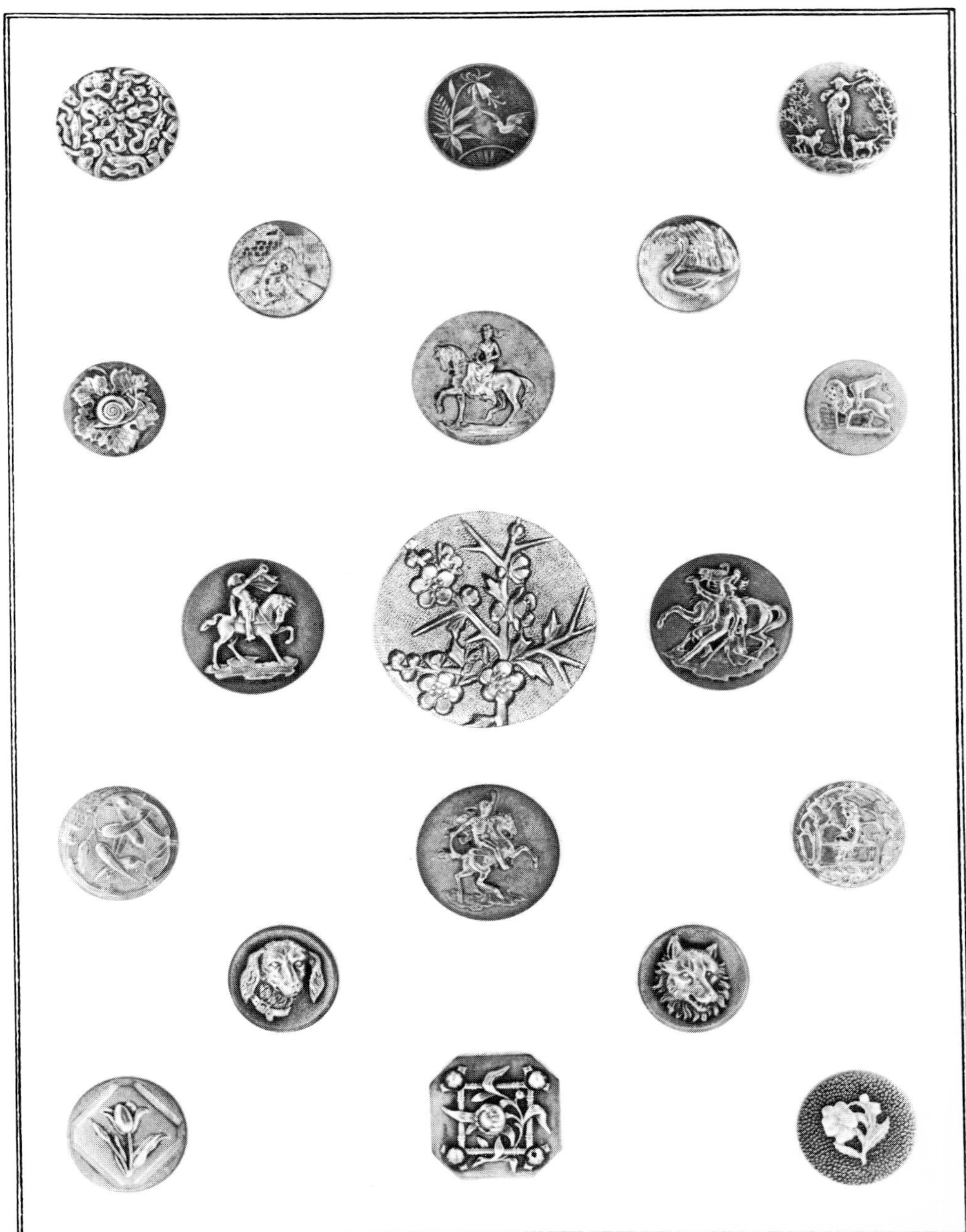

on the back. Now, collectors include all metal buttons marked "Paris," regardless of manufacturers' initials or names. There were many designs used on these buttons, including pictorials. The buttons were made with wire shanks or self-shanks, and ranged from 3/8" to over 1 1/4" in size. Occasionally, they bore a small applied design, but they were never made with a disk covering the complete face of the button. The T.W.&.W. firm changed its name several times; therefore, even buttons marked with other names may have been made by them.

PARKER, N., & COMPANY. *See* N. Parker & Company.

PASSEMENTERIE BUTTONS. A term used for fabric buttons decorated with beads and fine braids in the manner of passementerie (dress trimming). Most passementerie buttons found today were made in the eighteenth century. However, in the late nineteenth and early twentieth centuries, dressmakers made buttons to match the passementerie trimming fashionable on women's dresses at the time. Buttons made over wood or metal molds were decorated in this manner. The term is sometimes used also for buttons of faceted glass riveted to metal backs. *See* Beads for nineteenth-century passementerie buttons.

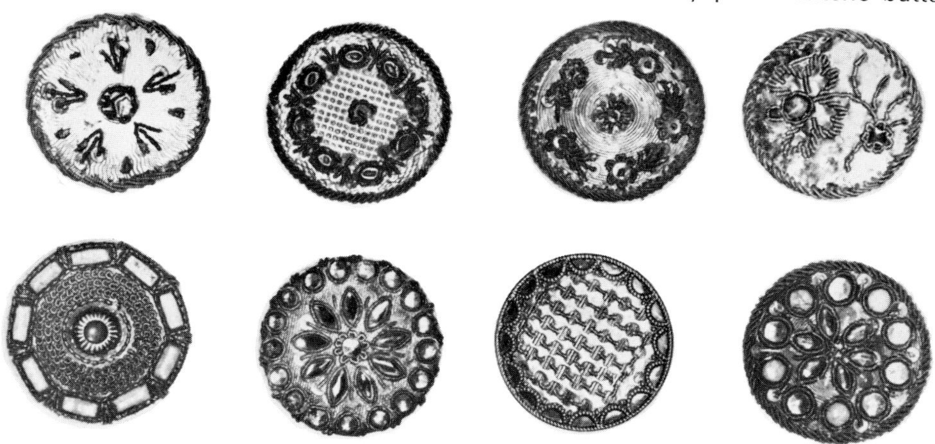

Passementerie buttons. Eighteenth century.

PASTE. This hard bright glass, often called rhinestone, is cut similarly to the way diamonds are cut, and is used in the same manner. Paste does not have the power of reflecting from the interior as diamonds do, and therefore foil is placed on the back of each piece. The paste used in decorating eighteenth-century buttons was put in sunken settings with cuplike indentations; later, prongs were used to hold the paste "stones" in place. Occasionally, button collectors refer to this material as "Strass."

PATENT OR PATENT PENDING. (Also, such abbreviations as Pat., Patt., Pat. Pend.) Frequently, one of these terms was stamped or molded on the backs of buttons to indicate that the maker of the buttons had applied for or received a patent for a method of manufacture or an improvement in manufacture or decoration. If a year accompanies the term on the back of a button, the button was made after that date.

PATENT BUTTON COMPANY. Manufacturers of glove, metal overall, and plastic buttons, Waterbury, Connecticut, 1870's to present. Many of the firm's buttons were made with patented fasteners for attaching the buttons to garments by machinery. The company made some aluminum buttons that are heavily covered with paint. *See also* Platt Brothers Company.

PEACOCK'S EYE. A button that has a foil decoration under glass imitating the blue-green eyelike spot on the tail feather of a peacock. Most of these buttons were made around 1900 or later. They are not plentiful.

PEARL BUTTONS. *See* Shell Buttons, Shells.

PEARLIZED BUTTONS. Glass or plastic buttons with an imitation pearl coating. The material used was made from ground fish scales mixed with a secret solution. Some pearlized buttons were made by Leo Popper & Sons, New York.

PEARLS. These gems come from mollusks. They are formed when the mollusk seals up a minute bit of any irritating substance that has found its way into the shell. Today, bits of foreign material are deliberately injected—to promote the formation of pearls, which are actually abnormal growths. Real pearls were seldom used in buttons. Pearls of irregular shape are called baroque pearls. Occasionally these have been used to trim buttons.

PEARY COAT BUTTONS. Frequently, button designs have been influenced by current events, particularly on such special occasions as the first successful trip to the North Pole, by the American explorer Admiral Robert Edwin Peary (1909). Peary buttons of brass were made in several sizes, ranging from $^{3}/_{4}$″ to $1^{1}/_{4}$″. They were constructed cheaply, with self-shanks or loops, and worn mostly on children's coats. They are already scarce.

Peary coat buttons. 1909–10.

PEASLEY, A. M. *See* A. M. Peasley.

PETOSKEY STONE BUTTONS. These buttons were made from fossilized crinoids found in Michigan near Petoskey. The word "crinoid" is derived from the Greek *krinoeides*, meaning "like a lily." There are about 2,000 species of fossil crinoids. The kind used for buttons has main stalk topped by a calyx with numerous branches, or feelers, through which it was fed. In cross-section, the calyx in Petoskey stone has beautiful markings.

Nineteenth-century enamels. All are painted and have cut-steel or champlevé enamel borders.

Liverpool transfers on porcelain (nineteenth century).

ɔme stones show pieces of the stalk or stem, and some show both side and top of ıe calyx. Colors vary from a light gray to dark brown. Buttons made from these stones ere highly polished to enhance their beauty. They were sold mostly to collectors.

ETTIBONE MANUFACTURING COMPANY. Ohio, 1880's. This name appears on the back uniform buttons.

EWABIC POTTERY COMPANY. Founded in 1906 at Detroit, Michigan, by Mary Chase erry, who later became Mrs. William Stratton, and A. J. Caulkins. Mrs. Stratton named e pottery works after the Pewabic Indians. Pewabic means "clay having copper color." ıe pottery produced here became noted for its fine glaze. Tiles and mosaics were also ade at the works, as well as a few buttons. Pewabic tiles were used in notable buildings -cathedrals and shrines, and the Detroit Institute of Art—and vases are in the Freer allery in Washington, D.C. The buttons made at the Pewabic pottery were molded of combination of blue and gray clay that was covered with a copper glaze.

Pewabic pottery buttons. 1940's.

EWTER BUTTON MOLDS. These molds made buttons complete with shanks. The molds emselves were made of bronze, sometimes with a design, at other times plain. Most olds made from one to five buttons with each pouring, and very often the size or ttern of each of the buttons differed. The top part of the mold, which had depressions r the shank, was divided so that it opened and closed. When it was closed, the hot olten pewter would flow down into the depressions for the button disks, filling the ank depressions at the same time, forming shelf-shank buttons. When the pewter was ol, the mold was opened and the buttons removed.

To date, only three molds have been found that make more than five buttons at a ne. These, which make nine, ten, and twelve buttons, are in Just Buttons Museum, uthington, Connecticut. When they were first used is not known with certainty, but was quite definitely before 1800. These large molds made men's buttons.

Only a very few molds have been found with military designs.

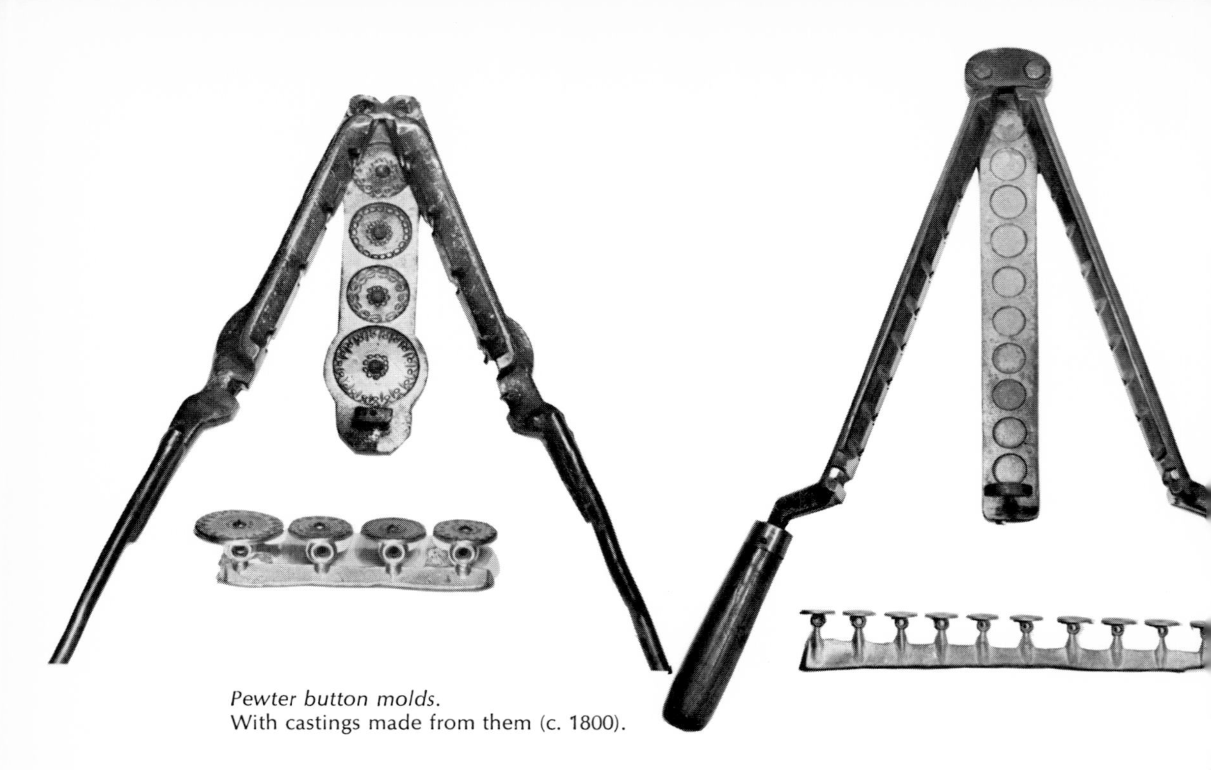

Pewter button molds.
With castings made from them (c. 1800).

PEWTER BUTTONS. Pewter was commonly used in the late eighteenth and earl nineteenth centuries for making men's buttons. It was used again after the middle c the nineteenth century for women's wear. Pewter is an alloy of tin and other meta such as antimony, bismuth, copper, or lead. Various combinations were used, but th best pewter was considered to be that made of at least 90 percent tin.

The first pewter buttons were probably made in Europe, and may have come to th United States with other pewter wares. However, although early histories mentio pewterers in several states who made buttons of this material, only buttons with Cor necticut pewterers' names have so far been found. A large proportion of pewter buttor have no back markings. The first pewter buttons were made in molds that included self-shank. (*See* Pewter Button Molds.)

About 1800, the Grilley brothers (*which see*) introduced a pewter button with an iro shank. From this time on, the pewterer's name more frequently appeared on the back of buttons. Local histories list Henry Grilley of Waterbury, Connecticut, as the first to sta a factory for the sole purpose of making buttons. Records of several other Connectic towns indicate that pewterers had shops of various sizes throughout the state, and wer also making buttons.

The following list shows some of the names of pewterers found on buttons:

A. Goodyear
Aaron Benedict
Anson Matthews
Bishop & Heminway
Booth Collins
Charles Yale
D. Pritchard
E. Scott
G. Scott
H. Grilley
H. Scott
Ives
Judd
Judd & Wooster
L. Merriam
M. Fowler
New Haven & Baltimore Co.
O. Pearl
S. Steel
Spencer & Hotchkiss
Steels Mfgr.

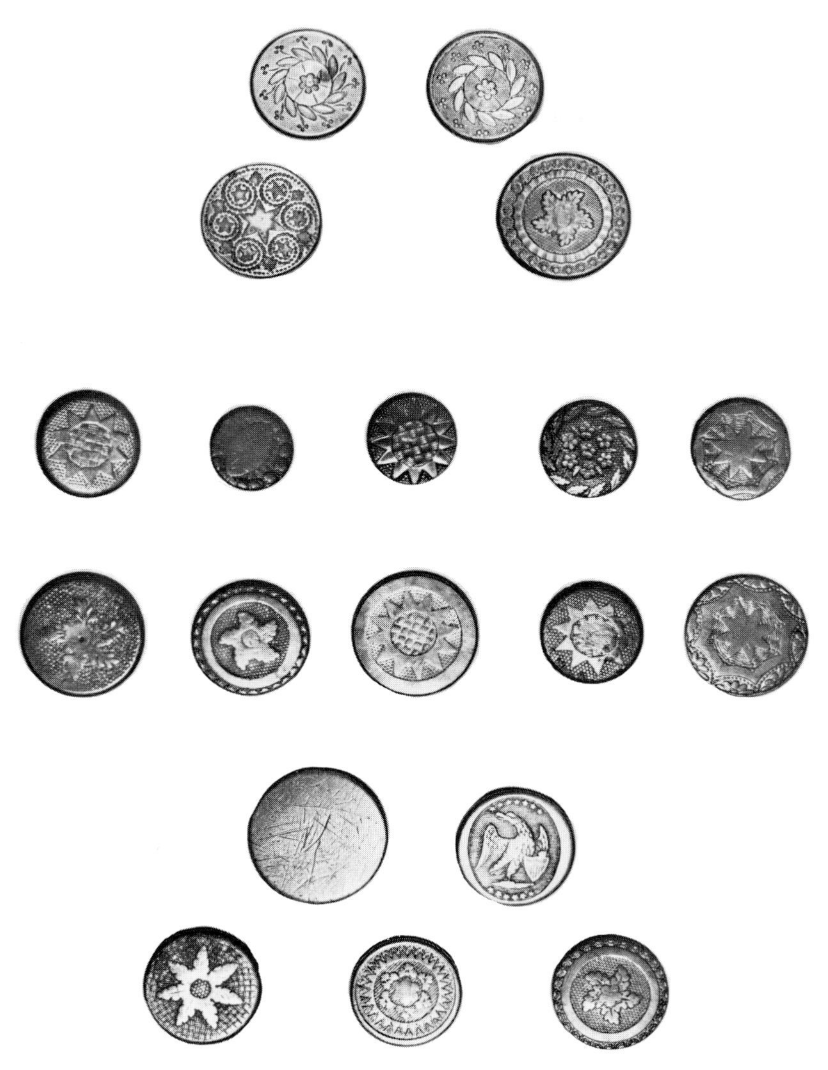

Pewter buttons. With wire shanks (1800–1820).

Massachusetts records state that Obed and Otis Robinson formed a partnership for aking pewter buttons in Attleboro, Massachusetts, but no buttons have been found ith these names.

About 1810, several pewterers shifted to the manufacture of brass buttons. With e popularity of brass buttons, the manufacture of pewter buttons ceased for a while.

In the last half of the nineteenth century, pewter and Britannia were introduced for utton making again. Much of the pewter used then was inferior to the pewter used the early part of the century because of its heavy lead content. Buttons of this nearly ad material were often painted or decorated with other materials, and this pewter itself as used to decorate buttons of other metals. Pewter buttons have continued to be made various shapes and sizes in the twentieth century.

PICK BACK or MARKS. Marks caused by a tool used to take a button out of a die c mold when it did not remove easily. Processed horn buttons most often show pick mark This is why, in the early days of collecting, these buttons were referred to as "pic backs." The term is seldom used now. Many horn buttons do not have pick marks, an buttons of other materials occasionally do have them.

PICTURE BUTTONS. All buttons having designs other than concentric, geometric, c conventional are called picture buttons. They range in size from less than 1/2" to over 3'

Picture designs have appeared on buttons from the earliest beginnings, made by ever art and craft, using every kind of material. The subjects are innumerable. Many seer peculiar for the particular garments for which they were made—for example, cupids fc men's coat buttons in the eighteenth century, and insects and nails for nineteenth-centur women's dresses. Popular designs such as flowers were used extensively for bot men's and women's garments.

More picture buttons have been made of metal than of any other material, but c course larger quantities of metal buttons of all kinds were made. It is becoming mor and more difficult to date metal picture buttons accurately. The designs were repeatec over the years, by different manufacturers, and old designs have also been reissued t make new buttons for collector-dealers. The first metal picture buttons were made in th middle of the nineteenth century, and the number increased considerably between 188 and 1900. Usually, gilt buttons dating from 1810 to 1850 are not included in thi grouping, although many have pictorial designs. When the design illustrates a particula story or a portion of it—a drama, fable, nursery rhyme, opera, poetry—the buttons ar called Story Buttons (*which see*).

Picture buttons can be classified in various ways according to materials, arts an crafts, or subject. The subject used for the design is popular as a means of specialize groupings. The list below gives examples of subject classifications.

Animals. *See* Animal Designs.
Architecture: arches, bridges, buildings, castles, gates, statues, towers, etc. *Se* Architectural Designs.
Astronomy: stars, crescents, comets, moons
Children (most commonly found in stories). *See* Story Buttons.
Circus: clowns, wagons, performers, etc. *See* Circus Designs.
Coins (and coin types). *See* Coin Buttons.
Cupids, including cherubs, gnomes, and fairies
Fables. *See* Story Buttons.
Fabulous Animals: griffins, dragons, unicorns
Fops
History. *See* Historical; Historical Wood Buttons.
Inanimate Objects: anchors, baskets, buckles, crosses, fans, feathers, horseshoes, nail pins, shells, shoes, screws, umbrellas and parasols. (*See* Crosses.)
Music: musicians and instruments
Mythology: characters and stories. *See* Story Buttons.
Oriental: flowers, masks, scenes, and stories. *See* Story Buttons; *also* Mask Buttons.
Pastimes: games and sports
People: men, women, heads, lovers
Plant Life: flowers, fruits (including nuts), leaves, grains, grasses, vegetables, etc.
Religion: characters, scenes, stories, symbols. *See* Story Buttons.
Scenes: land and water, identified and imaginary
Stories. *See* Story Buttons.
Symbols: conventional and traditional signs, mostly religious and political
Theatrical: drama, opera
Transportation: almost every mode of travel—airplanes, automobiles, balloon bicycles, boats and ships, engines and trains, trolleys, wagons, etc.
Zodiac. *See* Zodiac Buttons.

Picture buttons. Nineteenth century; of various materials.

Picture button. The die for a picture button
showing Red Riding Hood, and the button struck from it.

PIECRUST BUTTONS. A term used for one of the Small Chinas. It comes from the molde edge of fine lines resembling the edge of the crust on a pie that has been presse together with a fork (perhaps largely a New England practice). Many white piecru buttons were made with two, three, or four holes. Some were decorated with colore rings or bands, which were of one or two colors; the bands completely covered th piecrust edge. The buttons range in size from 3/8″ to 1″. Piecrust buttons should not b confused with sawtooth buttons. The lines on piecrusts do not go all the way to the edg

PIGTAIL SHANK. Some loop shanks have been found with one end loosened from th molded buttons—most commonly, the shanks on glass buttons. Many collectors believ this condition was caused by carelessness in the making of the buttons rather than b intentional construction.

PIN BACKS. A term given to buttons having a pin for fastening them to a garment. Recer campaign buttons are a good example of this type. The front has a metal rim; the pi has a loop that snaps behind the rim to hold the pin in place. A few very early ones ha a thin metal back that held the pin. There are collectors who specialize in collectin pin backs. Others do not accept pin backs because they were not made to fasten c decorate a garment. However, their use and purpose closely parallels that of many lape buttons. Early pin buttons were made by button manufacturers. Since 1896, there ha been a tremendous output of this kind of button.

Pin-back buttons. Celluloid; twentieth century.

PINCHBECK. An alloy of zinc and copper named for the inventor, Christopher Pinchbeck, who was a maker of watches and clocks in London in the early 1700's. In appearance, pinchbeck was so much like gold that it appealed at once as a substitute. Christopher Pinchbeck's son, Edward Pinchbeck, succeeded him. Although others tried to imitate this alloy, none was as successful as the Pinchbecks. Christopher Pinchbeck often called himself a toymaker, but he never made a toy as one thinks of toys today. Rather, he made many small articles, and one of his early lists mentioned buttons.

No buttons have been identified as having been made completely of this alloy. Buttons of horn and tortoiseshell were inlaid with designs of a metal that looks like pinchbeck. However, these buttons were manufactured long after pinchbeck ceased to be made. The metal used for the inlay work could have been made by Pinchbeck's imitators after the Pinchbecks died, and is probably some unidentified yellow alloy.

PINCHED CENTERS. A type of glass center for jewel buttons, made by heating the end of a glass rod and forcing it against a mold, then pinching it off. These small molded pieces were known as pinched centers. Not all glass centers for buttons were made in this way. When a glass center is mounted in a metal button, it is not possible to identify a pinched center. Glass centers are known to have been made by the Cheshire Manufacturing Company.

PINHEAD SHANK. A term used for a shank that was made with a wire having a head on it. The pinlike wire went through a hole in the button, and the end of the wire was bent up into the body of the button, forming a loop shank. The head may have been quite similar to a common pin, or had a design.

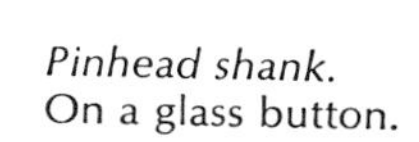

Pinhead shank.
On a glass button.

PINNA SHELL BUTTONS. Until very recently, these buttons were called Volute Shell buttons. The translucent material in the button continues to cause controversy because of the size and thickness of the buttons in relation to pinna shell, which is thin and narrow. It is argued that the shell could not be flattened enough to make buttons.

Pinna shell buttons are pinkish brown in color, with finely incised line designs on a flat polished surface, which has been filled with paint—silver, gold, or white. The buttons were probably made in the nineteenth century, perhaps of some unidentified composition. Several designs have been found. The buttons range in size from 1/2″ to over 2″, and are very interesting and scarce.

Pinna shell button.
Nineteenth century.

PIPESTONE. *See* Catlinite.

PLANT-LIFE DESIGNS. Real flowers, grasses, leaves, trees, and weeds were used t decorate buttons, as were pictures of them. When actual specimens were used, th buttons were often referred to as "habitat," especially the eighteenth-century button having plant life under glass. (*See* Habitat Buttons.) Grasses were made up into design under celluloid faces in the late nineteenth century. In the twentieth century, many di ferent specimens of plant life were encased in clear plastic. Plant life was also copie extensively by button designers, flowers being the most popular subject. *See also* Pictur Buttons.

PLASTIC BUTTONS. Many different moldable materials have been used to make button and were sometimes referred to as "plastic." In recent years, however, with the tremer dous growth of new materials, the word "plastic" has come to apply almost exclusivel to the synthetic products of chemistry. The ancestor of modern synthetic plastics considered to be celluloid, first made in the United States in 1869 by John Wesley Hyat but it was not until the discovery of Bakelite around 1907 that the real foundation c the modern plastics industry was laid. Makers of synthetic plastics set the date of th notable expansion at around 1930. *See also* Celluloid; Bakelite.

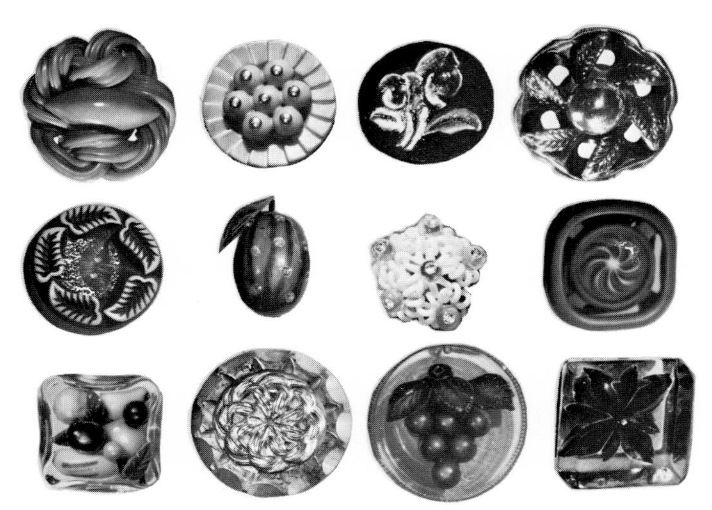

Plastic buttons. These were made in the 1940's.

When plastic buttons first appeared, the name of the plastics maker often appeare on the sales cards. Gradually these names were dropped, and all such buttons wer called plastics. Button manufacturers did not make the raw material themselves. It wa produced by plastics manufacturers, in various forms—powder, rods, and sheets; trans parent, translucent, or opaque; as well as in imitation of other materials.

The manufacturing and decorating styles and techniques used earlier, with natura materials, have also been used for plastic buttons, which have been carved, or molde to look like carving; trimmed or inlaid with other material; and shaped and decorated a glass buttons were. More and more, the collectors of plastic buttons are using the term that were coined for other materials.

Some of the early plastic buttons are already scarce; the earliest, in fact, were easil destroyed in laundering, and so few of them remain. Although new techniques hav made plastics more durable and corrected many other defects, there is still deterioratio of the original beauty of these buttons—even of those made as late as mid-century

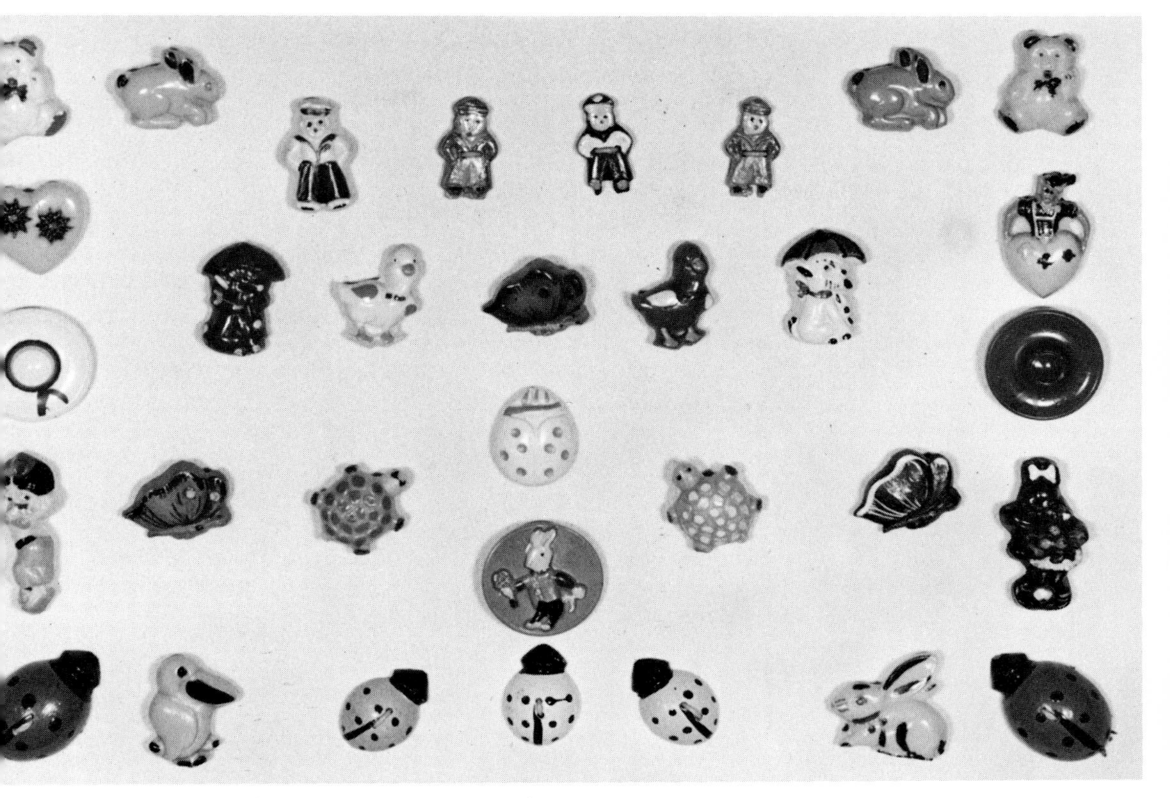

Plastic buttons. These are of the 1950's and 1960's.

PLATING. *See* Electroplating; *also* Sheffield Silver.

PLATT, A., & COMPANY. *See* A. Platt & Company.

PLATT BROTHERS COMPANY. Waterbury, Connecticut. The company originated in 1825. In the 1870's, it became Patent Button Company, manufacturers of metal buttons. *See also* Patent Button Company.

PLATT, CURTIS & COMPANY. Manufacturers of wooden buttons, Newtown, Connecticut, 1840's to 1850's. Although the records are not specific, it is believed that they manufactured mostly wooden button molds.

PLATT, L. L., and WILLIAM. Manufacturers of horn buttons, Newtown, Connecticut, 1840's to 1850's.

PLIQUE-À-JOUR. *See* Enamels, Enameling.

PLUMBAGO. A term for a white alloy consisting mostly of lead that was used for making buttons during the late nineteenth and early twentieth centuries. Plumbago, which easily becomes dull, is seldom used today. The material is sometimes referred to as a poor grade of pewter; at other times, as lead. Its exact composition is not known.

POLICE BUTTONS. *See* Uniform Buttons.

POLITICAL BUTTONS. Politics, as current events, has influenced button designs for almost two hundred years, perhaps even longer in the case of European-made buttons. (*See also* Picture Buttons, and *Punch* [Button Designs] for the influence of politics on button designs.) Buttons issued for political campaigns, inaugurals, and commemorations of these events are commonly included among "politicals," as they are called. Although a candidate or an event may have had only local interest at the time, the buttons made for the occasion are included in this large group. Of course, in some instances, a local candidate later gained state and national status.

Since 1900, most political buttons have been made with pin fasteners instead of shanks, and these have not always been acceptable to all button collectors. However, more collectors are now including all political buttons regardless of their construction or material. *See also* Campaign Buttons; Commemoratives.

Very few collectors include, among their political buttons, those with pictures of Presidents on fabric, jasperware, pearl, metal, or other materials that were made for other than political and commemorative events. When the production and sales of such a button have continued indefinitely, it is considered as belonging to the classification Presidential Buttons (*which see*).

POMEROY MANUFACTURING COMPANY. Manufacturers of paper buttons, Wallingford, Connecticut, 1840's to 1850's. E. M. Pomeroy of this firm secured a patent for paper buttons. The company name is found on paper buttons that are heavily coated with black japan. The buttons have four holes for sewing.

Paper button. Pomeroy Manufacturing Company patent.

POPPER, LEO, & SONS. *See* Leo Popper and Sons.

PORCELAIN BUTTONS. These white-bodied buttons were made of clay, and usually heavily glazed with transfer or painted designs. Fine porcelains had been made for several centuries, but records indicate it was not until nearly the nineteenth century that even the older potteries made buttons for the trade. Although each potter strove to keep his formulas and methods a secret, by 1859 porcelain buttons were being made in practically every country. In the seventy years between 1850 and 1920, they had several periods of being fashionable.

Collectors do not usually include Small Chinas, jasperware, or "Norwalk" and other coarser pottery in this group. Some do include Satsumas among porcelain buttons. (*See also* the separate articles on Small Chinas, Jasperware, Indian Pottery Buttons, "Norwalk" Pottery Buttons, Pewabic Pottery Company, Ruskin Pottery Buttons.)

It is difficult to date porcelain buttons more closely than as follows: pre-1800; 1850 to 1900; 1900 to 1920 (those decorated in American studios and homes, including shirtwaist studs); post-1940 (studio-made porcelains for collectors). Occasionally, porcelain buttons do have back marks, and these further substantiate the above dates; some also have names of potteries. Many European porcelain buttons were originally mounted on cards that gave the name of the pottery or the country, but by the time the buttons reached a garment, their source had been destroyed.

Delft button. A twentieth-century Delft "porcelain" button. Back mark is "Holland."

Porcelain buttons. Top row, eighteenth century. Second, third, and fifth rows are painted (note the silver trim on the third button in the fifth row). Buttons in the fourth row have transfer designs with gold backgrounds.

Hand-painted porcelain buttons. 1900–1920.

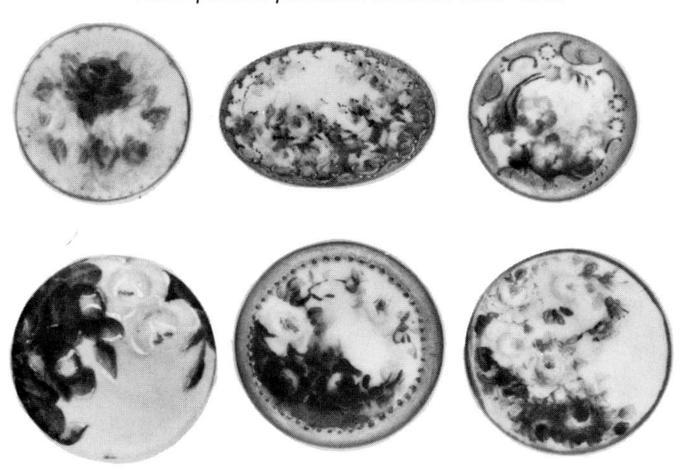

Most of the nineteenth-century porcelain buttons are of superior quality and beauty Many show the characteristics of certain specific potteries, but they could have been made in any of the well-known potteries. For example, the little flowers found on some buttons are typical of Dresden ware; and buttons with blue and lavender designs under clear glaze seem definitely of Delft origin.

A few porcelain buttons were made with colored glazes, deep blue being the color most commonly found, with bright designs and much gold; a few have been found with silver designs. Most early porcelains have transfer designs, often with some hand painting added. Occasionally, the transfers were not covered with glaze, and often the designs on these buttons have been partly destroyed by wear.

A rare find is a delicately painted porcelain button with a pinhead shank, credited to the eighteenth century. The pin usually had just a brass head; a very few had a pearl head or paste in a cup. The backs were usually unglazed, showing a gray-white body.

From 1900 to 1920, many buttons with self-shanks, and also shirtwaist studs, were hand painted. During this period, china painting was a fashionable pastime for young ladies. Plain glazed porcelain buttons and studs were purchased from a nearby pottery, and the designs were added in china-painting classes or at home. After the paint was dry, they were taken to be fired. The most popular design for these buttons was flowers with a border of gold; occasionally, transfers of heads or scenery were used.

Since 1940, porcelain buttons have been decorated in small studios. Artists sought out porcelain disks, or unfinished porcelain buttons with self-shanks, in small potteries having stock leftover from 1900. Buttons so decorated that bear the artist's name can be easily authenticated. Some were decorated to imitate buttons made in the early 1900's, the artist using transfers that had been made for jewelry centers in 1900. These buttons are confusing for collectors to authenticate. Current designs used on porcelain buttons include the astronauts, space capsules, and other recent subjects.

A very few porcelain buttons have been found with early potters' marks. *See also* Coalport Works; Sèvres Porcelain Buttons; Meissen Porcelain.

A Limoges porcelain button.
The back mark is "Limoges, France."

PORTER, ABEL. A pewterer of Southington, Connecticut, who probably began making pewter buttons before 1800. From the property he owned, it can be assumed he was a successful pewterer, and made many pewter buttons, but apparently with molds that produced buttons with self-shanks and no back markings. Waterbury and Southington histories lead one to believe that he went to Waterbury in 1804 to start what became the largest brass industry in the world, the Scovill Manufacturing Company. Pewter buttons have been found with Scott and Porter on the backs, but it has not been authenticated whether this Porter is Abel Porter. Histories do state that Abel Porter made pewter buttons before 1804, and was one of the earliest pewterers to turn to making brass buttons.

POTTERY BUTTONS. Although to some collectors all articles made of clay are considered pottery, to most button collectors only the coarser ceramic buttons are classified as pottery. These are usually more primitive in texture, shape, and glaze. For example, when the American-made "Norwalk" pottery buttons are viewed apart from the finer textures of other ceramic buttons, their own individual characteristics become interesting and, in their way, beautiful. Usually, coloring is in the clay (sometimes a mixture) as well as in the glaze. Pottery buttons were made with holes, with metal shanks, or mounted in metal frames. Most of them were made in small shops and are closely similar to other objects made of the same ceramic materials. Therefore, American pottery buttons interest collectors of American pottery as well as button collectors. *See also* "Norwalk" Pottery Buttons, Pewabic Pottery Company, Ruskin Pottery Buttons, etc.

PRECIOUS STONES. Diamonds, rubies, emeralds, and other precious stones were sometimes used to decorate buttons. These buttons are seen today mostly in museums, but more have been recorded in stories than have been found. Paste has long been used to imitate precious stones. Collectors have also found that the less valuable garnet and turquoise were more commonly used to decorate buttons than more costly stones. Garnets were set in prongs in the style of jewelry. Agates of several kinds, as well as various marbles, were used to make the body of buttons; these can be found from the eighteenth century, nearly always with a handmade rim and pinhead shank. *See also* Agate.

PREHISTORIC BUTTONS. Occasionally, objects resembling buttons have been excavated from early tombs. It is doubtful they were originally used as buttons, but they have shanklike apertures and are therefore sometimes referred to as buttons. It is more likely that they were worn on cords or chains; perhaps those with intaglio designs were used as seals. They have been found in both stone and clay, the clay ones frequently being in the shape of flowers or scarabs and tinted in colors.

Prehistoric buttons. Pottery and stone.

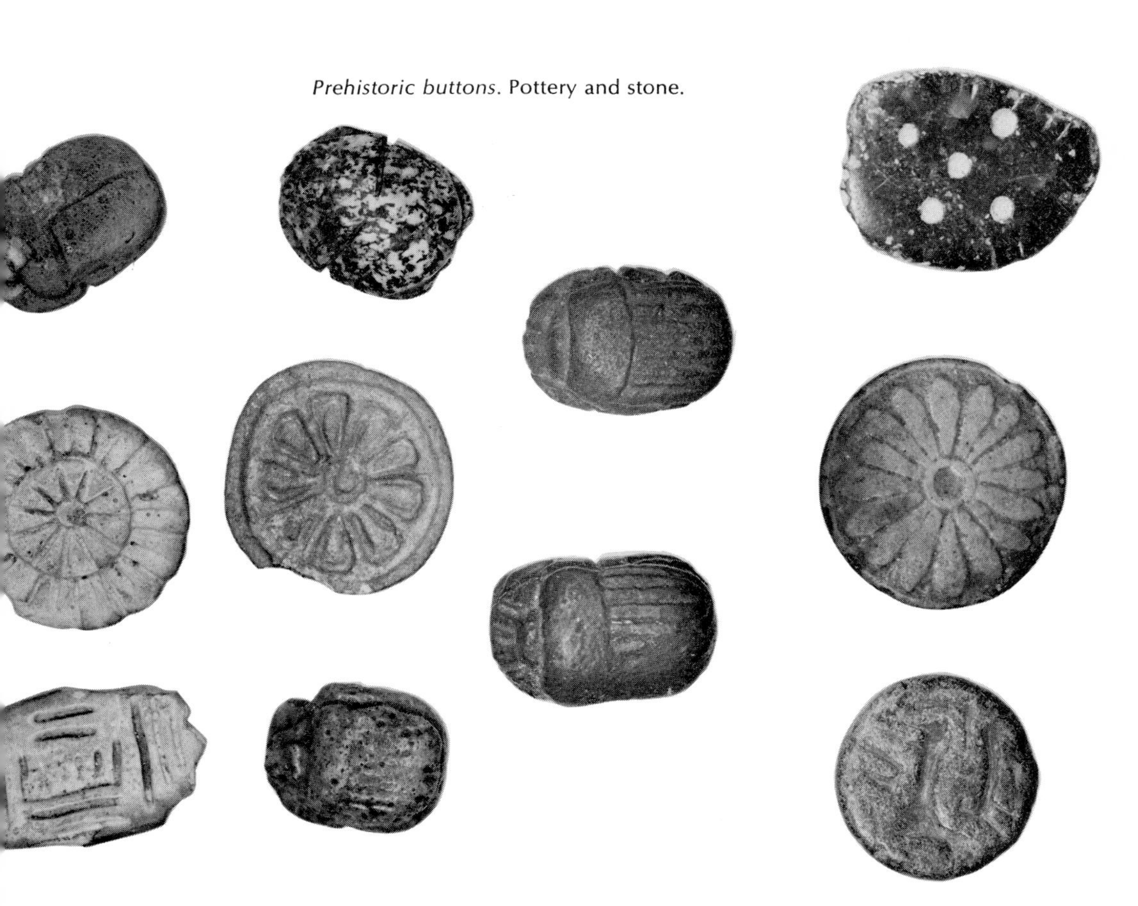

PRESIDENTIAL BUTTONS. All buttons with Presidents of the United States as the design subject. Buttons made for presidential campaigns and inaugurations are usually classified as Politicals (*which see*), but the buttons commemorating these events, or a President's birth, election, or death, are called Presidential Buttons. Many more buttons with a President as the design subject have been made *between* campaigns, or after other important events, than at the actual time. These are usually grouped as Presidentials. They were made of different materials and sizes and by various techniques. It is sometimes difficult to authenticate the date or purpose of a particular button.

Washington and Lincoln were the most popular subjects of the many Presidential buttons produced. Series of Presidents on buttons were made to be enclosed in cereal and tobacco packages, to encourage sales of the product. For occasions such as the "Civil War Centennial," U. S. Grant and other Presidents appeared on buttons. Sometimes, for money-raising programs, organizations have had buttons made with Presidential designs. And studio artists have made, and continue to make, buttons with portraits of Presidents or scenes from a President's life story.

There are almost as many varieties of Presidential sets as there are of single buttons. If a complete set is found, the last President in the set will help date it. In the 1960's, fabric having the Presidents' profiles, spaced far enough apart to be cut out, could be bought. Organizations and individuals purchased the material by the yard and covered buttons with it. The fabric came in three color combinations, the red, white, and blue being the most popular.

A collection of Presidential Buttons can be very large indeed.

See especially Lincoln Buttons; Washington Inaugural Buttons.

Presidential buttons. These were made in the twentieth century.

PRICES. *See* Values.

PRIMITIVE TYPE. A term used in the early days of button collecting to refer to two kinds of shanks found on eighteenth-century buttons. These self-shanks were formed by a "pocket" in one part of the button mold.

PRINCE ALBERT BUTTONS. A term used frequently by garment makers for the black fabric buttons worn on men's Prince Albert coats. Collectors seldom use the term.

PRINTING. As a method of decorating buttons, printing was used as early as the eighteenth century. Although the transfer method of printing was more often used, it is believed some of the printed button designs on paper were done by the direct method. Some eighteenth-century buttons have printed designs on paper or silk, under glass, in metal frames. Most printed designs on paper are scenes recognizable as definite places or actual buildings. Those on silk are generally classic Greek or Roman figures. *See also* Transfer Buttons.

Printed decoration. The printing is on paper, under the glass faces; eighteenth century.

PRITCHARD, DAVID. Probably a button salesman or distributor only, in New York City, from 1820 to the 1850's. He may have been connected with the other Pritchards who were in the button-manufacturing business in Waterbury, Connecticut, at the same time.

PRITCHARD, ELIZUR E. Manufacturer of gilt buttons, Waterbury, Connecticut, 1820's to 1850's.

PRITCHARD, LEONARD. Manufacturer of gilt buttons, Waterbury, Connecticut, 1820's to 1850's.

"PUNCH" (BUTTON DESIGNS). *Punch* magazine, published in England from 1841 to the present, is made up largely of political satire on the news of the day. Over the years, there have been many illustrated comments or cartoons of political issues. The characters from the 1840's magazines especially appealed to button designers, but it is not known when buttons with illustrations from *Punch* were made, or how many; so far, only twelve designs have been found. The back mark, "Treble Stan'd Extra Rich," indicates the buttons were made in England in the 1850's. They are two-piece brass buttons about 1" in size.

One smaller button has been found, with a design similar to that of one of the large buttons, with no caption, 5/8″ in size. *Punch*-design buttons are extremely scarce.

"Punch" designs. Buttons from the 1840's and 1850's with designs from *Punch.*

PYLES, IRENE. *See* The Tall Texan Lapidary.

PYROGRAPHY. Poker work—or "fire etching," as it has sometimes been called—is the art of decorating wood or other materials through the use of hot tools. By scorching the surface to a greater or lesser degree, effects of light and dark are produced. The technique was used mostly on wooden buttons, though some fabric buttons were decorated in this way.

Pyrography was among the ancient arts, as well as an art of the primitive tribes of more modern times. It was also a favorite pastime among young ladies in this country from the 1880's up until at least 1910. The instruments used were referred to as "pins and poking sticks of steel."

A 1903 book by Lilla E. Kelley, *300 Things a Bright Girl Can Do,* included decorating articles with pyrography. And a 1905 issue of the *Delineator* (a magazine) mentioned pyrography decoration, and showed illustrations of dress trimmings, including buttons, decorated by this method.

A salesman's box containing wood buttons and buckles to match has been found. Both the box and its contents are decorated in this manner, with bright paint added. Burned into the box is: "Stryper's Fancy Buttons—handmade. Amsterdam, Holland." It is quite possible the box and its samples were made in the beginning of the twentieth century; similar buttons with bright paint added appeared in American stores at about the same time.

Q

QUALITY MARKS. A term used for certain words found on the backs of buttons made after 1800. It is believed the purpose of the words was mainly to promote sales, as the differences in quality can seldom be noted. Most of these marks appeared between 1800 and 1850. Examples are "Rich Gold," "Superior Quality," "Treble Gilt," "Gilt," and "Rich Orange."

QUARTZ. *See* Agate.

R

R. & W. ROBINSON & COMPANY. In 1827, an invitation was extended by this firm "to visit the New Establishment in Attleborough, Massachusetts, to view and inspect the same and to partake of an entertainment." It was signed by Richard Robinson & Co. The "W" stood for Willard Robinson, son of Col. Obed Robinson, the early pewterer.

The Robinsons went from the making of pewter buttons into the manufacturing of brass buttons, as many of the New England firms did. They made gilt buttons of every description. Buttons are found with R. Robinson & Co.; Robinson, Jones & Co.; R. & W. Robinson; and R & W R. Co. on the backs. The reason for the changes in the firm's name is not positively known, nor are the dates. It is believed the Robinson family was in the business of manufacturing brass buttons from 1812 to the 1840's.

RADIANTS. *See* Glass Buttons.

RARIG, THERESA. Potter and glassblower, Minneapolis, Kansas. She has made porcelain buttons with polychrome transfers, and paperweight buttons, since 1955. Her paperweights have sulfide and cane designs.

Paperweight buttons. Made by Theresa Rarig in the 1960's, they have sulfide designs.

REALISTICS. A term used mostly for buttons made since 1935 that have realistic shapes. However, buttons have been made in realistic forms since the very first garment fasteners and ornaments. Over the centuries, realistic shapes were most commonly made of material that could easily be molded—clay, glass, metal, plastic, and so on. Some hard materials, such as bone, ivory, shell, and wood, were also cut into buttons of realistic shape—for example, the oldest realistics, which were shaped like flowers or scarabs.

It was near the middle of the twentieth century, when synthetic plastics were profusely used for buttons, before realistics were made in large numbers and in the maximum variety of shapes. By 1940, a large proportion of all buttons produced, no matter what the material, were realistically shaped. Often, realistics were offered in sets—for example, cards mounted with eight different vegetables, four different fruits, or two different birds. At the same time, such "deluxe" realistics were presented as a TV dinner on a plate complete with vegetables; or a piano or an armored tank. These buttons, which could be bought in all chain and department stores, ranged in price from eight buttons for ten cents to over a dollar apiece. At first, they were small (1/2" to 3/4"), but before the dress trade's interest waned, they were made in large sizes. Twentieth-century realistics were manufactured in almost every button factory and studio in every country.

Collectors with forethought for tomorrow's antiques shopped extensively, but many others remained reluctant to accept these newly made buttons—they called them "moderns." Since button fashions changed more rapidly between the 1940's and 1950's than they did a hundred years ago, twentieth-century realistics are already almost as scarce as those made in the previous centuries.

REBUS BUTTONS. Designs on rebus buttons consist of words or syllables, accompanied by pictures of objects whose names resemble the words or syllables; or, a riddle made up of such pictures or syllables. Buttons found with this kind of design usually bear French words and are delicately ornamented. Most such buttons were made in the last half of the eighteenth century. Among those found are metal disks with stamped rebus designs, painted designs on ivory under glass, and painted porcelains.

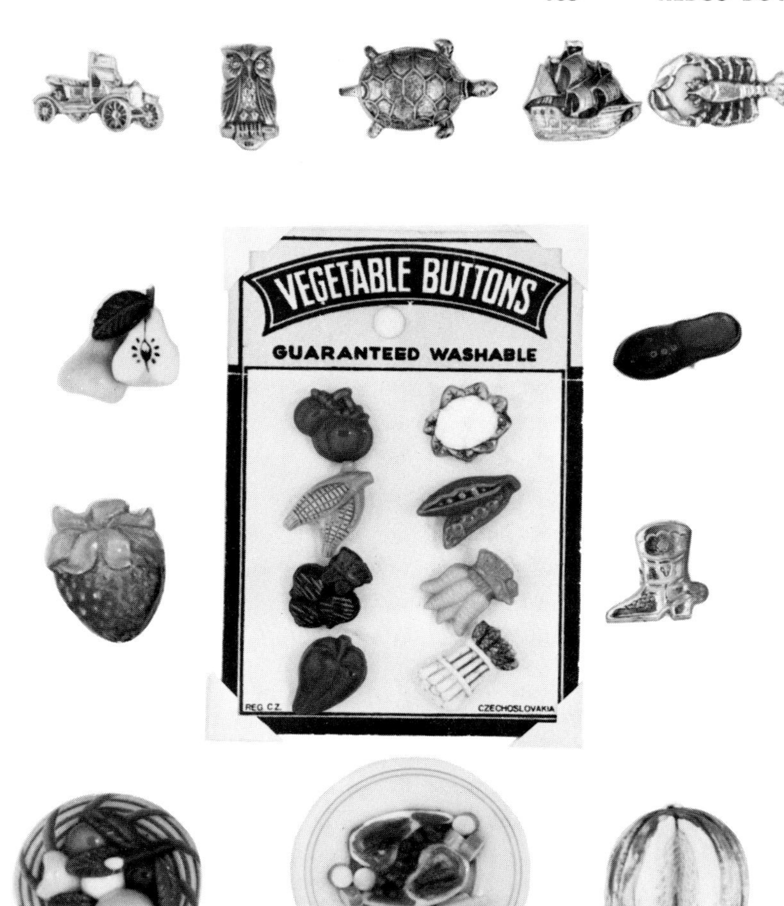

Realistics. Twentieth-century realistics of metal and plastic. The store card shows a complete set.

Rebus buttons. Two eighteenth-century rebus buttons of painted porcelain under glass:
(1) Love is without end.
(2) She was thinking of me.

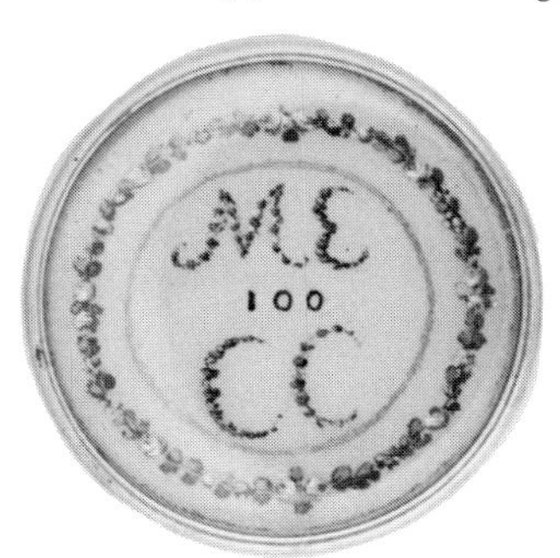

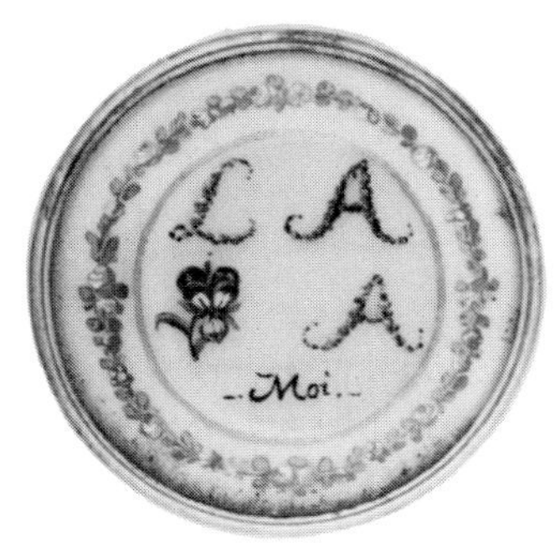

REEDS, JACOBS & SONS. Uniform makers, of the 1900's. The name appears on the backs of uniform buttons.

REFLECTORS. *See* Glass Buttons: Radiants.

REGISTRY MARKS. Marks found on the backs of British-made buttons. They have been found on ceramic, glass, horn, and metal buttons. A registry mark is diamond-shaped, with letters or numbers at the points of the diamond. At the top point is an extra circle with a letter. The letters and numbers indicate the material, month, day, and year the button was registered, and the bundle inspected. *See also* Back Marks.

Registry mark. Horn button showing an English registry mark. Nineteenth century.

REISSUES. A term used by collectors for buttons struck from old dies solely for the collector or the souvenir trade, long after the original use of the die was discontinued. Dies were frequently used for a long period of time, perhaps with interruptions because of changes in fashion; and such buttons, manufactured for the original purpose, are not considered reissues.

REPOUSSÉ. A method of creating a design in relief on metal by hammering or pressing from the reverse side. It is believed that very few buttons were decorated in this manner. Most hammering—or "sticking," as it is more commonly called—was done on the face of a button with a two-piece die. *See also* Dies.

REPTILES. *See* Picture Buttons.

REUSED DISKS. Some early one-piece button disks were reused. Often, the shank was removed from leftover stock, and a design was stamped on this plain side. Then a shank was placed on the side that held the original design. Reused buttons are more often found among early uniform buttons.

REVERSE PAINTING. A very early technique for decorating glass by painting on the reverse side. Fine work of this kind has been found on Chinese articles predating any work known in Europe or America. Eighteenth-century buttons were decorated in gold and black in the manner of églomisé (*which see*); there were also buttons with polychrome designs painted on the reverse side of the glass face. Very often, those painted with colors were left without a painted background on the glass, having instead disks of ivory or some other material placed against the back of the button, to serve as background.

In the middle of the nineteenth century, at about the same time that reverse painting was being done on glass panels for clocks in America, buttons were again decorated in this way. It has been suggested that the reverse painting on glass for buttons at this time might be called a revival of the art, rather than an imitation, as some have termed it.

The Scovill Manufacturing Company's records show that a French artisan was brought to the factory in 1868 to do glass painting for buttons, and remained until sometime in

Reverse painting. Set of buttons with polychrome reverse painting on glass. Eighteenth century.

Reverse painting. Buttons with reverse painting on glass. Nineteenth century.

the 1880's. The buttons made were mostly drum-shaped, in varying degrees of thickness, with reverse-painted glass faces. The hand-painted designs were applied one color at a time. The foreground was painted first; then other parts of the design were added, until the background completed what was almost a three-dimensional picture. Young ladies are said to have painted many of the clock panels, an American development, and it is likely that they also painted many button faces. The eighteenth-century reverse-painted buttons were mostly over 1″ in diameter; nineteenth-century buttons were mostly 1″. All are very scarce.

Imitations of this art were made by pasting paper with a printed design onto buttons. It is not always easy to distinguish these; however, the printed paper designs are more regular, and sometimes are found loosened from the glass.

RHINESTONES. Imitation diamonds made of colorless glass or paste, with foil backs; used to trim buttons, to make inexpensive jewelry, and for other decorative purposes.

RICHARDS, GILES. Manufacturer of pewter buttons and of combs for carding wool, Dedham, Massachusetts, 1788. Richards was born in Waterbury, Connecticut, in 1754, but no records have been found showing that he made pewter items in Connecticut. In fact, no buttons have been found with his name on the back. However, it was not until after 1800 that pewterers' names appeared on buttons. Giles Richards is on the records as having been in several manufacturing businesses in New York and Massachusetts. He was the inventor of many of the machines he used.

RICOLITE BUTTONS. Noel Cunninghan of Pinos Altos, New Mexico, is credited with being the originator of buttons made of Ricolite (1930–45). Ricolite is often referred to as the "gemstone of the serpentines"; its wide variety of colors and contrasting lines made it a very attractive material for buttons. The usually narrow lines were in tans, grays with black, light and dark greens with white. Ricolite buttons were made for the dress trade, and for collectors, in round, oval, and square shapes with self-shanks, 5/8″ to 1″ in size. They are already difficult to find.

RIDLEY, E., & SONS. *See* E. Ridley & Sons.

RIMMED TYPE. Buttons of this type were one-piece, completed by the addition of a metal rim, usually brass. This method of decorating began at least as early as the eighteenth century; large buttons of bone, copper, and horn have been found from this period. Rimmed buttons were more commonly made in the nineteenth century; these were small metal buttons, 3/8″ to 3/4″. The first small buttons were made of pewter with brass rims; then came brass buttons with brass rims. The buttons made entirely of brass were called Jacksonians (*which see*). Rimmed buttons of other materials appeared after the Jacksonians, but not in abundance. Collectors can also find rimmed buttons made in the twentieth century.

ROBBINS COMPANY. Attleboro, Massachusetts, 1892. The "new" Robbins Company was founded during this election year by Charles M. Robbins, who had become so interested in the presidential campaign that, in his own simple shed-workshop, he first designed and produced campaign buttons for his favorite candidates. This was the start of a business that increased to twenty general product lines.

ROBINSON, JONES & COMPANY. Button manufacturers, established May, 1831, in Attleboro, Massachusetts, by Richard and Willard Robinson, William H. Jones, and H. M. Draper. They manufactured metal buttons by horsepower in a small shop, and later built a brick building where the machinery was operated by waterpower.

At first, they manufactured "common gilt" buttons, which competed, to a degree, with those of English manufacture. Later, they produced all varieties of brass buttons—Navy, military, fancy, and sporting buttons, which were considered superior to any on the market in beauty, finish, and durability. The company received three medals from the American Institute of New York, the first one in 1833. The firm's full name, or "R. J. & Co.," is found on the backs of buttons.

ROBINSON, O. & O. Colonel Obed and Otis Robinson formed a partnership for making pewter buttons in Attleboro, Massachusetts, in 1812. *See also* Pewter Buttons.

ROBINSON, R. & W., & COMPANY. *See* R. & W. Robinson & Company.

ROBINSON BLACKINTON & CO. This company's name and its location (Paterson, New Jersey) have been found on the back of one-piece sporting buttons of fine workmanship. Paterson records give this information: "In 1832, there was one Gilt Button Factory, employing twenty hands, manufacturing 9,000 gross a year, average $4.50 a gross. Superior workmanship and elegance of finish, unsurpassed by any gilt button imported from Europe." However, the record gives no name or address. Genealogical references indicate that Robinson Blackinton was related to the owners of the R. & W. Robinson firm of Attleboro, Massachusetts, which was also well known for excellence in gilt buttons. Very few buttons have been found with "Robinson Blackinton & Co." on the backs. Another reference indicates that a company by this name was founded in 1862 in Attleboro, Massachusetts, and made silver and 14-karat gold novelties until 1900.

ROCHESTER BUTTON FACTORY. Wisconsin; Wellsville, Rochester, and Akron, New York. 1900's. Buttons made at Rochester were of vegetable ivory. At the Akron plant, casein buttons were made, the casein being imported from Norway and Germany.

ROSARIANS. A term, adopted from the word "Rosary," for glass buttons made with a hole through the center like that in a bead. The shanks of the older buttons were usually made of a heavy flattened brass wire, which was run through the hole, both ends being fastened to the knob on top. This knob was most often a plain flattened disk, but some were made in fancy shapes with star or floral designs. Most of these buttons have a loose metal ring around the shank. The term "Rosarian" is not used as commonly as in the early days of collecting; now, Rosarians are more frequently called Pin-Shank Buttons.

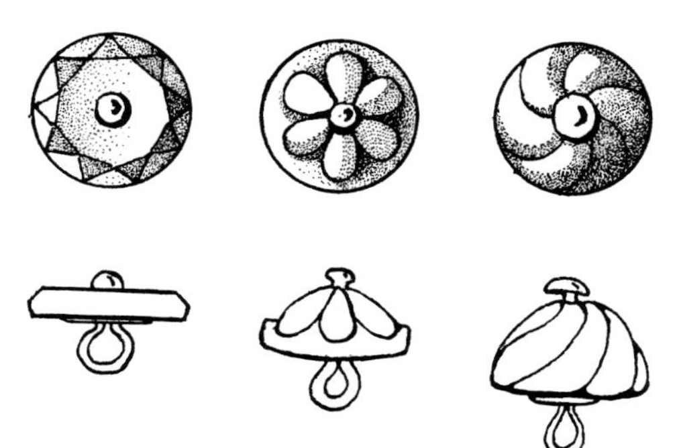

Rosarians. Pin-shank glass buttons dating from the nineteenth century.

ROSETTE SHANK. This classification of button takes its name from the unique shape of the metal shank plate, which has also been called a "spider-back" or a "claw shank plate." Rosette shanks, or rosette backs, are found on glass buttons of almost every color. These buttons range in size from 3/8" to 5/8".

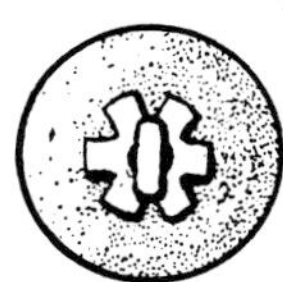

Rosette shank. At the left is a back view. Side view is at the right.

RUBBER BUTTONS. In the last half of the nineteenth century, many buttons were made of rubber. Those recognized as rubber buttons have the name Goodyear on the back. Others may seem to have rubber content, but collectors consider and treat them as composition buttons.

Buttons bearing the name Goodyear may also have other words, such as the button manufacturer's name, and "Patt." or "Patent, 1851." The date 1851 has no bearing on the date the button was manufactured. It was the year Nelson Goodyear secured his patent for an improvement in the manufacture of hard rubber. Buttons with the combination date "1849–51" can also be found.

Rubber buttons. Nineteenth century.

Rubber buttons.
Salesman's sample case.
Nineteenth century.

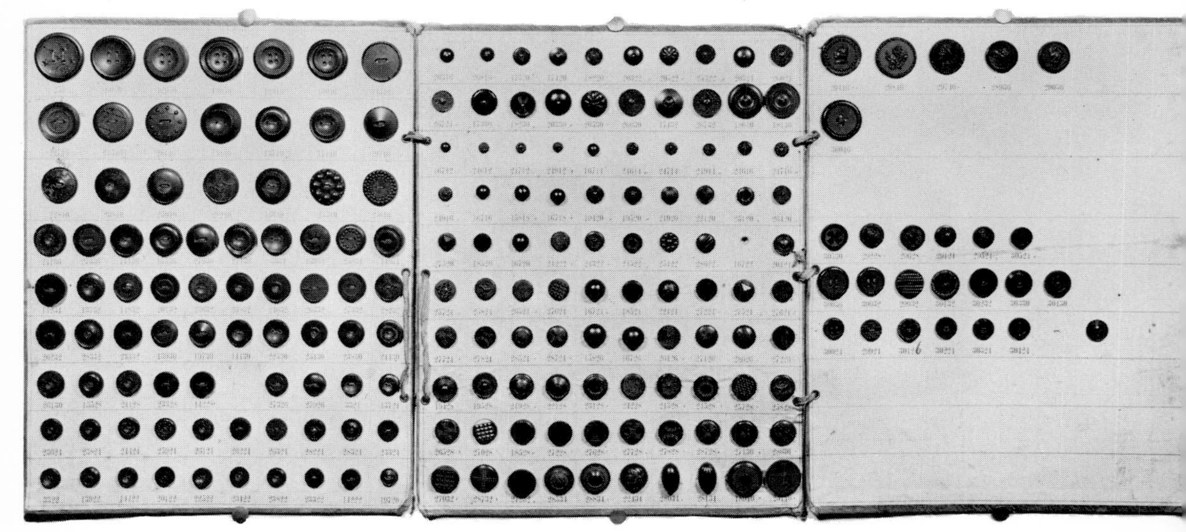

On rubber buttons, the designs are mostly concentric and geometric, but a few flower and animal designs were used. Only one story button is known to date. One or two have firm names on the front. And there is one Navy button made of rubber, and two campaign buttons.

Rubber buttons were made round, oblong, square, and melon-shaped. Most were black, though a very few reddish brown were made. They range in size from 1/2″ to over 2″, have wire shanks, self-shanks, or holes.

RUSKIN POTTERY BUTTONS. Pottery buttons made in England in the early 1900's. Advertised as having a leadless glaze, these buttons had a colored glaze on the front and then a nearly clear glaze over the complete button, including the shank. The colors were medium shades of blue, green, brown, or purple; some buttons were mottled. They ranged in size from 1/2″ to 1 1/2″. "Ruskin" was stamped under the glaze.

RUSSELLS. Manufacturers in Prospect, Connecticut, 1825–? The father, Ranson Russell, and two sons, Rufus and Edward, made bone buttons, and a recent excavation of their old factory site has turned up evidence that they also made ivory buttons. At one time they were associated with David Hopkins.

RUTTER, WINFIELD. Glassblower from 1890–1940's, in Millville, New Jersey. Rutter made paperweight buttons in the 1940's, especially for button collectors. Most of his buttons had colored bases, sometimes more than one. His preformed designs were mainly roses made of his own canes. During World War II, he made a few buttons with a "V" in the center on a white base, with red and blue added. A very few of his early buttons had two-way box shanks, but most had wire shanks.

S

SPARS. *See* Armed Forces, Women's Services.

SAFE-EYE BUTTON. A patent was granted Charles Goodyear of Philadelphia, Pennsylvania, on January 12, 1831, for an improvement in the manufacturing of what were called "safe-eye buttons." This patent was for enclosing pieces of cloth, leather, or other substances that could be penetrated by a needle, between plates or disks of metal. The disks had a hole 1/4″ in diameter punched in them to serve as an eye through which the sewing could be effected. The piece of cloth or other material was supposed to keep the button from cutting the thread that fastened it to the garment—a fairly common complaint.

SALT DECORATION. A term sometimes incorrectly used for the finely crushed glass decoration found on glass buttons. The fact that white opaque glass was most commonly used probably prompted the use of the word "salt." However, some crushed colored glass was used. While the button was warm, the crushed glass was sprinkled on it, creating a rough surface. *See also* Glass Buttons: Spatter Trim and Coralene, for further information on the application of fine-crushed glass as a surface decoration.

SAND CASTING. One of the earliest methods of decorating metal, sand casting was practiced by the ancient Greek and Roman craftsmen. Crude examples have been excavated from ancient sites. Modern methods have transformed sand casting from a crude art into an exact science, but the basic principles remain unchanged, and the molder of today uses methods similar to those employed by the early artisans.

Castings were made from patterns that were exact facsimiles of the buttons to be produced. Pressed into sand, a pattern left its impression when removed. Into this impression (or mold), molten metal was poured and allowed to cool. When the metal button disk was removed, it had the same shape as the mold, but was slightly smaller owing to the contraction of the metal. The sand used for the mold had to have certain properties, such as grains of a particular size and shape. The final step was a polishing process done with files, chisels, sandpaper, and emery cloth. The only buttons known to have been made with this method of decorating were made in the 1950's by John Eutzy, Pennsylvania.

Sand-cast aluminum buttons.
Made by J. Eutzy in the 1950's.

SANDERS, B. (Father and Son.) *See* B. Sanders.

SANDERS TYPE. *See* B. Sanders.

SANDLAND, H., and SANDLAND & EAVES. Early gilt buttons have been found with these names, but very little has been learned about the men. Sandlands were listed in Waterbury, Connecticut, and Attleboro, Massachusetts, directories as button makers. The construction of the buttons dates them between 1830 and 1850. It is also recorded that a Mr. Sandland came from Birmingham, England, to work in the Scovill plant in Waterbury, Connecticut. *See also* Draper & Sandland.

SATSUMA WARE. A Japanese pottery or semiporcelain first made in the province of Satsuma, from which its name is derived. It dates back to the fifteenth century, when one of the Satsuma princes invaded Korea and brought back several Korean potters as prisoners. The crackle glaze was developed in the sixteenth century. Satsuma ware has a feldspathic glaze of a light straw color with a network of fine cracks. Shades of red and green and dulled gold were employed, mostly on the early articles. Satsuma buttons sometimes have a deep-blue border and back. All have self-shanks.

Many buttons have been made of Satsuma, and—like all articles made for export—they vary in quality. When the very first ones were made is not known. Most of those made in the twentieth century are of a very low grade of workmanship. Satsuma medallions were occasionally mounted in metal with wire shanks. Unfortunately, some hatpins and buckles with Satsuma medallions have been converted into buttons.

It is doubtful that any Satsuma buttons were made before the last half of the nineteenth century. The earliest ones have exquisite painted designs with fine details. Gold outlining is never absent. The value of the buttons must be determined by the fineness of the decoration. Marks on the back are not dependable—many have been forged. Buttons of Satsuma ware varied from 3/8″ to over 2″ in size. The fine early ones are highly prized both by button collectors and by collectors of this ware.

Satsuma buttons. Nineteenth century. Two oval buttons have metal mountings with loop shanks. All others have self-shanks.

SAWTOOTH BUTTONS. A term used for one of the Small Chinas. It comes from the resemblance to the fine teeth on a saw. A narrow border of fine lines goes all the way to the edge of these buttons. Most sawtooths have a white body and two, three, or four holes; a few have paint on the fine lines, and some have a colored body. On some sawtooths, the lines are slanted or on the bias, and these buttons are referred to as Bias Sawtooths.

SCHMIDT, GEORGE E. Made inlaid wood buttons, mostly for the collector trade, in Collingdale, Pennsylvania, in the 1960's. Many different colored woods were used, and the buttons were generally carved by jackknife.

Inlay. Wood buttons made by George E. Schmidt; twentieth century.

SCHWANDA, B., & SONS. *See* B. Schwanda & Sons.

SCISSORS BACK. A term used for the backs of molded glass buttons that have a ridge of glass across the button. The ridge was caused by the closing of the mold. The shank was made of thin wire.

SCOTCH PIPER'S BUTTONS. Diamond-shaped metal buttons worn on the pipers' jackets and vests. Most of the buttons were diamond-shaped; although some seem square, the design is so placed that the button appears pointed. There are gilt buttons, and also buttons with white metal finish (some, thinly silver-plated). Among the various designs are a rampant lion, a thistle, and a Scotsman. The buttons worn on the jacket matched those on the vest, but were usually a little larger.

All military pipers had their own regimental crest on their buttons. Today, pipers wear such buttons mostly for the annual festivities, "the gathering of the clan." Gatherings of the clans have been traced back to the year 1040, but the feudal characteristics of the early years have been replaced by friendly rivalry in sporting events such as running, the tug-of-war, tossing the caber, and dancing; the music of bagpipes was played for dancing by kilted pipers. The dancing today is strictly by men, except for girls under sixteen, who are the only females allowed to wear kilts.

Sometimes these buttons have been called kilt buttons, but they were never worn on kilts.

Scotch piper's buttons. Nineteenth century.

SCOTT, E. (SCOTT & CO.). *See* E. Scott (Scott & Co.).

SCOVILL MANUFACTURING COMPANY. Waterbury, Connecticut. Scovill has made buttons since 1802, although originally under different names. The firm had its beginning in 1802 as Abel Porter and Company; it was made up of Abel Porter, Daniel Clark, Silas Grilley, and Levi Porter.

In 1821, the name of the firm was changed to Leavenworth, Hayden and Scovill. The owners then were Frederick Leavenworth, David Hayden, and James Mitchell Lamson Scovill. These names are the first to appear on buttons; "L. H. & S." also appeared on buttons from that time.

In 1827, the name changed to J. M. L. & W. H. Scovill (William H.). These names or initials appeared on buttons.

In 1840, the firm became known as Scovills and Company. Buttons with this name probably were made between 1840 and 1850. From 1850 to date, the concern has had the name Scovill Manufacturing Company.

The first buttons made by the company were of brass and gilt, and the company has never discontinued making brass buttons. They very early received government orders for uniform buttons; the back marks help to date their early buttons of this type. Since 1850, they have made uniform buttons of all kinds for this country and other countries. The company also makes many kinds of brass articles, and, at present, is probably making fewer buttons than at any time in its history.

SCREEN BACKS. *See* Wire Mesh Backs.

SCRIMSHAW. The fine carving on whales' teeth and bone, devised by New England whalemen. Scrimshaw is often called a "folk art." Said to be the only branch of art indigenous to America, it represents the striving of men, exiled on long whaling voyages, to attain something beautiful with the crude implements and materials at hand.

The carving on whales' teeth and bone was done almost exclusively with the jackknife. The tooth of a freshly caught whale was somewhat softer right at the start than it would be by the time it got to shore, since ivory becomes harder and more brittle with age. The finely carved drawings were filled with soot from the stoves and kettles. Most of the articles carved and decorated by whalemen of the eighteenth and nineteenth centuries had utilitarian purposes, and were made as gifts for the women back home. A very few buttons have been found that can authentically be attributed to the whalemen. A similar manner of decorating ivory has been practiced in the twentieth century, but it lacks the charm of most of the whalemen's pieces.

Carving on ivory dates back to the very early days. Ivory buttons with fine line drawings were made in several countries as early as 1700. Today, some collectors include all finely carved ivory buttons as scrimshaw, but a collector of scrimshaw usually does not. There is a distinct difference between the New England whalemen's whittling and carving and the fine-line carving that was done by Eskimos, Europeans, and Orientals. Each shows up more effectively by itself.

Bone buttons. Said to have been carved by New England whalemen in the early 1800's.

SEEDS. Corn, wheat, sunflower, and rice seeds were used to decorate plastic buttons in 1956 and 1957. An adhesive was applied to flat or cup-shaped buttons of various colors, and then seeds were sprinkled on the front. The buttons were made in two sizes, 3/4" and 1 1/4". Although Paris and New York fashion designers gave them much publicity, by 1960 collectors found them very difficult to find.

SELF-SHANK. A term mostly used for shanks that were molded as part of the button. They are commonly found on buttons made of glass, composition, rubber, and other moldable materials made after the middle of the nineteenth century. Sometimes, when the backs of metal buttons have stamped-out shanks, these are also referred to as self-shanks.

SETS OF BUTTONS. Since the beginning of the eighteenth century, buttons have been made in sets as well as singly. The material, color, and construction of the buttons in a set were identical, but the subjects for the designs were each different, though usually related to one another. Sometimes, together, they depicted a story.

In the eighteenth century, sets frequently were sold in jewelry-type boxes having satin linings, five to twenty-five in a box. In the nineteenth century, sets were offered at store counters, and there was more variety to choose from; dressmakers could purchase part of a set. Button sets became popular again from the 1930's–50's, especially those with the realistic shapes. These might be offered on cards of three to eight or as singles.

It is very often difficult for collectors to secure a complete set from any of these periods of production—the buttons have been scattered so widely. Nor is it always possible to learn the exact number the button designer or manufacturer originally intended for a set. For example, sporting buttons, made between 1830 and 1870, have been found with twelve buttons to a set; however, in some cases, though the designs indicate that originally there were more, only two or three buttons have been found.

SÈVRES PORCELAIN BUTTONS. The more a button collector reads of the history of Sèvres porcelain, the less he believes that the buttons that have been found are true Sèvres. The porcelain first made in Sèvres was soft paste, but before any buttons were made, hard paste was used. On some of the buttons, the paint is heavier than on others. The gold on some is almost encrusted, and these are considered the oldest. The buttons have self-shanks. It is doubtful any of the so-called Sèvres buttons were made before 1860.

Sèvres porcelain buttons.
They have crossed L's on the backs.

SEW-THRUS. A term used for buttons of any material that have holes for the garment-maker to sew through when attaching the button to the garment, either by hand or by machine.

SHANK PLATE. A metal disk to which a shank has been applied. Sometimes the shank was put through a hole in the plate, and the ends of the shank were fastened on the inside. Such shank plates are usually found on buttons made of moldable materials, and are embedded in the backs of the buttons. There are flat metal collars around some shanks, and occasionally these are referred to as shank plates.

SHANKS. Button makers have devised many ways to attach buttons to garments, and regardless of their construction, the pieces added to buttons for this purpose are called shanks. Loop shanks are probably the most common type. They were made of wire of any metal—flat, round, or twisted. Several inventions were patented for attaching a loop shank to one- and two-piece buttons of almost every kind of material. Some of the loop shanks that were embedded in molded buttons have one end loose because of poor construction, and have been incorrectly called pigtail shanks. Metal wire was also used to reinforce other types of shanks—for example, self-shanks.

Although some shanks may date a button definitely, and a collector invariably turns a button to inspect the shank, the type of shank is actually of little importance. Buttons with the same design can be found with different shanks.

For further information on shanks, *see* Antiquarians; B. Sanders; Box Shank; Key Shank; Loop Shank; Pigtail Shank; Pinhead Shank; Rosette Shank; Self-Shank; Thread Back; Wedge Shank.

SHARK'S-TOOTH BUTTONS. Tourists have purchased these buttons, made of small teeth with added shanks, in several countries. It is doubtful they were made for the garment trade. Otto Bieber, an American maker of plastic buttons, embedded shark's teeth in plastic button disks.

SHEATH OVERLAY. *See* Glass Buttons.

SHEET OVERLAY. *See* Glass Buttons.

SHEFFIELD SILVER. This is a plate produced by fusing, with intense heat, a thin sheet of silver to one or both sides of a thick sheet of copper. The combined metal was then rolled down to the proper thickness for making silver articles. Plating with silver in this manner was invented by Thomas Bolsover (sometimes spelled Bolsouver) about 1743.

In the eighteenth century, Sheffield silver plate was used to make buttons for men's coats. The silver was usually only on one side, and the thicker copper sheet readily showed on the edges and the backs of the buttons. These buttons often bore simple stamped designs, similar to those of other eighteenth-century metal buttons. Sheffield plate was used for many livery buttons and a few sporting buttons in the nineteenth century. (*See* Livery Buttons.) It was no doubt also used for some of the one-piece uniform buttons of the early nineteenth century. However, the silver sheet was very thin, and most such buttons soon showed the copper through the front.

SHELL BUTTONS, SHELLS. Many kinds of shells have been used to make buttons, both deep-sea shells and freshwater shells. For years, manufacturers have called buttons made from some deep-sea shells "mother-of-pearl buttons." In the early days of collecting, great efforts were made to identify and classify buttons according to the shells from which they were made. However, button makers and importers of shells have pointed out that the identity of the shell frequently is lost once the button disk has been removed, since the inner layers of many different shells are nearly identical. The completed buttons were sorted in the factory according to shades of color, disregarding the kind of shell, and this has added to the problem of classification.

Today, most collectors choose a shell button for its beauty rather than for the type of shell from which it was cut. Many shell buttons never reach a collection because they lack interesting designs, although they demonstrate well the natural beauty of the shell.

Buttons made of freshwater shell are seldom collected. The original brilliance of freshwater shells is not so great as that of deep-sea shells, and it dulls more quickly. Freshwater shell is used mostly for making utilitarian buttons, which seldom have designs. Many of the freshwater shells used for buttons come from rivers in the United States, and the buttons are made here.

Ocean shells for buttons have come from many grounds. Importers and manufacturers today speak mostly of white shell, black mother-of-pearl shell, abalone, and their variations. The sources for these are explained below:

Abalone Shell. This is seldom used for button-making purposes. Abalone shell is fished off the California coast and the coast of Mexico's Baja California peninsula. It is, however, gaining in popularity, especially now that mother-of-pearl shell is scarce.

Black Mother-of-Pearl Shell. Buttons of this shell are also sometimes known as smoked pearls. The Society Island group produces the bulk of this material and the best qualities. The Cook Islands produce a similar shell, a little grayer in color, of a smaller size and not so heavy and thick as the Tahiti shell (which is what the Society Island shell is usually called). Shell from the Cook Islands is referred to as Manihiki shell. Black mother-of-pearl shell from these areas is found mainly around the atolls or in lagoons, at depths of from 20 to 60 feet.

White or Mother-of-Pearl Shell. The best varieties come from Broome, Port Darwin, and Thursday Island, Australia. Next source in importance is the Indonesian Aroe Islands, south of New Guinea. Third is the southern part of the Philippine Islands and the area around the Sulu Sea.

Egyptian Shell is next in order. It is produced in the Red Sea and the Persian Gulf. It runs about 30 to 40 percent white, the balance being a yellow-green or brownish color. Dark buttons made from this shell are usually smoked up and sold as smoked pearls. Up to about twenty years ago, a fair supply of a similar shell was received from La Paz and San Lucas, fished from the waters off Mexico's Baja California peninsula.

Irregular supplies of a shell that runs 25 to 50 percent yellow, and is known as Gold Lip Shell, are produced in the Solomon Islands, the Island of Ceram in the Indonesian area, Burma, and numerous other areas.

Green Snail Shell is fished in most of the South Sea Islands in lesser or greater quantities, but the most important source is the eastern part of New Guinea, North Australia, most of the Indonesian Island group, along the Malay coast and the southern part of the Philippine Islands.

Trocas Shell is produced in about the same areas as Green Snail, except for an inferior quality of Trocas that is fished in the Red Sea and the Persian Gulf.

Practically all the white or mother-of-pearl shell is fished by professional divers with modern diving equipment, since this shell is more plentiful in water as much as 30 to 40 fathoms deep. Green Snail and Trocas are found in shallow waters nearer shore, and therefore are fished by masked divers.

Shell buttons have been decorated in many ways, but probably more of them by carved or cut designs than in any other way. The carved designs range from fine lines to deeply gouged-out cameos (*which see*). Frequently, a pigment of contrasting color was added to the fine lines or paint was used to form a background to a raised design.

Shell disks were sometimes dyed for buttons, and often the design was applied with a stencil pattern. At other times, a design was cut through the dye to show the shell. Shell buttons were also decorated with inlay of other materials, mostly with shell of another color.

Frequently, in studios or small button shops, designs have been painted on shell buttons. The first came from European shops, but recently some have been painted especially for the collector trade. Some of the first painted shell buttons had portions of the design built up with a substance somewhat like plaster of Paris, before the paint was applied; a similar technique was used on painted horn buttons. All painted shell buttons were fragile, and when found now in button boxes, they are badly scratched or chipped, since no protective coating was added.

Transfer designs on shell buttons are likewise seldom found in good condition. Only a thin coating of protective lacquer was applied. It would seem that not many buttons

SHELL BUTTONS

Row 1: Numbers (1) White shell, finely carved and painted with gold and silver. (2) Green snail shell, cameo, background dyed light blue. (3) Black shell, carved open design; green snail background in steel mounting. (4) White shell, finely carved and painted design.

Row 2: Numbers (1) Cameo carved, showing dark and light layers of shell. (2) Stenciled design, background in brown color. (3) Design carved after button was dyed. (4) White shell, fine carving filled with black pigment.

Row 3: Numbers (1) Helmet shell, cameo, showing light brown inner layer, paste border. (2) Black shell with design cut into white layer, gold paint in fine design in background. (3) Black shell with applied white shell design. (4) Like Number 1.

Row 4: Numbers (1) Black shell, design cut through the layers white and black. (2) and (3) Transfer under glass center in white shell. (4) Black shell, finely carved design filled with white paint.

Row 5: Numbers (1) Black shell design applied to white shell button. (2) White shell button with applied brass design, cut steel in border. (3) Green abalone shell with white shell head design. Cut steel stars. (4) White shell button with design cut in outer dark layer, cut steel trim.

were decorated in this way. Most of them were approximately ³/₄", with an all-over poly chrome design; very few have been found as large as 1¹/₄".

Shell button disks have also had trims of many kinds added, such as escutcheons o rims of various metals, cut steel, paste, or other pieces of shell.

Shell buttons made over the last three centuries can be found for collections. They range in size from the tiny ones for infants' clothing to extra-large ones for coats. Almos all types of shanks have been used, as well as two, three, four, or five holes. For the tourist trade, island natives have sometimes added shanks to small shells, among them small conch, flamingo tongue, gold shell, and snail.

See illustrations under Abalone; Cameos; Cowrie Shell; Jordan Pearl Buttons; Pinna Shell Buttons, etc.

SHIELDS and DEVICES. Nearly all eagles on United States uniform buttons have a shielc on the eagle's breast or side; on it is a letter or device. In David Johnson's book *American Historical Buttons* he cites the following three variations: the Union Shield, the Spade Shield, and the Eared Shield. The Union Shield is the broadest of the three, anc usually has double upper corners. It may have stars, bars, lines, or letters. The Spade Shield, almost triangular in shape, has sides that come to a point at the bottom. It has horizontal lines in the upper part (chief), vertical lines in the lower part. The Eared Shielc is very much like the Union Shield, except that the upper corners extend up into long points, and very often the top is a straight line. *See also* Armed Forces Buttons.

SHIPLEYS. Makers of real stone buttons in the middle of the twentieth century, Minera House, Bayfield, Colorado. Most of the stones the Shipleys used were various kinds o chalcedony. Some of the buttons had silver loop shanks, and many stones were set ir silver mountings.

SHOE BUTTONS. These buttons, which were sewed on leather- and fabric-top shoes for fastenings, have been made of several materials. Most of them were dome shaped. Black and white were the two most popular colors because they were made to match the shoes; however, colored shoe buttons were made. The colored ones were usually coverec with paints, though some were made of colored glass. Unless the glass buttons are founc on shoes, it is difficult to differentiate them from small dress buttons.

SILHOUETTE TYPE. These buttons are similar to the Sanders Type. The front of the button, which includes a self-rim, has a cutout design. Under this, on the back of the button, is a background for the design. Most silhouette types are dress buttons, but the term also refers to uniform buttons, which in most cases were made in the twentieth century.

SILK BUTTONS. Silk buttons have printed or painted designs. *See also* Fabric-coverec Buttons.

SILVER, BEN. *See* Ben Silver Company.

SILVER BUTTONS. Scant records have been found concerning early silver buttons, and although there have been various stories about elaborate silver buttons in the sixteenth and seventeenth centuries, the collector will find it almost impossible to find one made before the middle of the eighteenth century. A very few eighteenth-century American-made silver buttons have been recorded. Some of these have reached museums, along with other American-made silver items, and some have never been located. However, silver buttons have been made in almost every country, and a wide variety can be collected, even though the numbers of some types may be limited.

Most solid silver buttons were made from sheets of silver; cast silver buttons were heavy and impractical. Perhaps the oldest silver buttons the collector will find are the toggle type made of large coins. (*See* Link Buttons.) Thin silver caps, like caps of other

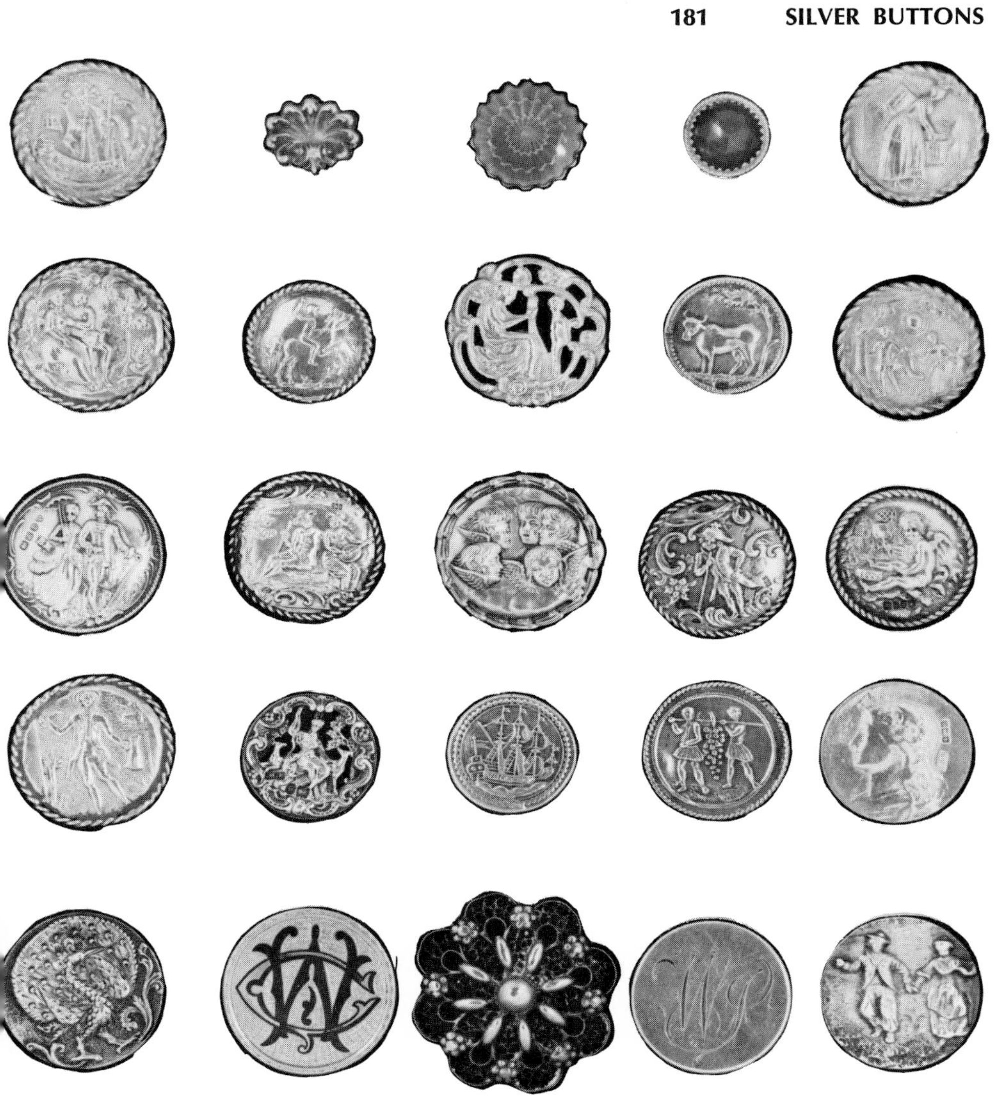

Silver buttons. Nineteenth and twentieth centuries.

netals, were used to cover bone, ivory, wood, and horn molds in the eighteenth century. n 1754, Judge Joseph Hopkins of Waterbury, Connecticut, a silversmith as well as a udge, made a set of nine silver buttons having a thin silver cap on horn molds. *See also* Covered Type.

In Philip H. Hammerslough's three books, *American Silver,* privately published in the 960's, are pictures of five different sets of silver buttons with back marks of American ilversmiths from 1750–1800. These buttons are frequently shown in the Wadsworth Atheneum in Hartford, Connecticut.

Silver buttons began to be made in wide variety in the eighteenth century. All over Europe, solid silver buttons were stamped with designs; large and small hollow buttons vere made with two thin sheets of silver fused together at the edges; silver buttons were set with paste and medallions of all kinds; sheets of silver were fused to thicker sheets of copper and rolled again for buttons. (*See* Sheffield Silver.) In the eighteenth century, most silver buttons were large because they were made for men's heavy fabrics; the few small ones found were made for breeches, or are cuff buttons with the links removed. Many silver buttons were fashioned of silver wire—almost every country produced silver filigree buttons. Silver wire was also used to decorate plain surfaces on silver buttons. *See* Filigree.

In the early nineteenth century, brass and gilt buttons replaced silver buttons in many countries, the yellow metal buttons becoming the most popular thereafter. However, the smaller silver picture buttons made for women's wear are not too difficult to find. Solid silver picture buttons usually have silver marks and makers' marks, indicating that most of those found today were made in the nineteenth century, as recently as 1900. The later they were made, the more thinly the silver sheet was rolled. These buttons usually have a rope edge of twisted wire soldered onto the disk. In the 1950's and 1960's, a considerable number of late nineteenth-century European silver picture buttons came onto the market; although they were attractive, the quality of workmanship on many of them is inferior to that on early silver buttons. Among the designs found on silver picture buttons are horses, cows, flowers, and biblical scenes.

Sporting buttons were sometimes made of solid silver. Most of the silver Scotch piper's buttons that have been found are thinly plated. Silver disks were used for enamel buttons and for niello buttons, and, of course, silver coins were frequently used for buttons for several centuries. *See also* Armed Forces Buttons; Coin Buttons; Enamels, Enameling; Indian Silver Buttons; Mexican Silver Buttons, Niello Work; and Scotch Piper's Buttons.

SILVER POINT DESIGNS. Fine line drawings were made very early with silver-pointed tools. The silver point was placed in a holder, similar to the holder for an ink pen, and

Silver point designs. Eighteenth century.

was sharpened according to the degree of fineness desired in the lines. To make these drawings with a silver point required a specially prepared paper called bone paper: a parchment with gesso, white lead, and oil on which moistened bone dust was evenly spread. Later, probably long before silver-point drawings were used for button designs, a "Chinese white" was discovered, and the work of making bone dust was no longer necessary.

The silver-point drawings used for buttons were drawn similarly to pencil drawings. The slight roughness of the prepared paper caused the silver point to leave a fine line of silver. The artist made a fine outline for his design and then repeated his strokes to leave broader or darker lines. These silver designs have tarnished somewhat over the years, adding to their beauty. The few buttons that have been found indicate they were made in the late eighteenth century. The designs were mounted under glass in metal frames with wire shanks. The buttons were about 2" in size.

SKIN BUTTONS. The skin most commonly used to make buttons is snakeskin, though some were made of alligator skin. The snakeskin buttons in collections were made since 1900—to match garment accessories such as belts, purses, and shoes. References have been made to chicken-skin buttons, but the very few that have been examined show a stretched material that is difficult to identify. On them are painted designs. These buttons were mounted in metal frames of eighteenth-century construction.

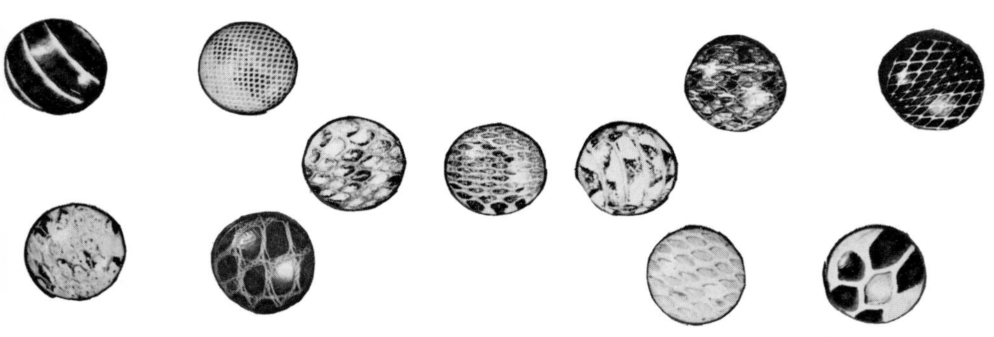

Skin buttons. Those shown are all twentieth century, and all of snakeskin.

SLEEPERS. A term used for certain black glass buttons by Mrs. Edith Fuoss in her book *Black Glass.* The term actually refers to the collectors themselves who failed to notice these buttons. Black glass buttons were usually molded round and had metal shanks. The dull fronts were painted with satiny concentric designs in deep greens or browns. Some had white enamel dots.

There are other black glass buttons with classic figures seemingly in the same texture of paint; perhaps a little ground glass was mixed with the paint. These buttons have the same colors as the "sleepers." The classic figures very often appear on square and rectangular buttons.

SMALL CHINAS. A term used by button collectors for a group of Small China buttons most of which were made in the 1860's. This group consists mostly of buttons ranging from 3/8" to 3/4" in size, decorated with transfer designs. Among the buttons in this group are calicoes, birdcages, bull's-eyes, hobnails, igloos, piecrust buttons, ringers, sawtooth buttons, and whistles. Most have a white body, but bodies of all colors can be found, including black. *See also* Birdcage; Calico Buttons; and so on.

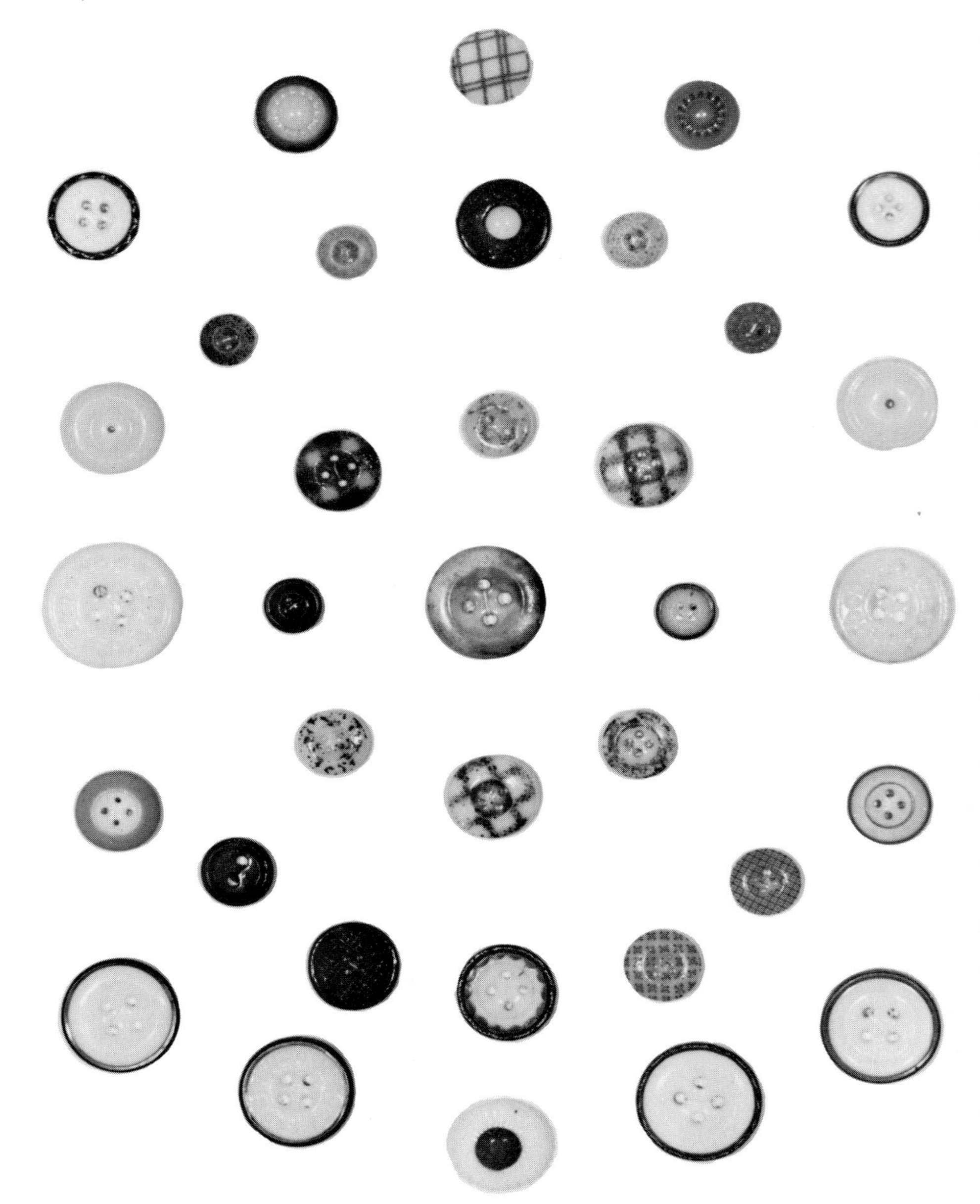

Small chinas. Nineteenth century.

SMITH, G. Pewterer, Connecticut, 1815. Name found on pewter buttons.

SMITH, H. Pewterer, Connecticut, 1815. Name found on pewter buttons.

SNAKESKIN BUTTONS. *See* Skin Buttons.

SOCIETIES. *See* Button Collectors' Organizations.

SOUVENIR BUTTONS. Many buttons were made for various souvenir purposes, to commemorate persons and events. (*See* Commemoratives.) Others were made to advertise merchandise, and were given away at festivities. Some were made solely for profit, and were sold at world's fairs and conventions of all kinds. Souvenir buttons date back into the nineteenth century. Usually, the design itself dates and authenticates a souvenir button, but some had the dates on them.

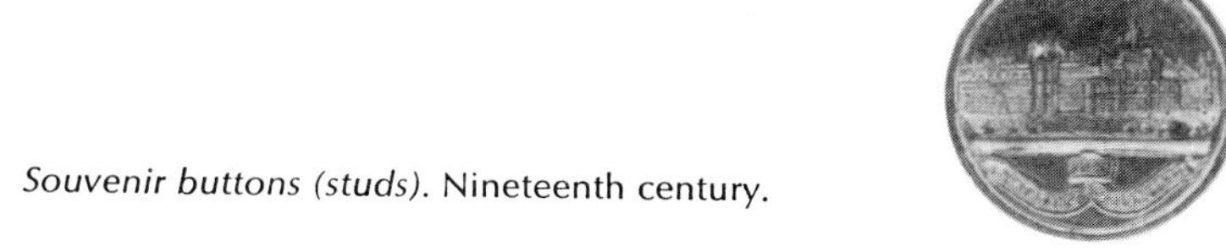

Souvenir buttons (studs). Nineteenth century.

Souvenir button.
A Lafayette presentation button, made in the early 1900's.

SPATTERS. A term used for small white china buttons decorated with spatters of colored paint, sometimes with more than one color. These buttons are frequently included in the calico group (*which see*).

SPENCER, HOTCHKISS & CO. American makers of brass and gilt buttons, 1812–30.

SPENCER & TERRELL. American makers of brass and gilt buttons, 1815.

SPORTING BUTTONS. The designs on these buttons depicted such sports as hunting, boxing, fishing, bicycling, and cockfighting. Many sporting buttons were made in sets from five to as many as eighteen buttons.

Metal sporting buttons. Nineteenth century. Each row contains a set.

Sporting buttons date from the eighteenth to the twentieth centuries, but most of them were made in the nineteenth century. In the present century, they have been made mostly as singles, only one design being worn on a garment—golf clubs, tennis rackets, bowling pins and balls, baseballs, or footballs. Sporting buttons have been made in vest and coat sizes, depending on button styles at the time.

Until quite recently, sporting buttons were made for garments especially fashioned for sportswear, not for casual clothes of all sorts. For example, ladies and men would wear garments especially designed for bicycling, and on them would be buttons with bicycles, never a football or any unrelated sporting item. Sporting buttons should not be confused with buttons made for sports-club members.

Sporting buttons. Finely carved ivory.
Early nineteenth century.

SQUARE SHANKS. *See* Box Shank.

STAFF TYPE. A term used for uniform buttons having the front and back pieces held together with a separate rim. The front was usually domed and the rim plain. The staff type was originated in the 1830's, and derived its name from the use of the buttons. They were made mostly for the United States General Staff from 1832–1902. Sometimes the backs were of brass; at other times, of tinned metal.

Staff-type shank.

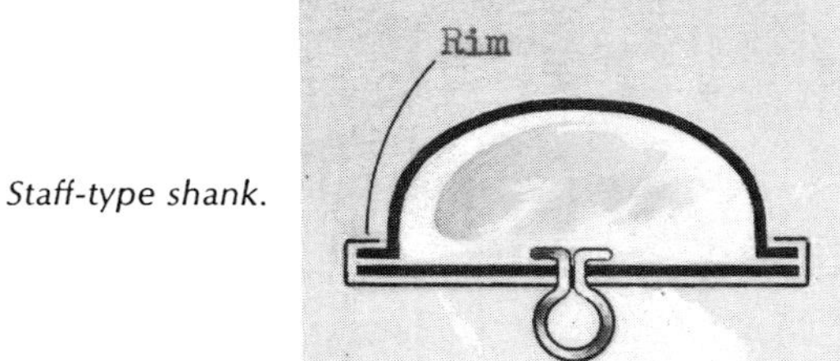

STAPLE SHANKS. *See* Antiquarians.

STEEL BUTTONS, "CUPS," TRIMS. Steel was used to a considerable extent in the eighteenth and nineteenth centuries for making buttons. In the eighteenth century, the disk was made of steel, and sometimes was trimmed with faceted steel pieces (*see* Cut Steel). At other times, medallions of various materials were fastened to the front; a pinhead shank was frequently used to hold the medallion in place. Steel collets were also used to trim eighteenth-century buttons.

In the nineteenth century, steel disks were stamped or engraved with designs for buttons. Saucer-shaped steel disks were made in this century, too. In these, trims of all kinds were placed, and the buttons themselves were sometimes called "steel cups."

A steel button can be picked up with a magnet. This is a good means of identifying steel if the material is in doubt. Steel rusts very easily; hence, steel buttons should be handled as little as possible, and fingermarks and moisture should be avoided.

Flat steel buttons. Those with cast designs are shown in the top row.
Buttons in the bottom row are etched and dyed.

STEELE & JOHNSON (S & J MANUFACTURING CO.). American button manufacturers, 1858–1920. Names frequently found on uniform buttons.

STENCILING. A method used to apply designs on buttons and other articles. Much skill was used in cutting a design into a stencil of metal or paper. This was placed on the button disk, and paint was spread over the cutout stencil, creating a design on the button. In the early days, the paint was applied by hand; in more recent years, it has been sprayed on. Small Chinas with stencil designs are called Stencils. Stenciled designs were placed on buttons of such materials as shell, metal, horn, glass, and porcelain. Hand-painted and stenciled designs are frequently confused; however, brushmarks are not usually visible on stenciled designs, and the edges of the design are more pronounced. *See also* Aluminum Stencils; China Stencils.

STENCILS. *See* Aluminum Stencils; China Stencils.

STEVENGRAPHS. A name given to buttons covered with silk having varicolored woven designs. In the 1880's, Thomas Stevens of Coventry, England, invented an improved process for weaving designs in a continuous repeated pattern on ribbon. These ribbons were called Stevengraphs, and some were used to cover a very small quantity of buttons.

(Most of the woven fabrics used for covering buttons were damasks.) *See also* Damask; Jacquard Looms.

STONE SETTINGS. Both real stones and glass imitations have been used to decorate buttons. They were set in various ways. In the eighteenth century, most stones were placed in cuplike settings. In fact, cup settings have been used for stones from the beginning right down to the present time. Sometimes a stone was set as a solitaire; sometimes stones were set in clusters or as a border. Since the middle of the nineteenth century, prong settings have also been used. On some buttons, the stones in prong settings completely cover the button frame; on others, they are mounted in clusters or singly.

STONEWARE GLASS. A term used for a dull black glass having a pebbly appearance on the back. The buttons are usually dome-shaped; sometimes they were molded to have a cut-effect design. The pebbly back looks somewhat like stoneware. The term was used in early reference books, but is seldom used now.

STORAGE. Storing a large collection of buttons can be something of a problem. Even when a collection is of modest size, it is necessary to have adequate temporary storage space—a place to keep the collection between hobby hours. Some collectors choose the size of their mounting cards with this consideration in mind. They use boxes that will fit conveniently into closets or chests of drawers. A shallow box may hold only one card. If deeper boxes holding two or more cards are used, soft paper or cloth should be cut to fit and placed between the cards. These linings or separators will absorb any moisture and also serve to cushion the weight of the cards above. In any case, never pile many cards of buttons on top of one another. The weight can crack glass buttons, which often are weak at the shank center, or crush two-piece metal buttons. Fasten a list of contents to each box.

File cabinets are excellent for storing buttons. Choose a cabinet with a sufficient number of drawers, according to the quantity of buttons to be stored. The cards of buttons can be put into folders like correspondence, and the folders labeled. This is an ideal arrangement because the buttons do not rest on top of one another. Be careful not to crowd the cards tightly together.

When the storage space permits, mounting cards can be put into wooden frames, and the frames set on shelves like books. The end of each frame should be labeled. Storage frames are available with glass fronts and removable backs.

The above methods are suitable in homes where the temperature is fairly even and the collection is going in and out of "storage" frequently enough to be checked. Long-time storage is another matter—it does the most damage to a collection. Sometimes a collector becomes inactive in the hobby and lets even his finest specimens go unchecked, while the days turn into years. Or heirs quickly pack up a collection while the estate is being settled. Actually, if a collection is to be stored for more than a few weeks, it should be packed with extra care. Each card should be wrapped in clean paper, and the cards should be stood on an end or side. And, as usual, a list of the contents should be attached to each box, or the boxes should be numbered to coincide with contents lists. Then they should be put in a dry place, as evenly heated as possible. Deterioration takes place under poor conditions: metal rusts, ivory cracks, glass shatters, mold discolors many materials, moths eat horn and some fabrics—to mention just a few of the possible mishaps.

Never use plastic containers for long-term storage. Sometimes a chemical action takes place between the container and its contents. It is hard to pinpoint the real cause of the trouble because so many varieties of plastic are used for containers.

STORY BUTTONS. These buttons are decorated with designs depicting identifiable nurs-

Metal story buttons. Nineteenth century.

ery rhymes, fables, poetry, drama, and the like. Many button designs suggest stories, but unless these can be identified by the illustrations, the buttons are not usually included in the Story group; instead, they are referred to as unidentified Picture Buttons.

The nursery rhymes and verses pictured on buttons include Little Jack Horner, Mary Had a Little Lamb, Little Bo-Peep, Hey-Diddle-Diddle, Old King Cole, Jack and Jill, Three Little Kittens, See-Saw, and Ring the Bells. There are also story buttons with scenes from such children's favorites as Red Riding Hood, Puss in Boots, and Jack and the Beanstalk.

Story buttons in other categories include the following:

Drama and Music: Rigoletto, Lohengrin, The Merry Widow, The Mikado, Carmen.

Fables: "The Fox and the Crane," "The Fox and the Crow," "The Fox and the Grapes," "Le Roman de Renard."

The Bible: Rebecca and Eleazer, Rebecca at the Well, Moses in the Bulrushes.

Story designs have been used for at least two centuries, and can be found on buttons of various materials. Most frequently, they were used on metal buttons, and some collectors are referring only to metal buttons when they use the term.

STRASS. *See* Paste.

STRAW. Sometimes used to decorate buttons. Many of the buttons with straw trimming were plastics made in the twentieth century. Few were made. The straw was woven across the center of the button.

STUDIO BUTTONS. Since early days, craftsmen have made buttons in their homes and in small shops. Such enterprises often represented the beginning of a large business firm. However, it is seldom possible to tell which of the early buttons were made in the home or a year or so later in the factory. (*See* Williston and Knight Company.) The term "studio" refers mostly to twentieth-century buttons made in the home, purposely for the collector trade since 1930. These buttons were not usually worn on garments.

Several of the twentieth-century craftsmen, both men and women, began their button making as a creative hobby. They worked in a room in their homes, and in some cases gave their first buttons to collectors in the family or to friends. These craftsmen used many different materials such as aluminum, clay, glass, plastic, and wood. In most cases, they made buttons only when in a creative mood; hence, the production of studio buttons has been small. Even though many of the buttons were beautiful, some craftsmen were discouraged because of the seeming lack of interest in their product, and discontinued making buttons. This has often been a source of regret to collectors. Some studio buttons are already bringing higher prices than when they were offered by their makers. Although twentieth-century paperweight buttons were made in homes and small shops, they were not made as a creative hobby; they were all made purposely for the collector trade. *See also* Twentieth-Century Buttons.

STUDS. This type of button consists of a button-like disk that has a built-up post and a smaller disk, or a patented fastener of some kind. The fastener always has some post-like portion, and this has given the name "stud" to the whole button. Studs are not so popular with collectors as buttons with smaller, less clumsy types of fasteners.

Studs were made for several purposes: to fasten cuffs at the wrist; for men's vests; for ladies' shirtwaists; and to be inserted into the lapel. The studs for cuffs and vests were similar to jewelry in construction, and often in decoration as well. The studs made for ladies' shirtwaists between 1890 and 1920 were made completely of porcelain and decorated with hand-painting. Lapel studs might be anything from souvenirs items, to those associated with political campaigns, to "emblems" signifying membership in a lodge or fraternal group. *See also* the illustration under Souvenir Buttons.

Studs. First and second rows are commemoratives of the 1870's. The third row contains hand-painted porcelains of the 1900's. The fourth row shows campaign studs.

SULFIDES. Objects preformed of a special clay formula that fuses with glass when enclosed by it and subjected to the correct, very high temperature. When the glass article has cooled, the so-called "sulfide" inside it has a silvery appearance. Since 1940, sulfide designs have been used in paperweight buttons. Most of the designs are busts, though sometimes a full figure appears. A very few eighteenth-century copper buttons have been found with sulfide designs in glass centers. It is not known in which European country they were made.

Credit for inventing this type of decoration is sometimes mistakenly given to an Englishman, Apsley Pellat. In 1819, Pellat took out a patent on his process of making sulfides. However, the French had long been using this art, with varying degrees of success. But Pellat's process was reputed to reduce the costs, and there were differences in the degree of heat used.

It is believed that twentieth-century glassblowers have had to experiment and develop their own process of making sulfides, since the earlier methods were kept so highly secret that detailed information about them is lacking. *See also* Glass: Clear and Colored, Mechanical Makeup.

SWIRL BACKS. The backs of some glass buttons show swirls that were made when the wire shank was inserted while the glass was still soft. Such swirls appear more often on glass buttons of the nineteenth century, but they are not an actual proof of age. "Swirl back" is a term used less frequently today because it is known that the swirl was caused accidentally rather than purposely.

SWIRL PATTERNS. Designs made on the fronts of glass buttons by an overlay pattern of fine glass-cane swirls. The swirls were usually of contrasting colors on clear or opaque glass. Goldstone was often used.

SYROCO. A trade name for buttons made in Syracuse, New York, 1918–25. Syroco buttons were compression-molded of a mixture containing 90 percent ground wood. Most were sprayed with paint in shades of brown or in various other colors. Silver and gold paint were also used. These buttons are similar to the Burwood buttons made in Michigan about the same time. In fact, collectors find it difficult to differentiate between them. Probably the only difference is in the nature of the adhesive used with the ground wood. (*See* Burwood.) The designs were usually molded to look like carving, but some of the buttons have cutout designs. Syroco buttons range in size from 1″ to 2″. Most of the backs are rough.

Syroco buttons.
Made of ground wood (1918–25).

T

T. W. & W. *See* Paris Backs.

TAGUA NUT. *See* Vegetable Ivory Buttons.

THE TALL TEXAN LAPIDARY. Irene Pyle and Joe Hettler, cutters and producers of gemstone buttons, in San Antonio, Texas, 1950's and 1960's. These artists have worked with American gemstones from several states. Their business started with jewelry, but gradually they included buttons for the collector.

TALLY-HO. A term sometimes used for sporting buttons, especially those with designs depicting hunts.

TAPA CLOTH. A unique material made from the soft inner bark of certain trees growing on the South Sea Islands. The finest grade comes from the paper mulberry tree; the second from the breadfruit tree. Whatever bark is used, the method of producing the cloth is the same. The outer bark is first scraped off with a shell. The inner bark is then removed in strips, dipped in seawater, and left to ferment. Next, it is placed over the hollow trunk of a tree and beaten with wooden mallets until the bark fibers are as closely blended together as if they had been woven on a loom. The cloth can be beaten to different thicknesses, even as thin as gauze. It can be bleached in the sun, but the natives revel in color; they often dye it with dyes they make from roots and leaves. Designs are often sketched on the fabric and filled with color. Sometimes, a design is impressed by using ferns, leaves, and flowers that have been dipped in dye.

In the middle of the twentieth century, tapa cloth was used for covering buttons that were sold in South Sea Islands tourist shops. The buttons found to date are mostly in shades of brown, and range in size from 1/2" to an inch.

TAPESTRY. A woven material used very little for button making. True tapestry, always woven by hand, was made in many countries long before the loom was invented. In very recent years, imitations have been woven by machines. The design of a hand-woven tapestry is the same on both sides, except that there are loose ends on the back or wrong side. The woven cloth found on buttons that are sometimes called "Tapestry" was made on Jacquard looms. It has a slight resemblance to imitation tapestry. *See also* Jacquard Looms; Fabric-covered Buttons.

TEARDROP. A term used for the small mound on the top of molded glass buttons. This round tearlike mound is also sometimes called dewdrop. It is found mostly on glass buttons in the Reflector category. *See also* Glass Buttons; Radiants.

THORVALDSEN, ALBERT BERTEL. Sculptor, Copenhagen, Denmark, 1770–1844. Copies of his creations of mythological subjects have often been used as a decoration on buttons. They can be found on nineteenth-century metal buttons and twentieth-century jasperware buttons.

THREAD BACKS. Buttons sometimes had crisscross threads in place of shanks. The black, brown, or white threads were wound over and across the cup-shaped back many times until it looked as if they radiated from the center. A thick soft cardboard was then pressed into the inside of this thread-wound back to hold the threads tight. Over this, the front was placed; either it was rolled over the back to hold the three pieces together or an extra rim was used to fasten them together. Among the many styles and materials found with the thread backs are tole, crystallized tin, stamped gilt, inlays, glass, metal pictures, beaded fabrics, and lithographs. The various fronts indicate these buttons were made from 1820–1900. However, the threads are now old, and even when found in seemingly perfect condition, they are fragile and require special handling. Many times the fronts are worthy of preservation even when the threads are gone. These buttons were made from ½″ to over 1″ in size.

Thread-back buttons. Nineteenth century.

THREAD CENTERS. A term used for buttons with a center design made of threads. Thread centers may consist of tufts of thread or crochet over rings that fill a cavity made in the body of the button. Thread centers are found mostly in glass and vegetable ivory buttons.

TIN. Tin was used to cover the fronts and backs of buttons in the nineteenth century, and these buttons are often referred to as "tinned." The very thin plating is frequently found nearly worn off. Some two-piece eighteenth-century buttons were tinned on the backs. This was done mostly to prevent rust. *See also* Crystallized Tin, a method used to decorate buttons.

TINGUE BUTTON. A term coined for a particular glass button with a preformed foil and glass decoration. At first, it was believed the body of these buttons was made only of black glass, but they have been found in almost all the popular glass colors, clear and opaque. Most of these buttons, regardless of the color of the body, first had a small piece of gold or silver foil set into the "cavity" made on the top of the button for the decoration. On this foil was placed a faceted piece of clear glass, which had been flashed with color. So far, only red, blue, and green flashings have been found. The bodies of Tingue buttons usually were faceted too, and all have self-shanks. They were made in ball, domed, octagon, and square shapes.

TINGUE BUTTON COLLECTION. This collection of 90,000 buttons was given to the State of Connecticut in 1886 by Senator Tingue of New York State. The senator, intrigued by a charm string of 1,000 buttons that he saw that year at the Connecticut State Fair in Danbury (where the annual state fairs were then held), authorized the *Seymour Record* to say that he "would give a check of fifty dollars to any three young lady readers of the *Record,* under twenty years of age, who would collect a similar string, viz: 2700 buttons, no two alike, and all with shanks, and bring them to him within thirty days." The offer made by Mr. Tingue in the columns of the *Record* was copied far and wide. The buttons began to come in, and within thirty days he had 90,000 buttons, mostly from Connecticut young ladies. Mr. Tingue had the buttons strung on wires and the wires fastened vertically in three glass cases. He presented them to the State of Connecticut.

By 1942, some of the wires were broken, and the Acorn Button Club, through the efforts of Sally Luscomb, was given permission to restore the collection. They mounted a representative group of the buttons, restrung the balance, and moved the collection from the State Capitol, where it had been since 1886, to the State Museum in the State Library. The collection consists mostly of brand-new buttons made in Connecticut factories in the 1880's.

TINSEL TRIM. On February 1, 1881, J. H. Johnson was given a patent "for decorating buttons and other articles by drilling, or forming cylindrical, or other holes, in the face; coating the interior of the holes with adhesive material, and then applying powdered or finely divided tinsel, or other glittering material. The tinsel, etc., being sunk below the face of the button, is completely protected." Buttons made of shell, vegetable ivory, composition, and glass have been decorated in this manner. In many cases, the tinsel has disappeared or has lost its sparkle.

TINTYPE BUTTONS. *See* Ferrotypes.

TOGGLE BUTTONS. *See* Link Buttons.

TOLE BUTTONS. *Tôle* is a French word meaning "sheet iron." Used as a term for buttons, tole refers to metal buttons having disks that were first tinned and then decorated with

Tole buttons. Nineteenth century. Those in the top row are tinned and decorated. (The buttons in the bottom row are brass with painted designs.)

lacquered designs. Sometimes collectors use the word for all-metal buttons treated with a lacquer. Most tole buttons were made in Europe, although many have Oriental or New England designs. The first coat of lacquer was usually black; then bright painted designs were applied, or the surface was treated to show a design in crystallized tin (*which see*). A very thin coat of clear lacquer covered all the designs. Tole buttons are either one- or two-piece buttons, and range in size from 3/4″ to 1 1/2″. The decorated tinned center of the two-piece button had a brass rim holding front and back together. These buttons are often found badly scratched; one in fine condition is a rare find. They greatly interest collectors of toleware as well as button collectors.

TOMBAC BUTTONS. Buttons made of tombac, a variety of brass, seem to have originated in the late seventeenth or very early eighteenth century. In the early days of collecting, most buttons of this material that were found had similar construction; therefore, the term "tombac" was used to designate a type. As research progressed, it was learned that buttons made of tombac metal were not all made alike; they were constructed and decorated differently, like the other metal buttons made in the eighteenth century.

Tombac buttons are mostly large and one-piece. Some were hand stamped with punch tools, others cast in domed and concave shapes; still others were decorated with gilt and applied brass designs. Most of the shanks are flat iron wires, but applied in different ways. A very few two-piece buttons made of tombac have been found. The size of tombac buttons ranges from 1/2″ to over 2″. Many of these buttons have no designs.

There are also white metal buttons, a deep gray in color, without the yellow tint of tombac but with the same hard, brittle texture. Although they have similar designs, they were made of a different alloy, which has not been identified and should not be confused with tombac.

Tombac buttons. Eighteenth century.
Four different backs are shown in the top row.

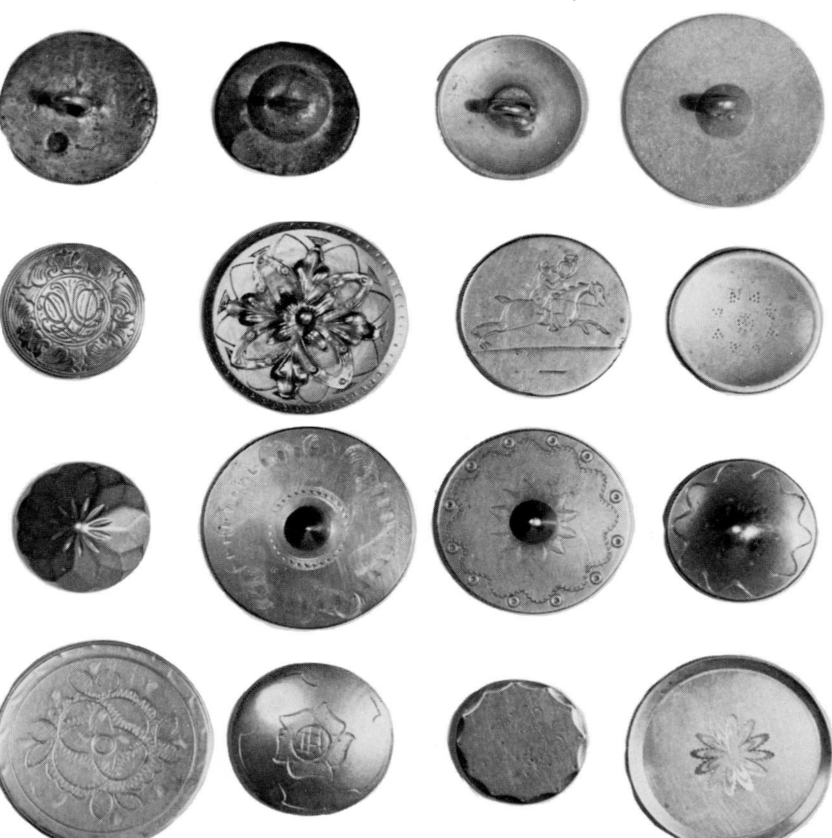

TOPICAL COLLECTING. Topical collecting is practiced in many hobbies. In button collecting, the variety of topics is almost limitless, including such subjects as historical events or places, the arts, architecture, transportation, political campaigns, and economics. Button designers apparently had a free hand, for they pictured on buttons such things as castles, barnyard scenes, hunters, dogs, game, sportsmen and numerous sports, musicians and instruments, actors and drama, religious symbols, and biblical scenes.

Collectors find that many of the topics used for button designs are closely related to other collectibles, to which buttons make an interesting addition. And some button collectors add related items such as political medals, jewelry, and badges to their button collections.

Various arts and crafts have been beautifully demonstrated in buttons: mosaic, inlay, glassblowing, metalworking, carving, painting, weaving, photography, and others. The works of artists and illustrators have also frequently been copied (*see* Kate Greenaway, Thorvaldsen, and others).

Coins and stamps have been used to make and decorate buttons, as well as copied for designs. Often the designs on coins and stamps are identical or commemorate the same event.

Manufacturers' products and histories can be traced by the names and places on the backs of buttons—in many cases, almost from the day they began to the date they took on a new partner or went out of business.

Topical collecting sometimes can limit the size of a collection, but this depends on the length and breadth of the particular topic. However, frequently, a collector who begins with one topic finds that it leads to other topics, and before long he has spread into a more complete coverage of buttons.

TORTOISESHELL BUTTONS. The tortoiseshell used for making buttons came from one species of the more than 200 tortoises, the hawksbill turtle. Tortoiseshell consists of a horny matter, but is harder, more brittle, and less fibrous than ordinary horn. Its beauty depends on the rich mottled colors and on the high polish this shell takes and retains. A tortoiseshell has thirteen sections; the color is yellowish above, mottled with chestnut brown, and a yellowish white below. Old turtles (tortoises) have a thin yellow plate on the belly; this shell is much sought after.

Finished tortoiseshell articles were entirely handmade products, no machinery being used. The tools of the trade were simple and few in number. The rough shell for a button was carefully scraped to clean the surface, then sawed into pieces of proper dimensions. If the button was to be thicker than the original shell, two or three pieces were molded together. This was done by laying pieces, one upon the other, tying them with thread, and wrapping in wet cloth. The package was placed between two pieces of wood, then between flat iron plates already heated to the necessary temperature. The whole was then subjected to pressure in what appeared very much like a massive copy press. In about ten minutes, the pieces of tortoiseshell became one. The process required great skill. The final step was polishing and decorating the button disk. Most of these buttons were left undecorated because of the natural beauty of the shell itself. A few have been found with applied metal pieces, inlay of gold, and other trimmings. Tortoiseshell buttons were made in a variety of sizes and shapes.

Tortoiseshell has also been used to decorate buttons of other materials. A veneer of shell on another material sometimes resembled a button entirely of tortoiseshell, especially when the veneer was placed on horn.

Very few tortoiseshell buttons were made in this country, and buttons of this material are extremely rare today. Some were made in a horn button shop in Rhode Island in the 1860's, but most have been brought back by tourists during the last hundred years.

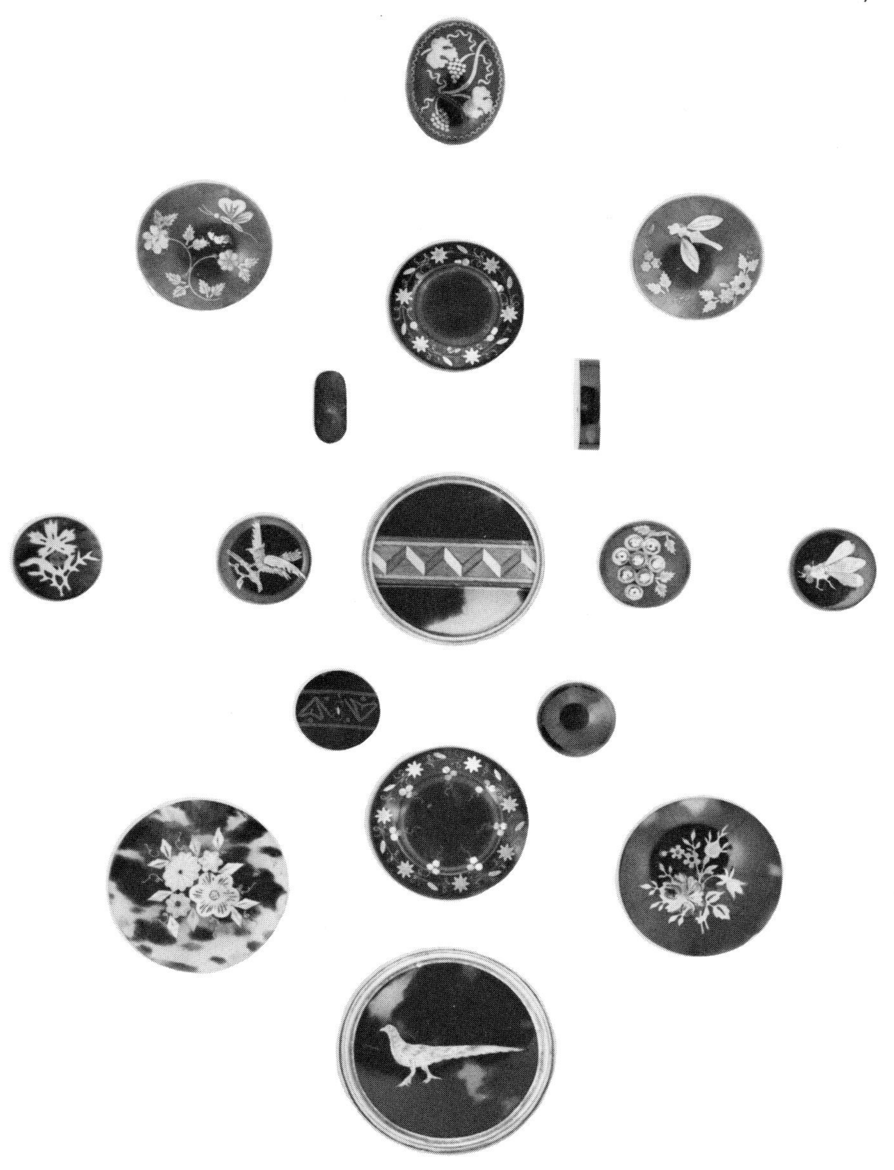

Tortoiseshell buttons. Inlaid with wood, metal, and pearl.

Fewer and fewer people seem to bring them back now, and it must be assumed that the art of working with tortoiseshell has fallen into disuse.

TOWNSEND, IRMA. Ceramist, Rhode Island, 1940's–50's. Most of Miss Townsend's buttons were hand shaped and had molded raised designs. They were sold by George E. Adams, and have sometimes been called the Adams buttons. Very few bore the ceramist's initials.

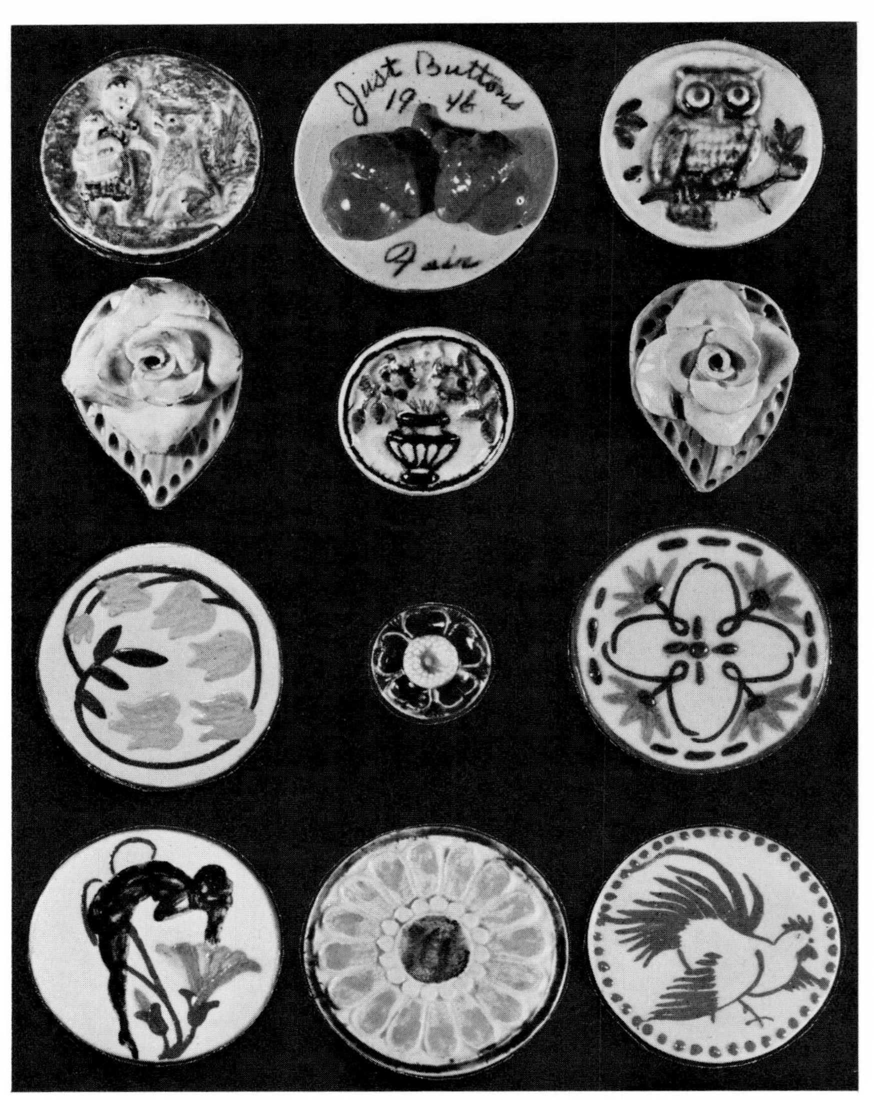

Porcelain buttons.
Made by Irma Townsend in the 1940's.

TRANSFER BUTTONS. The term "transfer" is used more frequently for designs on buttons than "decals" is. However, it refers to the same process of transferring designs from paper to a button. (*See* Decal.) Transfer buttons include buttons of any material having a transfer design. Porcelain and shell buttons were the ones most commonly decorated in this way. Transfer designs were sometimes so finely made and so well applied that they closely resembled hand painting, but careful examination of transfer designs will reveal that they have definite edges that painted designs do not have.

One of the finest of transfer-decorated buttons is the type called Liverpool Transfer (*which see*).

TRANSPORTATION BUTTONS. These are buttons made for the uniforms of employees of transportation companies. They were made in various uniform styles, for coats, vests, and sleeves. There were stock patterns, such as brakeman's, trainman's, conductor's, gripman's, and baggageman's, that could be used by any company, but most companies had their own designs. These were sometimes changed, and so a collector may find more than one design used by a single company. Transportation buttons were made for railroads, steamship lines, airlines, trolley companies, and others. Many transportation companies were small, and merged after a very few years of service; their buttons are very scarce. *See also* Uniform Buttons.

TRANSPORTATION DESIGNS. Modes of transportation have been used for button designs for at least two centuries. The vehicle depicted on a button does not always represent a clue to the age of the button. For example, a 1900 model automobile may appear on a button made for car coats in the 1950's; an eighteenth-century ship may have been used as a design on a nineteenth-century button. Transportation designs were used on buttons of almost any material. The most commonly found design is the automobile. First, automobile buttons were made for the linen dusters that were worn by both men and women in the early days of open cars and dusty roads. In the 1960's, automobile designs were used again for car coats. The first buttons with bicycle designs were especially made for suits for both men and women bicycle riders.

Transportation designs. Celluloid, metal, and wood buttons of the nineteenth and twentieth centuries.

TRIFLES (Pewter). A term used in the early days for all small articles, including buttons, that were made of a cheap grade of pewter.

TUNBRIDGE TURNERY. A type of polychromatic woodwork used for making buttons in the twentieth century. It derived its name, Tunbridge Turnery, from a small market town in England called Tunbridge. Making wooden articles was one of the industries of Tunbridge during the seventeenth and eighteenth centuries. As the craftsmen who did this work passed away, it became a lost art.

In the middle of the twentieth century, Mr. E. E. Brown of California, an ardent wood collector, learned of the art through research concerning woods. With his knowledge of the various characteristics of woods, and some experimenting, Mr. Brown was able to produce inlay buttons of many woods and colors in the manner of the early Tunbridge craftsmen.

Tunbridge Turnery. Twentieth-century wood buttons made by E. E. Brown.

TURN-AGAIN BUTTONS. A term used for buttons having a design that is the same when turned. They remind one of the designs children used to make with ink on paper, which, when neatly folded, would be repeated on the other half of the paper. The designs on buttons are less crude. They usually are found on black glass buttons with finely incised patterns. The term was first used by Mrs. Edith Fuoss in her book *Black Glass* (1945). The designs are scarce, and the term is not used often.

TURNER BUTTONS. These buttons have a design with four repetitions of the letter "F." The four "F's" were a sign of health in Germany. The stand for *Frisch, Fromm, Froh,* and *Frei*—fresh, loyal, happy, and free. This was a political as well as an athletic symbol in the days of Friedrich Ludwig Jahn, who founded the first Turnverein in 1811. The Turnvereins were German gymnastic and weight-lifting societies that flourished in the middle of the nineteenth century. The first American Turner Society was organized in Cincinnati on November 20, 1848. A number of the outstanding members organized the first gymnasiums in high schools and colleges.

Although several black glass buttons have the four initials of this society's emblem, the exact purpose of the buttons has not been determined. There seems to be no society record of the buttons; they were no doubt made in the late nineteenth century.

TURNVEREINS. *See* Turner Buttons.

TWENTIETH-CENTURY BUTTONS. Thousands of buttons have been made since 1900. The invention of new machines and the creation of new materials have added to the variety. Although many of the small nineteenth-century shops were gone long before 1900, other shops cropped up, and in them were made the buttons collectors call Studio Buttons. Commercial manufacturers continued to make some of their stock patterns too, and it is difficult for the collector to know when these were made. Some collectors' organizations have tried to establish dates for old and new buttons, and this sometimes confuses the new collector, especially as the twentieth century grows older.

Many twentieth-century buttons will become tomorrow's antiques, and therefore the quality buttons of this century should be collected and preserved while they can still be found. The dearth of storage space in modern homes discourages today's housewives from saving things as their grandmothers did. There will not be many treasure-filled old button boxes for tomorrow's collector to explore. And old store stock will not be found tucked away much longer either. Collectors of twentieth-century buttons have already discovered that the search is less productive than it was just a few years ago.

The synthetic plastic button is the one entirely new, twentieth-century button. Modern plastics lend themselves well to imitation of earlier buttons, but many plastic buttons are thoroughly twentieth-century in style and design. These will be exceedingly interesting in the next century. The collector should watch not only the button departments in stores and shops but especially garments. Many twentieth-century buttons have never reached button counters; they were, and still are, often made solely for garment manufacturers.

Many handsome buttons were made in studios during the first half of the twentieth century, but sometimes only a very small quantity of any one button was produced. Collectors were slow to buy studio buttons, sometimes mainly because they were of twentieth-century manufacture, and so the artist would discontinue the line. The only source for these buttons is the collections that come on the market from time to time.

Many twentieth-century buttons are beautiful additions to a collection. Others are interesting for other reasons—the type of workmanship or material or the designs themselves—just as buttons of other centuries were and are.

U

UNDERGLASS BUTTONS. A term used for metal buttons with glass centers and designs under the glass. The term most frequently applies to buttons made in the late nineteenth and early twentieth centuries. These cuplike buttons were usually made of brass, and had self-shanks or loop shanks. The glass was sometimes domed, sometimes flat on top with built-up sides; it was transparent, either clear or colored. Many collectors include in this category all metal buttons constructed in this way, regardless of their age. The designs under the glass may be of any material.

Underglass designs of cupids. Eighteenth century.

UNIFORM BUTTONS (Nonmilitary). During the period of Reconstruction following the Civil War, and well into the 1900's, nonmilitary uniforms with especially designed buttons were worn in abundance, as symbols of progress and prestige. Brass buttons were strictly "in fashion" for employees of both public and private enterprises, to indicate their particular occupations. Changes in styles and customs, plus constantly rising costs of tailoring and insignia, have lately placed considerable restrictions on the use of uniforms by people in civilian pursuits. Especially desirable are the buttons of obscure transportation companies, hotels, department stores, and other business ventures no longer in existence. These are now treasured heirlooms of olden, golden days.

There are many methods of classifying these various specimens in correlated subject groups. Obviously, a collector can break down the broad general classification into specific subclasses of his personal choice. Possible categories of this sort are Government, Commemoratives, Transportation, Protection, Societies and Institutions, Business, Entertainment, Travel, Celebrations. The range is extensive; the choice, a matter of personal inclination.

For military uniform buttons, *see* Armed Forces Buttons; *also* Confederate Buttons.

UNIFORM BUTTONS

Government: (1) Consular or Diplomatic service. (2) Federal agency. (3) State administration. (4) County administration. (5) City department.

Communication: (6) Postal service. (7) Telephones. (8) Telegraph and cable lines. (9) Printed matter—newspapers, magazines, books. (10) Wireless broadcasting—radio, television, Telstar. Other more remote means will suggest themselves.

Transportation: (11) Railroad systems. (12) Street transit lines. (13) Steamship lines. (14) Passenger and commercial airlines. (15) Bus and trucking companies. Also obsolete ferries, "L" lines, horse and cable cars, bicycles, balloons—even the new monorails!

Protection: (16) Frontier and customs officials. (17) Police forces and (18) prisons. (19) Old volunteer fire companies. (20) Organized municipal fire departments. Sheriffs, detective agencies, private guards are included in this category.

Education: (21) Schools. (22) Military academies. (23) Collegiate organizations. (24) Athletic associations. (25) Recreational facilities. (Owing to space limitation, this row combines Education with other activities. In practice, however, each subject warrants a separate classification).

Societies and Institutions: (26) Fraternal organizations. (27) and (28) Veterans groups. (29) Public charities. (30) Social service—health and hospitals.

Business: (31) Heavy industry. (32) Retail stores. (33) Food products. (34) Financial institutions. (35) Public utilities.

1
U.S
L.S.S
2
STATE
CAPITAL
3
PROVIDENCE
COUNTY
4
MUNICIPAL COURT
5
U.S.M
6
7
8
THE
LONG ISLAND
NEWS CO.
9
WORLD WIDE
WIRELESS
10
11
MEMPHIS
12
13
14
DEARBORN
COACH
CO.
15
BORDER
US
PATROL
16
CHICAGO
POLICE
17
KENTUCKY
18
DAVY
1
CROCKETT
19
FIRE DEPARTMENT
20
21
MILITARY ACADEMY
22
BAND
23
24
ROLLER SKATING
25
B.P.O.E
22
26
27
28
NEW JERSEY
HOME
DISABLED SOLDIERS
29
STATE
SD
HOSPITAL
30
CARNEGIE
STEEL CO.
31
Filene's
32
Armour
33
NYSE
34
CITY
E.L.D
35

UNION LEAGUE CLUB. A patriotic and political organization formed in Philadelphia in 1862. The members were strong backers of Lincoln's administration, and were active supporters of the Republican Party for decades. Buttons made at this time with the words "Union" or "Union and Strength" are believed at least to have been influenced by this movement, possibly worn by the members. The buttons were made of metal and black glass.

Union League buttons. 1860's.

UNITED BUTTON COMPANY. *See* Williston and Knight Company.

UNITED CONFEDERATE VETERAN BUTTONS. These buttons were worn by the United Confederate Veterans' Association on the uniforms of their organization. The buttons have a Confederate flag in the center, and the initials U C V, with "1861–1865" at the bottom. The organization was formed in 1887.

U.S. BUTTON COMPANY, UNITED STATES BUTTON COMPANY. The history of these companies is still not unraveled. Anderson's *History of Waterbury, Connecticut* speaks of the "firm as occupying a certain shop between 1865 and 1875." Another reference, giving no source, mentions the date 1837 for the U.S. Button Company. There have been only a few of their buttons found (two designs to date) with names on the back. These gilt buttons are larger than the usual gilt buttons of that period, ranging from $1\frac{1}{4}''$ to $1\frac{1}{2}''$ in size. They have the same fine quality of construction and material as the other gilt buttons.

V

VALUES. Estimating values and setting prices are more difficult for buttons than for other collectors' items. Button collecting, a comparatively new hobby, formally only about thirty years old, is as yet somewhat naïve in its organization and inexperienced in its market. To a greater extent than in the case of other collectibles, the price of buttons depends on fluctuating factors—vogues set by button societies, clubs, or magazines; the often purely personal judgment of the seller or dealer; or the quantity of a particular button that has been unearthed. An unusual old button might be of value for its rarity, but if a store stock or private collection were to be discovered that yielded a supply of the same button, its value would immediately drop. Beauty of design and quality of material and construction are also factors to be considered in setting a value. However, more often it is the age, the history, the rarity, and/or the demand among collectors that really establish the worth of a button.

A handicap in attempting to set up a price guide for buttons is the impossibility of creating any inclusive catalogue of buttons or of ascertaining how many buttons of any one type were produced. The number found today depends on the popularity of the design or size when it was originally made, but it is also contingent on such accidentals as survival and discovery.

Although early buttons were largely ornamental, and often as artistic and as valuable as jewelry, relatively few of these have been found ("so far," it must be added!). Certainly any buttons from the eighteenth century or earlier are rare and valuable, with their prices determined by their history, their art, or in some cases their actual material worth. The majority of button collectors do not have many early buttons in their collections. They concentrate, rather, on the more available, more reasonably priced buttons from the nineteenth or even the twentieth centuries. But even for buttons from these more recent and familiar centuries, setting a price is a not too scientific matter. Here, too, price fluctuates and is a more or less personal decision or a matter of agreement between seller and buyer. Within a single category of buttons, prices may range from a penny to twenty-five dollars.

New mounting suggestions and prize lists, encouraged by button clubs and societies, cause brief inflations, invariably followed by a decrease in demand, and usually ending in a period of devaluation and no sales. As in the case of other antiques or other collecting hobbies, prices change according to supply and demand.

Transient overenthusiasm for a particular kind of button, increasing new classifications and discoveries in the growing hobby, and newly uncovered stocks and caches also create fluctuations in values that make it impossible to prepare a price guide that would be valid for any length of time.

Buttons made of ivory and other precious materials and decorated by talented and famed artists probably will never come into price brackets. In price, they can more nearly be compared with fine jewelry, miniatures, oil paintings, vases, and figurines. Each button will command its own price and will always have a market.

Collectors and dealers soon become familiar with the many kinds of buttons that can be added to a collection. In this field, as in all collecting hobbies, there are periods when enthusiasm runs high for a single category or type of item and causes short-lived inflations. That is not the ideal time to buy unless the pleasure of adding the particular piece to one's collection outweighs the cost of the investment. The dealer should be wary of a period of overenthusiasm when purchasing for long-range investment.

For the collector, experience is definitely the best teacher. A new collector can, to a considerable degree, rely on his own interest, taste, and instinct to determine the value of buttons. He can also rely on the growing number of books about buttons, and on dependable dealers and experienced collectors, in attempting to estimate what are fair current prices.

Offered below are a few guidelines and approximate ranges of value within the major button categories.

Eighteenth-Century Metal Buttons. (Sometimes called Colonials.) These handmade buttons of copper, brass, or tombac were extremely reasonably priced in the early days of collecting. Prices increased steadily until perhaps 1950–55; since that time, they have dropped and collectors can now buy these buttons for less than the 1955 price. Of course, the situation could change quickly with a little more interest in them on the part of new collectors. An increase in interest is not unlikely, since these buttons do have quality and beauty of material and design.

Enameled Buttons. Each type of enameled buttons has its separate price bracket. For example, plique-à-jour buttons are so scarce that they are almost priceless. Prices of the various types depend on size, design, and trimming. Scenes, heads, and people are in the greatest demand, and are often priced higher than scarcer enameled buttons. The same designs trimmed with an encrusted beadlike border, paste, or cut steel command higher prices. In the case of cloisonné buttons, the nineteenth-century ones are much scarcer than twentieth-century buttons and usually bring higher prices. At one time, small enameled buttons were in demand for making jewelry, and they were then very scarce and high priced.

Glass Buttons. Some of these buttons are very plentiful, especially black glass buttons. Here is another example of how the style of garments affected the quantity of buttons that are found today. At times, the buttons on a garment might number in the dozens, and so old button boxes may yield strings of from one to three dozen buttons of a single design of that period. These buttons are no less beautiful or interesting, but consequently they *are* easier to find. On the other hand, glass buttons are fragile, and some did not stand the abuse as well as others. Some types are seldom found in perfect condition, and of course this affects their price.

Hundreds of designs were used on glass buttons. It may be safe to say that there were thousands of designs and that one design may have been made in ten or more sizes, in every color. So enormous is this one field in the hobby that a price guide might be more confusing than helpful. As this book was being written, the controversy concerning Carnival glass and early iridescent-painted black glass buttons caused the latter to soar several hundred percent in price—to a figure considered ridiculous by button collectors, but highly profitable to some antique dealers.

Historical Buttons. At present, campaign, presidential, and inaugural buttons are soaring very high in price. Recently, the increased interest in politicals has created a condition of real inflation; most collectors believe this will level off. Other historical buttons such as Armed Forces buttons have had their inflation and are already leveled to normal prices as worthwhile collectibles. Only the scarcest of uniform buttons bring high prices. There are many very reasonably priced, as low as a few cents apiece.

Horn Buttons. Unless natural horn buttons have much hand carving, they are very reasonably priced. Many of the processed horn buttons are also moderately priced, twenty-five cents to a dollar apiece. Picture buttons are numerous; a very few identified story buttons will be found priced as high as $50 each. Colored processed horn buttons will be priced a little above black ones with the same designs.

Metal Picture Buttons. These buttons have been, and no doubt always will be, one of the most popular types and—fortunate for collectors—one of the most plentiful. This, of course, causes a steadier demand and price. However, there are a few designs that to date still seem scarce, such as one of the Red Riding Hood designs, William Tell Shooting the Apple, Skating in Central Park; these probably will always be priced higher. Another factor to note is the difference that size and construction make in the prices of buttons having the same center design. The price of small sizes of the exact same button seldom increases in proportion to the price of the large size.

Pewter Buttons. Pewter buttons made around 1800 are fairly plentiful. Those with no back markings can be found for a few cents apiece. The early pewter button bearing pewterers' names create the most interest; so far they are not expensive. Pewter buttons made later in the nineteenth century and in the early 1900's have very little demand and are inexpensive.

Plastic Buttons. The collector's interest in buttons made of this material, to date, is so slight that prices are below the original dress-trade prices. However, some plastic buttons have already become scarce, especially those made in realistic shapes. These had a period of soaring in price as a result of a short-lived demand. Both the demand and the prices have leveled, but prices are still higher than the original ones. Other types of plastic buttons will no doubt receive more interest in due time, as they grow older, and then their prices will increase. Many plastic buttons can now be purchased for less than twenty-five cents apiece.

Porcelain and Pottery. Buttons of these materials made in the nineteenth century or earlier are scarce—too scarce to set up price suggestions. However, at present their prices are not high considering their scarcity and workmanship. Those being made right now are inexpensive.

Rubber Buttons. The prices of these buttons have remained low; very few cost more than they did in the early collecting days. Except for the one with the Falcon Huntress design, most of the few rubber picture buttons are very moderately priced. Of course, rubber buttons bearing the heads of political candidates are priced comparably with other campaign buttons. Among the different back markings, some are scarce and sometimes priced a little higher; this is especially true of buttons having the dates 1849–51 on the back.

Small Chinas. These buttons come in many shapes, designs, and sizes, and their prices have the widest range of all types. To date, small chinas having only bands or colored rings are very plentiful; there is almost no demand for them. They can frequently be found on strings selling at 100 for a dollar.

Calicoes are the most popular buttons in this category, and the size and construction of the button have the most influence on its price. Calicoes measuring 1/2" to 5/8" evidently were the most popular when they were being made (a hundred years ago), and can now be bought for as little as ten cents apiece. Calicoes smaller or larger in size range from fifty cents to twenty dollars each, especially those with metal rims.

To illustrate the temporary demands and inflations that occasionally occur, take the small chinas called igloos as an example. A few years ago, this button was in almost no demand—it was considered clumsy and uninteresting by most collectors. Then a project for mounting china buttons was designed that included an igloo. In a matter of months, this button that had been priced at ten cents in poke boxes went for thirty-five dollars in an auction. Undoubtedly the price will level down in a short time, since the qualities of the button do not warrant the high price.

Vegetable Ivory Buttons. These are much more plentiful than the demand, except the ones with picture designs such as cats, dogs, scenes, people. During a period of widespread interest in several mounting projects, the demand suddenly increased, attention being given to the construction and trimming. As a result, vegetable ivory buttons having thread backs or crocheted centers experienced inflated prices for a short period. The picture designs in this material will always be scarce and higher in price than the many tweed and mottled patterns.

VAN WART, SONS & CO. Button manufacturers, 1860's. Name found on uniform buttons.

VEGETABLE IVORY BUTTONS. These buttons were made from nuts of the corozo or tagua palm. Very shortly, the trade name became Vegetable Ivory to distinguish this material from tusk ivory, especially in the case of buttons made from the white nuts. The nuts fell to the ground when ripe and hard, and were gathered by natives of South America, who carried them out of the jungle to shipping points along the river. When they arrived at the factories, the nuts were irregularly round in shape, about the size of large eggs, brown and rough in appearance, the bark being cracked and brittle. They were kiln-dried for ten days, then put into tumblers to remove the bark; it required hand chipping to finish the job.

Next, the nuts were sawed into slices for buttons, the face, the part nearest to the bark, being the choicest section. Buttons made from the part near the core of the nuts show tiny cracks. There was much waste in manufacture, approximately 50 percent. Button blanks (disks) were graded by "shaders," girls who sorted the blanks according to shades of natural color: white, yellow, and amber (the latter two were dyed). These nuts were so close in texture that it was difficult for the dye to penetrate, and often the buttons are found today with the colors faded.

Vats were used to dye the solid colors. Mottled or multicolored buttons required

Vegetable ivory buttons. Nineteenth and early twentieth centuries.

special machines, a machine for each different color, the buttons being carried on conveyor belts. A stencil or chart was laid on each button face, and the dye was spread on, the darkest color first. The last color was set by the solid-color vat method.

A very few uniform buttons were made of vegetable ivory; most of the buttons were for civilian wear for both men and women. Vegetable ivory buttons were decorated by embossing or stamping, carving, stenciling, or transferring designs. A native garnet from Watertown, Connecticut, was used for producing a dull satin finish, sometimes called sandblasting. Vegetable ivory buttons range in size from less than 1/2″ to over 1 1/2″. The larger buttons are very scarce, since the nuts were not usually big enough for making large buttons.

VENETIAN GLASS BUTTONS. A term used for glass buttons that somewhat resemble Venetian beads. Twisted glass cane was festooned over a preformed glass button having a wire shank, and then heated to fuse it to the button. The fine, ropelike glass covered the top of the domed or cone-shape button—sometimes irregularly, at other times in a pattern. A few buttons made similarly in the twentieth century have self-shanks.

VEST BUTTONS. In the nineteenth century, smaller buttons were worn on men's vests than had been worn on the eighteenth-century long waistcoats, especially after 1850. Sometimes these vest buttons were set with jewels, but more often with molded glass, printed pictures under glass, and so on. The shanks were usually larger than on the similar buttons worn by women, which are called Jewel buttons (*which see*).

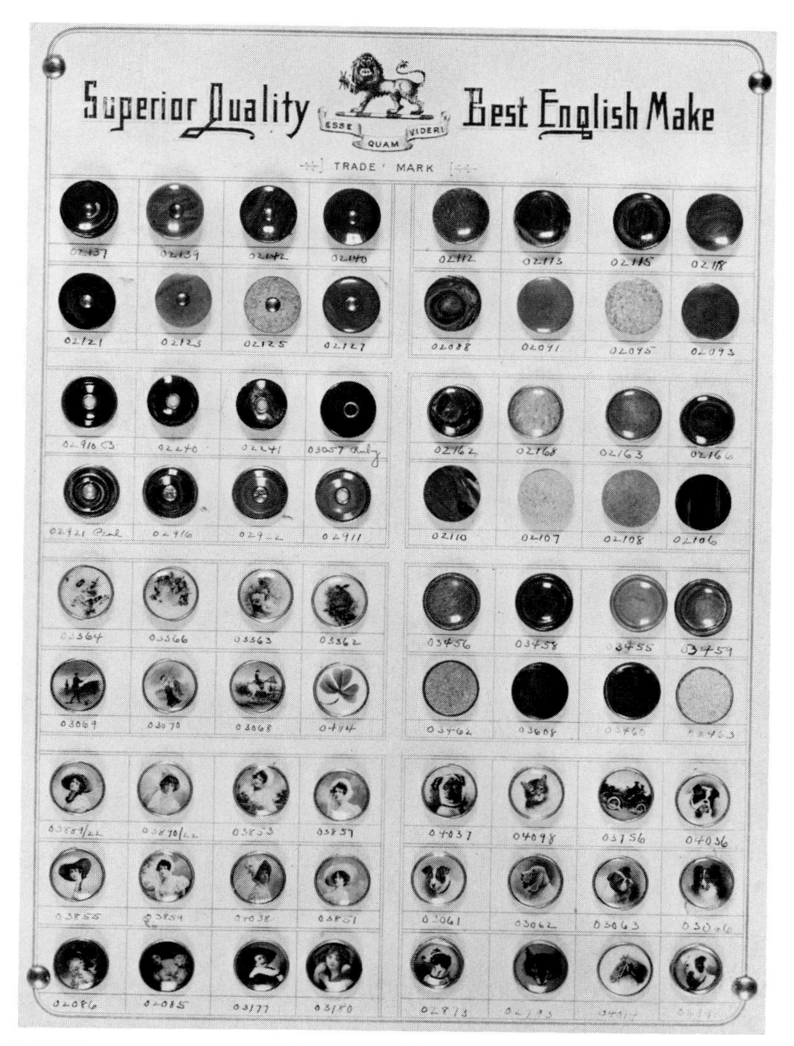

Vest buttons. Salesman's sample card dating from the nineteenth century.

VICTORIAN BUTTONS. A term used loosely for several different types of buttons made between 1850 and 1900. Molded glass buttons with raised designs and much gold are frequently called Victorian. Too many types of buttons were made in the period for the term Victorian to be effective. It is being used less and less.

VICTORIAN JEWELS. A term used for large jewel-type buttons with glass centers, made mostly for coats. Some of these buttons are identical to smaller ones; therefore, the term is confusing. There are many types among the large jewels to which the term could apply, such as drums with raised heads, modified drums, domed jewels, faceted jewels. These buttons have wire shanks or flexible shanks; a very few have self-shanks.

Victorian jewels. Button centers are milk-white glass. Nineteenth century.

VOLUTE SHELL BUTTONS. *See* Pinna Shell Buttons.

W

WAAC. *See* Armed Forces Buttons: Women's Services.

WAC. *See* Armed Forces Buttons: Women's Services.

WAF. *See* Armed Forces Buttons: Women's Services.

WASP. *See* Armed Forces Buttons: Women's Services.

WAVES. *See* Armed Forces Buttons: Women's Services.

W. C. MINTZER. *See* Mintzer, W. C.

WADHAMS, THE. Manufacturers of brass buttons, 1800's. The history of the Wadhams in Torrington, Connecticut, has proved impossible to unravel accurately. They produced many fine specimens of gilt buttons, and their names appear on one- and two-piece buttons. The earliest mark found to date is Wadhams, Coe & Co. A partnership was formed in the early 1830's that consisted of George D. Wadhams, Ashael Coe, and two Abernathys. In 1838 Mr. Coe left the business, and the firm became Wadhams, Webster & Co. (Martin Webster). About 1847 Webster sold his share, and the firm became Wadhams & Co. It is believed that, because of less demand for gilt buttons by 1850, the firm ceased making buttons. Records state they manufactured papier-mâché at about this time, but there is no mention of buttons. However, other manufacturers were making japanned papier-mâché pants buttons at the time.

WADHAMS, COE & CO. *See* The Wadhams.

WADHAMS, WEBSTER & CO. *See* The Wadhams.

WAFER BUTTONS. *See* Glass Buttons: Wafer Buttons.

WAISTCOAT (WESKIT) BUTTONS. In the eighteenth century, men's waistcoats (garments corresponding to vests) were often elaborately embroidered, even the buttons. When a coat had metal buttons, the waistcoat did, too. The button designs on the waistcoat did not always match those on the coat during the eighteenth century. The buttons on the leg of the breeches were the same size as those on the waistcoat; hence, it is not always possible to be sure whether a small button of this period was worn on the waistcoat or the breeches. However, very few small embroidered buttons have been seen on breeches. Although there were ten or more small buttons on the waistcoat, and eight or more on the breeches, these small eighteenth-century buttons are much scarcer than the coat size.

There are definite distinctions between eighteenth-century buttons and those made later. Although men continued to wear fancy buttons for another half-century, button styles changed very definitely with the beginning of the nineteenth century. Copper and tombac buttons ended quite abruptly in 1800, and the brass for buttons became a different alloy. The use of embroidery on men's coats and waistcoats also seemed to stop, and small embroidered waistcoat buttons ceased to be used. The shanks on eighteenth-century waistcoat buttons were heavier than those on buttons for vests in the nineteenth century.

The embroidered buttons of the eighteenth century were sometimes very elaborate and had gold and silver metal threads, sequins and foil; at other times, they were dainty and in pastel colors. Waistcoat buttons were embroidered before the fabric was used to cover the horn, bone, ivory, or wooden molds. The material was gathered, then fastened

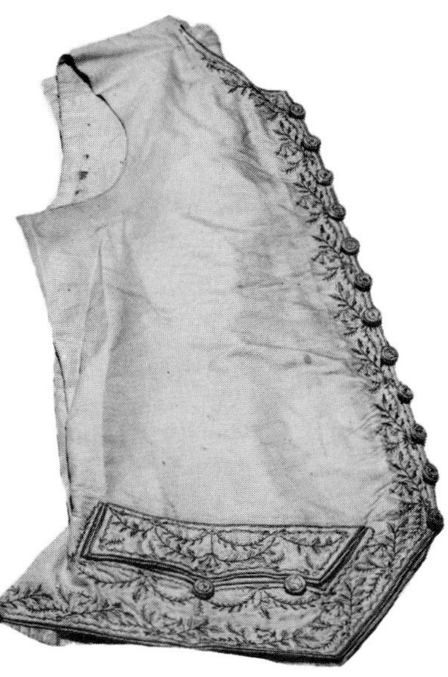

Waistcoat buttons. A handsomely decorated coat and matching waistcoat of the eighteenth century.

tightly on the back with heavy homespun thread, usually linen; often, extra stitches were made to reinforce the fabric for sewing the button to the garment. Waistcoat buttons ranged in size from $^1/_2$″ to $^3/_4$″.

WANAMAKER, JOHN W. Merchant, Philadelphia and New York, 1861 to 1960's. John Wanamaker had a partner, Nathan Brown, a brother-in-law. Until 1885 the company was known as Wanamaker & Brown. Some of the employees wore uniforms, and five different styles of buttons were used on these over the years. The imprint of Wanamaker & Brown on the backs of buttons signifies the firm's early interest in contract outfitting. Both staff and Sanders-type uniform buttons have been found with their names.

WASHINGTON INAUGURAL BUTTONS. These buttons especially made for delegates to wear to George Washington's first and second inaugurations are to collectors what the United States flag is to the citizens of this country. There is a special affection for them—and a place in every collection that no other button could fill. It hardly seems possible that any other button will ever reach such distinction. The first two inaugurations were very important occasions in this country's history. It must be remembered that few people were able to travel to inaugurations in 1789 and 1793, and each delegate represented many citizens. Every little ornament, including buttons, representative of Washington's inaugurations has become a treasure. (These buttons were also worn to important functions during Washington's first term.)

The buttons for coats were made large—in the fashion of the day—of copper, brass or Sheffield silver plate. Small buttons were made of the same materials. The only ones seen to date on an original garment are twelve copper buttons found on breeches of hand-woven material, favorably matching a coat-size button having the same design. The other known small buttons may also have been worn on breeches or perhaps waistcoats. No references have been found to indicate that the buttons were made anywhere except in the Colonial States, although the metal may have come from Europe. They were probably made by makers of "hardware" or "coin makers," as was true of other metal buttons in the eighteenth century.

Washington inaugural buttons were hand stamped. To date, twenty-two different patterns have been found, and five of the twenty-two are small-size buttons. There are

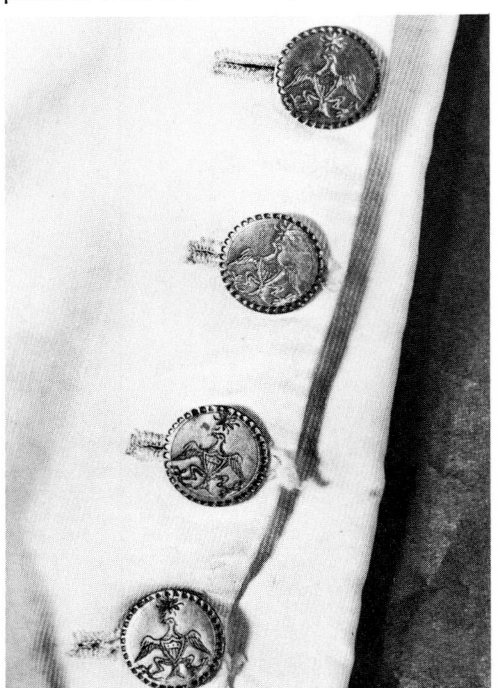

George Washington Inaugural buttons. Close-up of original old breeches with George Washington Inaugural buttons in small eagle and star pattern.

variations in several of the patterns—spaces between the letters, the size of the letters, and other slight differences.

Following is a list of the patterns:

1. Liberty Cap on Pole 1789
2. Profile of Washington 1789 (Smithsonian, not shown here)
3. Pyramid of 13 stars, "G.W.," and "LONG LIVE THE PRESIDENT"
4. Dated Eagle
5. G W in Oval
6. Rayed Pattern
7. Sunburst
8. Grant
9. Linked States. Found in varying colors, greenish brass, gold-brass, copper, and intermediate shades.
10. Script G W
11. Plain G W
12. Elder 13 Stars. Found with thirteen, fourteen, or fifteen stars and various flower groups.
13. Small Wreath
14. Wreath and Star
15. Darby, 15 Stars
16. Fifteen Stars, small (20 mm.)
17. Eagle & Star, small, brass or copper (*see* breeches in the illustration)
18. Eagle and Sun
19. The Majesty
20. Pater Patriae, copper face, pewter back.
21. Unity Prosperity Independence
22. Counterstamp "G W Long Live The President." Die strike was applied to both Colonial and English coins and to various metal disks, round and octagonal.

George Washington Inaugurals: Pattern numbers 1, 4, 5, 7, 8, 10, and 11, with variations in metal, die strikes, and border counts.

Row 1. Cobb Numbers: 1. Liberty Cap on Pole, 1789, copper, 34 mm. 4. Dated Eagle, brass, 34 mm. 4a. Dated Eagle, copper, 34 mm. 5e. GW in oval, no legend, brass, 28 mm. 5. GW in oval, narrow spacing, copper, 34 mm.

Row 2. Cobb numbers: 7. Sunburst, 23 pyramidal flames, brass, 31 mm. 7a. Sunburst, 24 pyramidal flames, brass, 31 mm. 8. Grant, 33 punch marks, copper, 33 mm. 8b. Grant, 32 punch marks, closed spaced rays, copper, 33 mm. 8a. Grant, 32 punch marks, wide-spaced rays, copper, 33 mm.

Row 3. Cobb numbers: 10. Script GW, brass, 35 mm. 10a. Script GW; design shows through back; brass, 35 mm. 10b. Script GW, copper, 35 mm. 11. Plain GW, regular W, brass, 36.5 mm. 11a. Plain GW, narrow W, brass, 36.5 mm.

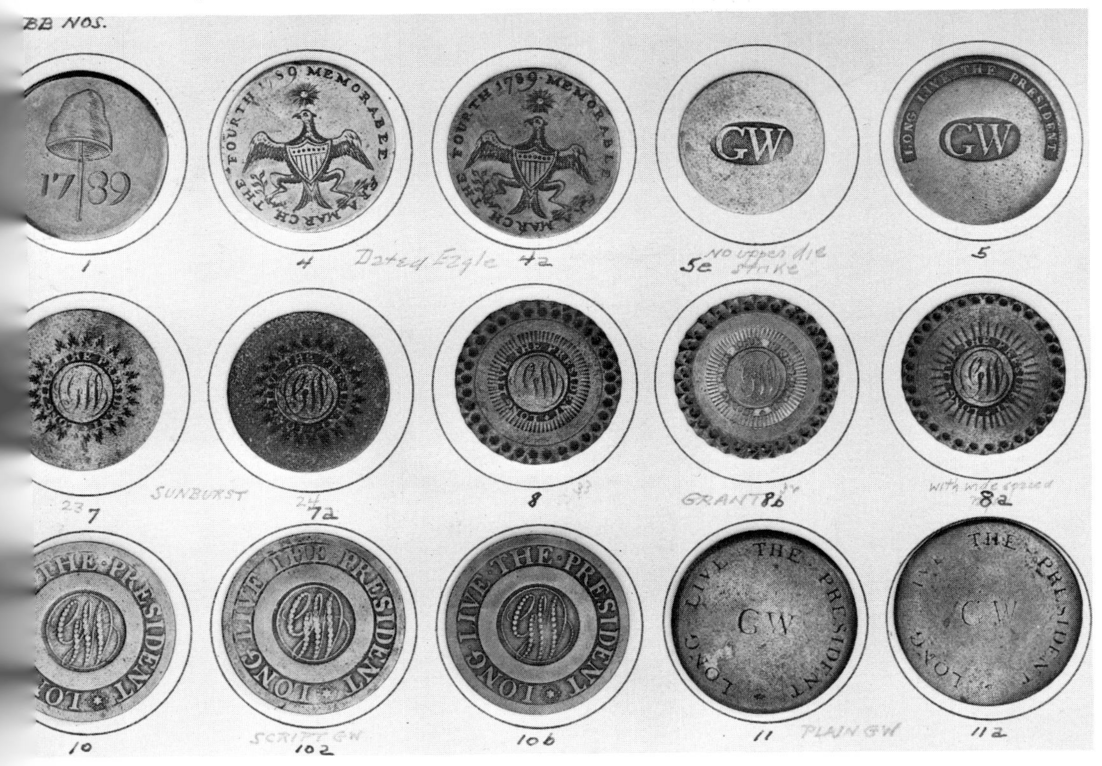

George Washington Inaugurals: Pattern numbers 5, 6, 9, 12, 13, 14, and 15, with variations in metal, die strikes, and the spacing of letters.

Row 1. Cobb Numbers: 5a. GW in oval, medium spacing, copper 34 mm. 5b. GW in oval, wide spacing, copper, 34 mm. 5c. GW in oval "Emilio," copper, 34.5 mm. 5d. GW in oval with date incised, 30 April 1789, copper, 34 mm. 6. Rayed, copper, 32 mm.

Row 2. Cobb numbers: 9b. Linked states, three indentations between links at border, brass, 34 mm. 9. Linked states, brass, 34 mm. 9a. Linked states; design shows through back; brass, 34 mm. 9c. Linked states, gold color, brass, 34 mm. 9d. Linked states, copper, 34 mm.

Row 3. Cobb numbers: 12. "Elder," 13 stars, gold color, brass, 34 mm. 12b. "Elder," 15 stars, gold color, brass, 34 mm. 13. Small wreath, brass, 15 mm. 13a. Small wreath, copper, 15 mm. 14. Wreath and star, copper, 20 mm. 15. Star "Darby," 15 stars, brass, 15 mm.

George Washington Inaugurals: Pattern numbers 16, 17, 18, and 22, with variations in metal, and items counterstamped.

Row 1. Cobb Numbers: 16. Star, 15 stars, brass, 20 mm. 17. Eagle and star, 37 impressions in border, brass, 18 mm. 17b. Eagle and star, 36 impressions in border, copper, 18 mm. 17A. Eagle and star, 37 impressions in border, copper, 18 mm. Continental Navy, c. 1789, brass (found on white breeches with No. 17a). 17g. Eagle and star, 63 impressions in border, brass, 34.8 mm.

Row 2. Cobb numbers: 17i. Eagle and star, 63 impressions in border, bronze, 34.8 mm. 17k. Eagle and star, 72 impressions in border, copper, 34.8 mm. 17l. Eagle and star, no border, brass, 30 mm. 18. Eagle and sun, 21 punch marks in border, copper, 34 mm. 17x. Unlisted.

Row 3. Cobb numbers: 22e. Counterstamp, Long Live the President; GW, 13 stars on Connecticut colonial cent, copper, 29 mm. 22. Counterstamp, Long Live the President; GW, plain, on Connecticut colonial cent, copper, 29 mm. 22b. Counterstamp, Long Live the President; GW, on English two pence, copper, 34mm. 22c. Counterstamp, Long Live the President; GW, on octagonal planchet, copper, 27 mm. 22d. Counterstamp, Long Live the President; GW, with border of dots, brass, 29 mm.

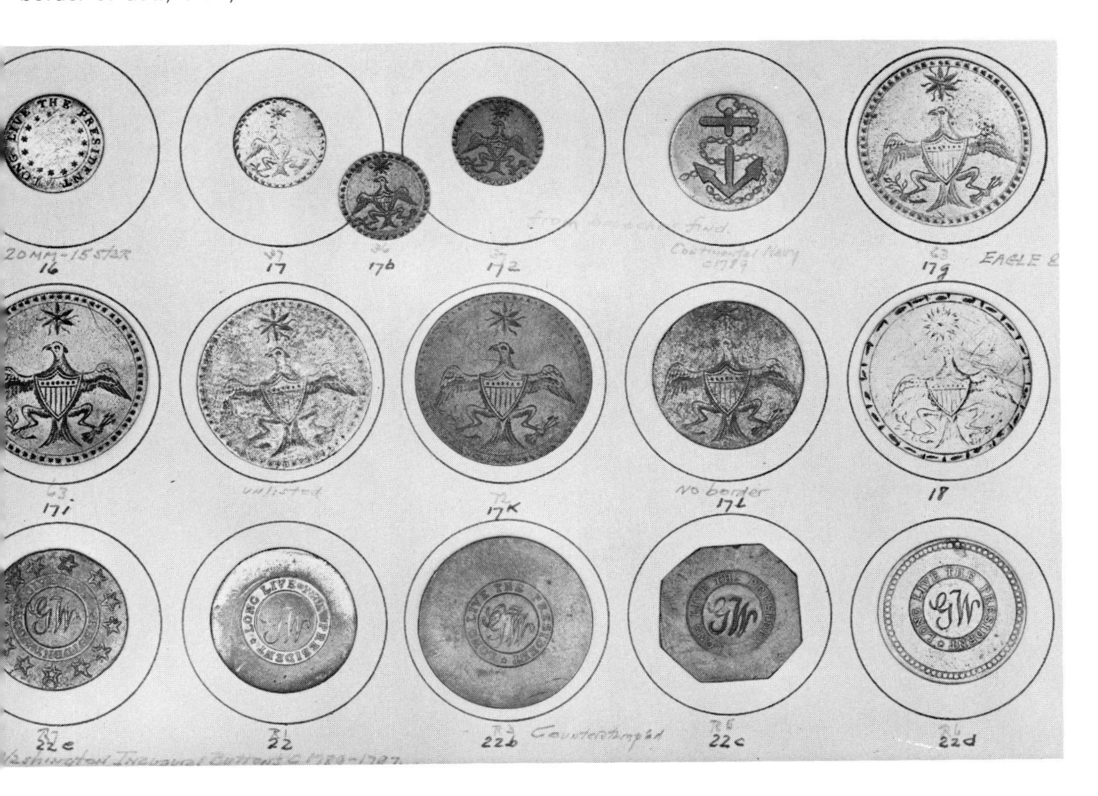

George Washington Inaugurals: Pattern numbers 17, 18, 20, 21, and 3, with variations in die strikes and border counts. English counterparts, c. 1776 and c. 1789, issued for George III.

Row 1. Cobb numbers: 17h. Eagle and star, 63 impressions in border, design shows through back, brass, 34.8 mm. 17j. Eagle and star, 63 impressions in border, copper, 34.8 mm. 17d. Eagle and star, 54 impressions in border, brass, 34.8 mm. 17e. Eagle and star, 54 impressions in border, bronze, 34.8 mm. 17f. Eagle and star, 54 impressions in border, copper, 34.8 mm.

Row 2. Cobb numbers: 18c. Eagle and sun, 27 punch marks in border; design shows through back, brass, 34 mm. 18b. Eagle and sun, 27 punch marks in border, brass, 34 mm. 20. Pater Patriae, pewter back, copper, 25 mm. 20a. Pater Patriae, bone back, cutout shank (not shown), copper, 25 mm. 21. Unity Prosperity Independence, no face showing, brass, 34 mm. 21x. Unity Prosperity Independence, with face, 34 mm.

Row 3. Cobb numbers: 3. Pyramid of thirteen stars, Long Live the President, GW, 1789, brass, 34 mm. "Washington in Star," brass. Long Live the King, c. 1776; "The Daddy of the GW's," George III, copper, 38 mm. Long Live the King, c. 1789, copper, 38 mm. Long Live the King, c. 1789, silvered, 38 mm.

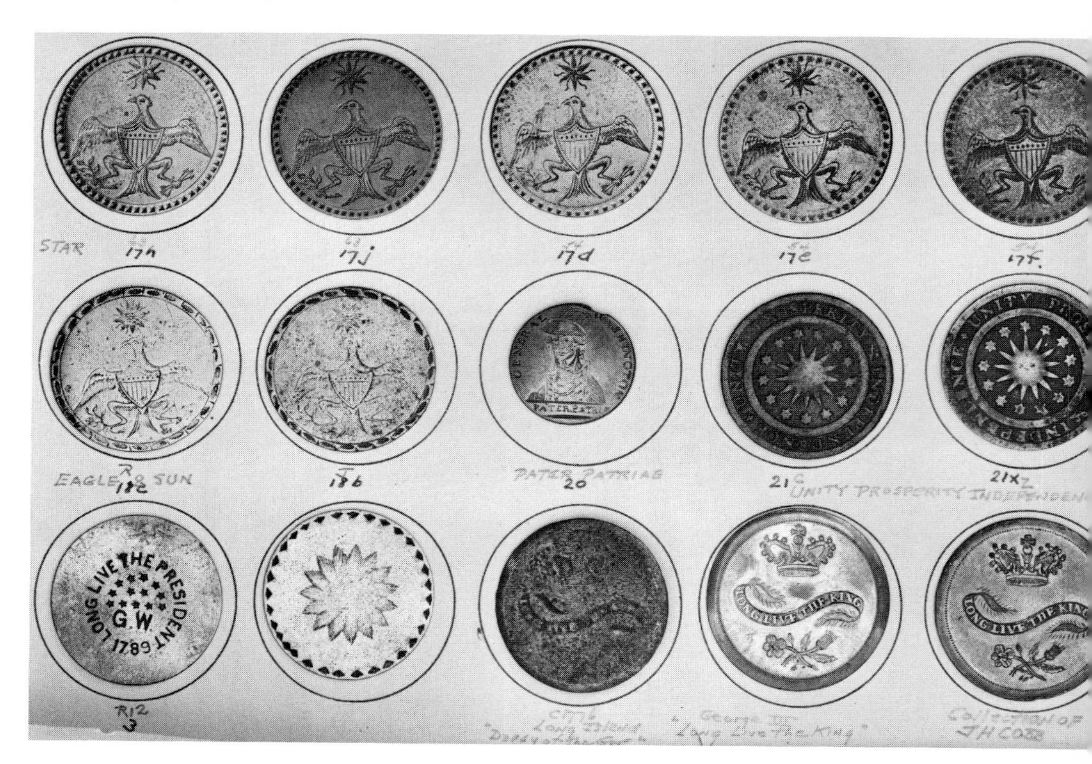

The most complete compilation of research on these buttons was privately published in 1963 by J. Harold Cobb and limited to one hundred copies, which he gave mostly to museums and libraries. With Mr. Cobb's permission, this listing here is the first time such extensive coverage has been presented to all collectors and students of Washington memorabilia.

Unfortunately, a few fakes, reproductions, and other undesirable specimens have shown up in recent years. The Collectors of Historical Buttons have arranged an educational display of noncollectible specimens that can be seen at Just Buttons Museum (open by appointment). Recently, an attempt has been made to establish the origin of Nos. 12 and 22, but to date no actual proof has been found. *See* Collectors of Historical Buttons.

WATCH CRYSTAL BUTTONS. A term used for a type of button with a very thin glass face —thin as a watch crystal and usually slightly convex. The glass disk has reverse-painted designs, which were painted in black and gold. Most of the designs consisted of stripes, circles, or flowers. A few rare buttons had bird designs. The backs of these buttons were flat metal disks with loop shanks; on the inside of the back, a cream-color cement-like material was placed, and on it, small pieces of pearl shell. These pieces show through the glass front, making an attractive background for the black-and-gold design. The front and back are held together with a black substance called "pitch." Often, over the years, it has dried and cracked, allowing the button to fall apart. A very few watch crystal buttons are sew-thrus; they have one hole in the glass and across the back, and instead of a shank there is a metal bar. The threads for fastening go to and from the front on each side of the bar. These buttons range in size from 3/4" to over 1".

WATCHCASE BUTTONS. A term used for one type of two-piece gilt buttons shaped similarly to the hunting case of a watch. The manufacturers' names on the backs of the buttons indicate they were made between 1835 and 1850, but hunting watchcases were actually made later. Processed horn buttons have been found with similar shapes and designs.

The top of the gilt button is flat, except for a very low-relief design, which is sometimes chased. The deep edges or sides are not perfectly straight, the back of the button being a trifle larger than the front. Very often, the edge of the button is elaborately stamped. Very few small buttons have been found. Watchcase buttons were worn by men, and are the rarest of the gilt buttons.

Watchcase buttons.
These are Golden Age specimens (1830's to 1850's).

WATERBURY BUTTON COMPANY; WATERBURY COMPANIES, INC. This concern, known as Waterbury Companies, Inc., since 1944, has a long history. It began in 1812, when Aaron Benedict began to make bone and ivory buttons in Waterbury, Connecticut.

In 1823, A. Benedict and Co. was formed, with Aaron Benedict, Nathan Smith, William Bristol, David DeForest, and Bennet Bronson as partners. By this time, they were making brass and gilt buttons, and the firm name has been found on such buttons.

In 1829, the company became known as Benedict & Coe. The partners were A. Benedict, Israel Coe, B. Bronson, J. DeForest, Alfred Platt, and James Croft. Benedict & Coe has been found on gilt buttons.

In 1834, the name was changed to Benedict and Burnham (Gordon W. Burnham). These two names have been found on buttons; also B & B Co.

In 1849, the firm became the Waterbury Button Company, and in 1944 (as already noted) Waterbury Companies, Inc. Since 1820, the main product has been metal buttons, but in the 1950's they also made plastic buttons. The various company names on metal buttons help to date them.

WATERBURY MANUFACTURING COMPANY. Some confusion still exists about this name, since there were at least three companies in Waterbury, Connecticut, that operated under it. They must not be confused with the Waterbury Button Company and Waterbury Companies, Inc. The first Waterbury Manufacturing Company was organized in 1814, and it may be the one that marked the back of its buttons. Another firm of the same name was formed by Scovills in 1849 for the production of "German Silver goods," which was later moved to Wallingford; they probably did not make buttons. Still another company started with this name in 1873, but no buttons are known. Buttons found with this company's name indicate the firm was in the button business in the 1840's; although larger than the usual size, these are included with early gilts. The buttons have high relief designs, and are of fine quality in material and workmanship. They are extremely rare.

WATERVILLE MANUFACTURING COMPANY. Manufacturers of buttons in Waterville, Connecticut (a section of Waterbury), from 1825 to the 1850's. The firm began as Hayden, Webster and Bond, about 1825. In 1829, it became Leavenworth and Kendrick (Mark Leavenworth and Green Kendrick).

In 1837, the firm became Ives, Scott & Co. (Dr. Ambrose Ives and Herman Scott). Kendrick retained a financial interest.

Some time later, the concern was named Ives, Kendrick & Company. In 1847, the name was changed again to the Waterville Manufacturing Company. Some very fine specimens of sporting buttons have been found with this company's name on the backs.

WEBSTER & WOOSTER. Manufacturers of metal buttons in Waterbury, Connecticut, 1840's.

WEDGE SHANK. These shanks were cast or handwrought with the body of the button. They were always flat or wedge-shaped, and had a hole drilled by hand after the button was finished. Sometimes buttons with these shanks were called Wedge-Type Buttons. The wedge shank has been found on bronze, brass, and white alloy buttons made in the eighteenth century.

WEINMAN, FRANK X. Glassblower, 1890's–1950. He began his trade about 1895, working in shows and carnivals, making small glass items. He also had a shop in Olean, New York, in 1895, where he made men's fancy collar and cuff buttons, hatpins, and desk paperweights. Mr. Weinman exhibited in the Pan-American Exhibition, Buffalo, New York, in 1901. After that, he did very little with glass until the 1940's, when he learned of the button-collecting hobby. Then, in a shop in Boston, Massachusetts, he began to make paperweight buttons. Most of these were flat, slightly domed, or cone-shaped. On a colored base formed around a wire shank he placed preformed glass pieces or disks, which he fused together in a Bunsen burner. He used pieces of goldstone profusely. Over the designs he built up clear glass. He advertised his buttons, which are already very rare, as Aventurine Glass Art.

WESSEL BUTTONS. In the 1950's and 1960's, in Pennsylvania and Indiana, Harry Wessel made enameled, stainless-steel buttons with designs enclosed by glass faces. In each button was placed a picture, or tiny objects, to make the design. In some, seaweed or small shells were arranged similarly to the manner of eighteenth-century habitat buttons. Real flowers were enclosed in some; bright foil glistened in others. Some Wessel buttons had pictures of such historic subjects as Abraham Lincoln and his family; others showed famous sculpture or Philadelphia scenes. His buttons were usually $1^{1}/_{4}''$ in size.

Enameled steel buttons. Watch-crystal face.
These were made by Harry Wessel in the 1940's and 1950's.

WHEELMEN, LEAGUE OF AMERICAN. *See* Bicycle Buttons.

WHISTLE BUTTONS. This term was coined for a particular two-piece small china that had one hole on top and two on the back. One-piece buttons with a similar arrangement of holes for sewing have gradually been included. Hence, the use of the term has broadened. Small china whistles range in size from less than $^1/_4$″ to nearly 1″.

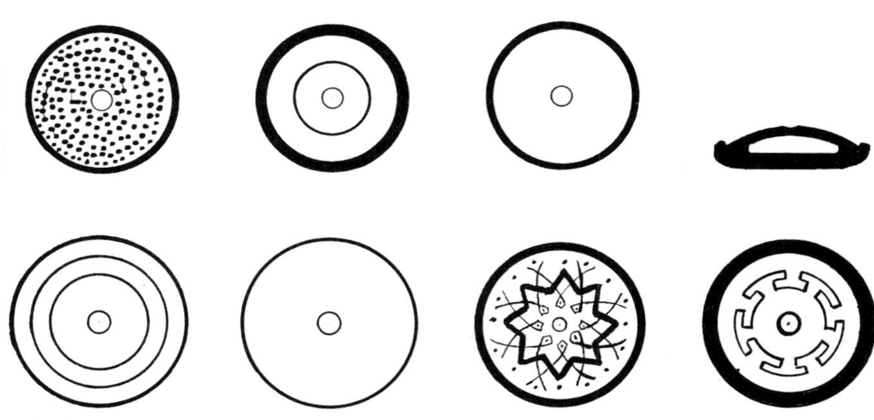

Whistle buttons. A type of small chinas (late 1800's).

WHITBY JET. *See* Jet Buttons.

WILLIAM EAVES & SONS. William Eaves was brought to this country from Birmingham, England, by the L. M. L. & W. H. Scovill Company, Waterbury, Connecticut, in 1829. He worked for this company until he went into business with his two sons in Wolcottville (now Torrington), Connecticut. There are only scant records of Eaves and his sons, John and Joseph, while in Wolcottville, and these are somewhat confusing. Most of the buttons found to date are fine-quality, one- and two-piece gilt sporting buttons. It would seem that the manufacturing done by the Eaves family was between 1842 and 1849, when William Eaves went into the Methodist ministry. Back markings found are J. J. Eaves & Sons; or Eaves & Sons, Wolcottville.

WILLISTON and KNIGHT COMPANY. The history of this Massachusetts firm actually began with Mrs. Samuel Williston, who decided to make covered buttons by hand in 1826. She purchased bone and wooden molds, "lasting" (a material for a lining), and silk. The enterprise was started in the Williston home, but it soon reached out to other housewives, who made buttons in their homes for the Willistons, until a shop was opened by Samuel Williston in 1827. Mr. Williston traveled to New York, selling the buttons to New York merchants.

Upon finding some new machine-made British buttons in the New York market, Williston decided to shift from handmade to machine-made buttons. He sent someone to England in an effort to obtain rights to manufacture in America by the new methods. When the negotiations failed, Williston prevailed upon Joel Hayden and his brother Josiah to invent and perfect the necessary machinery. The date was about 1833. A Francis Sidney of England helped them to perfect the process further.

In 1843, a young man, Horatio G. Knight, was given the status of partner in the button business, which continued as S. Williston from 1847–49. Mr. Williston changed his product about 1849, and Williston and Knight Company was then known as Horatio Knight. Within five years another partner was taken, Seth Warner, and the company name was changed to Williston, Knight and Company. Machine-made buttons have been found with Samuel Williston, S. Williston, and W. K. Co. on the backs. In 1852 and 1853, Samuel Williston and Company opened offices in New York City; the manager was H. G. Knight. In 1865, when the partnership agreement had run out, a stock company reorganization took place and the company took the title of National Button Company; the backs of their buttons showed N. B. Mafg. Co.

After the death of Mr. Williston in 1874, settlement of the estate and refinancing led the company to revert to the name Williston and Knight Company in 1880. About 1905, the business was reorganized under the name of United Button Company. The company moved to New York and, in 1922, was finally liquidated.

WILLISTON, SAMUEL. *See* Williston and Knight Company. A very few buttons have "S. Williston" on the back.

WIRE MESH BACKS. Commonly called Screen Back Buttons by collectors. A patent for this invention was issued to Albert M. Smith, Brooklyn, New York, January 28, 1873. The invention related "to making a button of a vitreous substance and combining with it a metallic back for increasing its strength so as to prevent it from breaking when in use, and at the same time embedding in it a flat shank, all at the time of pressing (molding) the button." This back was made of wire woven in the manner of cloth, and usually termed "wire-cloth." It allowed the glass, while in a hot plastic state, to be forced or squeezed through, or into, the holes in the wire and become embedded in it.

Although the patent was issued in this country, it is not known that buttons were made with this wire mesh in the United States. Most of those found with wire mesh backs are black glass, except for a very few colored glass ones. They are usually 3/4" in size. Wire mesh backs should not be confused with larger glass buttons having a molded meshlike pattern on the backs.

Wire mesh back. Front and back view of a black glass button with a wire mesh back (nineteenth century).

WOMEN'S LAND ARMY OF AMERICA BUTTONS. These were worn by the officers on the uniforms of the Women's Land Army of America, 1918–19. This group supervised women who replaced male farm workers called to serve in our Armed Forces in World War I. The button was designed by Paul Manship, nationally known sculptor, for Gorham, the New York jeweler. In the center of a round bronze button was a raised shield design in the shape of a "V" for victory. It enclosed WLAA in a banner motif surmounting a sheaf of grain resting on a sickle. Not many of these buttons were made, for the war was near its end. The making of the uniforms ended in 1919.

WLAA (Women's Land Army of America) button. Worn in 1918.

WOOD BUTTONS. Almost every known wood has been used to make buttons since at least the eighteenth century. Many wooden buttons have mellowed with age, and the kind of wood in them cannot be determined without cutting them; others were painted and lacquered. Eighteenth-century wood buttons frequently had pinhead shanks, and seem to have been made more for utilitarian purposes than for adding beauty to garments.

In the nineteenth century, wooden buttons were decorated in many ways—inlaid with other woods or other materials, carved, painted, or trimmed with escutcheons. The great variety of wooden buttons continued into the twentieth century, and then plastic was added to the list of trimmings. Many wooden buttons have been made in studios specializing in inlay and marquetry, as well as in factories, during the nineteenth and twentieth centuries. Wooden buttons generally range in size from $^{1}/_{2}''$ to over 2″.

Nineteenth-century wood buttons. Those in the top row have metal escutcheons. The first two in the bottom row have carved pearl centers; the third has inlaid wood of several colors.

WORK-CLOTHES BUTTONS. These were worn on the jackets or coats called "jumpers," which were made to wear with overalls. They are sometimes called overall buttons, but were never worn on overalls. The face of the buttons was made of brass. The backs were usually made of iron, with black lacquer or tin, and a loose wire shank. Some have holes instead of shanks. A few have patented fasteners. These buttons are about $^{3}/_{4}''$ in size. Many have designs, slogans, or garmentmakers' names. They were made in quantity in this country beginning in the late nineteenth century by prominent button manufacturers, but some found on American-made garments were made in other countries.

Work-clothes buttons lack quality, but the unique designs are attractive to some collectors. Hundreds of different designs have been found.

WOVEN BUTTONS. *See* Fabric-covered Buttons; *also* Jacquard Looms.

YALE, CHARLES. American manufacturer, 1830's.

Work-clothes buttons. A salesman's sample card.

YALE, E. R. *See* E. R. Yale.

YOUNG, H. American button maker before 1833. Name found on buttons.

YOUNG, SMITH, & CO. American button makers, 1833–44. *See* Young, H. This Young could have been in the Young, Smith & Co. firm.

Z

ZODIAC BUTTONS. In the twentieth century, zodiac symbols and signs have been very popular as button designs. They consist of the following:

Aries, the Ram
Taurus, the Bull
Gemini, the Twins
Cancer, the Crab
Leo, the Lion
Virgo, the Virgin
Libra, the Balance
Scorpio, the Scorpion
Sagittarius, the Archer
Capricornus, the Goat
Aquarius, the Water-Bearer
Pisces, the Fishes

Three different styles of one-piece nineteenth-century metal buttons have been found with zodiac signs. To date, no complete set of the twelve signs has been found in any of the three styles. Gemini is missing in all three sets. This seems strange and unaccountable.

Twentieth-century buttons decorated with zodiac signs have been made in almost every material and by several kinds of artwork. Although most were made by button manufacturers and sold to the garment trade, a smaller quantity was made by hand in studios. They have been made in several other countries as well.

Metal zodiac buttons. Twentieth century.

Twentieth-century zodiacs. These pearl buttons were hand-carved in the Holy Land.

Cloisonné zodiacs. Made in the present century.

Enameled zodiac buttons.
With foil under glass; twentieth century.

INDEX

Page numbers in italics indicate an illustration of a button on a different page from where the text about it appears.